DIRECTING FOR THE STAGE

A Workshop Guide of 42 Creative Training Exercises and Projects

TERRY JOHN CONVERSE

MERIWETHER PUBLISHING LTD
Colorado Springs, Colorado

Meriwether Publishing Ltd., Publisher
P.O. Box 7710
Colorado Springs, CO 80933

Editor: Arthur L. Zapel
Typesetting: Lou Ann Neal
Cover design: Tom Myers

© Copyright MCMXCV Meriwether Publishing Ltd.
Printed in the United States of America
First Edition

Library of Congress Cataloging-in-Publication Data

Converse, Terry John, 1945-

    Directing for the stage : a workshop guide of forty-two creative training exercises and projects / by Terry John Converse.
    p.   cm.
    Includes bibliographical references.
    ISBN 1-55608-014-2
    1. Theater--Production and direction--Handbooks, manuals, etc.
I. Title.
PN2053.C63   1995
792' .0233--dc20

           93-35414
           CIP
           AC

1 2 3 4 5 6 7 8   99 98 97 96 95

To my treasured family:
Sheila, Kathleen, and Ryan
with all my love

CONTENTS

PREFACE

Taped to the wall of my office, torn from a magazine or newspaper long since forgotten, is the following irreverent saying:

Directing is like sex
in that you never see anybody else do it
so you don't know whether you're doing it right.

The humor comes from the shock of recognition that there is an element of truth to the comparison. "Doing it right," implying that there is only *one* way to "do it," is doubly absurd with both activities, but it is kind of fun to think about what would happen without any previous knowledge whatsoever with both pursuits. Would the hours and hours of inevitable fumbling be justified as part of the "creative act," or would there be a better, more enjoyable way to go about it? How many of us have fumbled in the dark theatre of our minds, frustrated with the knowledge, but not the means, that there must be a better way of training beginning theatre directors?

The sexual simile is easily applied to teachers of directing. Until somebody writes the directorial equivalent of Eva Mekler's *The New Generation of Acting Teachers*,[1] much of what happens behind the closed doors of directing workshops will remain a worldwide mystery. Mekler interviewed twenty-two master teachers of acting across the country, allowing them to discuss in their own words their philosophies of acting, and the specific exercises and techniques they use in their teaching. Had Mekler interviewed instead twenty-two master teachers of directing, we would now have a much better sense of what specific techniques are currently in practice.

The progressive series of exercises in this book were created out of a very definite need. There were workshops to conduct with very eagerly awaiting students, and in the heat of this need, the exercises (or variations of the ones now in this book) were given birth. Many times ideas for specific exercises sprang out of something we were working on that was totally unrelated to the exercise itself, but which demanded recognition and further exploration. Other times, exercises arose from discovering that it was too great a jump, too great a step, to get from one conceptual place to another. There was also an immediate need to put the exercises down on paper because time in the workshop is much better spent in the doing rather than in the talking about the doing.

Inasmuch as they are the kinds of exercises I would have wanted to have had in my early training as a director, they are, in a sense, belated wish fulfillments. I had stellar teachers at both the University of Minnesota and UCLA; teachers who were, in many cases, true mentors. But even at the time, I felt that there was something missing.

---

[1]Eva Mekler, *The New Generation of Acting Teachers,* (New York: Penguin Books, 1987).

There had to be a more efficient and thorough way of learning directing. Like many others, I suspect, I learned via a scene study approach, but what was missing was a step-by-step, progressive approach allowing for the possibility of learning one concept at a time. True, not being able to see behind closed doors makes it impossible to say with confidence exactly what is happening in today's directing classes, but what can be said with certainty, is that nothing yet written provides a sequential series of exercises.

Acting texts abound with progressive, practical exercises, yet not so with directing texts. Outrageously unfair — yes, except that the injustice is a fairly pure reflection of the fact that directing itself is a remarkably recent phenomenon. The modern concept of the director emerged only within the last 140 years or so. It wasn't until 1860 with the formation of the Duke Georg II of Saxe-Meiningen's company in Germany that the director in the modern sense of the term began to emerge. Actors have been around seemingly forever compared to the Johnny-come-lately directors, so we are deservedly last in line to get our exercises.

Creating an exclusively exercise-driven directing text is the single-minded point of this book. The sacred precepts of theatre directing that one would hope to find in a basic text are still here to be found, but the approach is totally experiential. Basic concepts are meant to be actively, not passively discovered; only by ripping them out of their carefully wrapped problem-solving packages will the student really learn directing. This book offers suggested pathways of learning, providing challenging excursions, each of which is meant to culminate in miniature, but complete "pieces" of art. The exercises make very specific demands, and present very specific problems, but never should it be assumed that there is only one way to direct; to assume so is to hark back to the slogan in my office, which is meant for laughs only. Searching for a style of directing best suited to the individual should be a primary concern of any training method.

A word of appreciation needs to given to the many students at Washington State University who have worked through the various incarnations of these exercises, and to to my colleague Dick Slabaugh for his figure drawings and perspective sketch. Special thanks to Jack Thornton and Sheila Converse for their incredibly constructive criticism and proofing, and to Arthur Zapel of Meriwether Publishing for recognizing the value of this work. As I type these very words, my young children, Ryan and Kathleen (ages 5 and 8), are nearby contentedly drawing marvelous creations; it has become a ritual; Dad sits staring at the screen, while the children hover about with their creative projects. All I have to do is suggest something like, "What kind of Halloween board game could you make?" and they are busy literally for hours. Later, after silently enjoying each other's company, we have loads of fun as a family playing the games. How similar all this is to what the book itself wants to do — plant seeds for the many magic gardens ahead. My thanks to them a thousand times over for reminding me daily to never lose sight of the fun and fascination of creating.

CHAPTER 1

CREATING THE DIRECTING WORKSHOP

What's wrong with the following exercise for the beginning director?

> Read the chapter in the text on blocking, and then direct a ten-minute scene from Eugene O'Neill's *Long Day's Journey into Night*. Use direct, secondary, duoemphasis, and diversified emphasis as well as direct, counter, and indirect focus by carefully blending all the concepts discussed in the chapter such as stage area, body position, plane, level, contrast, spatial distance, and balance.

Nothing at all is wrong, assuming that it is meant to be a culminating showcase representing months and months of specialized, segmented work. But all too often beginning directors are deluged with similar exercises too early in their training. Just the amount of reading alone in this kind of exercise is daunting, not to mention the time that would be needed for script analysis. Sure, it is always beneficial for the beginning director to read as much dramatic literature as possible, but it is a misdirected use of time and energy when the objective at hand happens to be learning the visual skills of staging. Theatre is by nature a synthesis of the arts, but no matter how bright the student, there is a limit to how much can be assimilated at a given time. Apparently the vision behind this kind of exercise is that of beginning director as magician, able to pull out of a hat in a single synthesizing bound, a theatrical bunny worth watching. In truth, what this kind of exercise does best is set up the beginning director to fail. Yes, some learning may happen, but if it does, it will happen in spite of the exercise, and no matter what the outcome, it is far from an efficient way to learn.

There is by no means a dearth of basic directing books — many very fine texts are currently in print — but there is very definite need for a segmented, sequential series of exercises that invite the beginning student to experiment with concepts one at a time. Books abound with exercises of this type for the actor, and music and art students expect step-by-step exercise work for their training, but somehow this approach for directors has been basically overlooked. Many directing texts simply don't have any exercises at all, and those that do generally tend to ask too much too soon, failing to provide the student with a step-by-step approach.

1

Step by Baby Step

To date, still the most comprehensive and illuminating book on staging principles is Alexander Dean's and Lawrence Carra's *Fundamentals of Play Directing*, which does happen to be filled with many exercises, but the vast majority of them take the form of demonstrations more than actual exercises; a typical demonstration, for example, is:

> Place a figure onstage; have a second figure stand below and to the R, focusing on the first figure. We have direct visual focus. Now have the DR figure turn to the R in a three-quarter body position. The focal emphasis of the first figure is now just as strong if not stronger than before.[1]

Demonstrations such as these can be very valuable, but they do not actively involve the student director. When Dean and Carra do actually provide exercises rather than demonstrations, the exercises tend to be like the following: "Each member of the group analyze in writing the mood of a scene from a play of his own choosing. Stage the scene, conveying the mood by means of line, mass, and form."[2] And so even with step-by-step demonstrations, we're right back where we started by asking for sleight of hand, synthesized magic.

A successful director is someone who can give both actors, designers, and his audience a different way of looking at the world. Before such vision is even remotely possible, however, the student director must acquire a vast array of skills. The complexity of this task is exacerbated by the fact that the skills are inextricably connected to one another. Effective directing exercises must be able to isolate specific skills for study while keeping a window open in the background that allows at least a momentary glimpse of how the isolated skills relate to the whole. Each exercise brings the director more tools with which to work, and one step closer to seeing how each part relates to the whole. Deciding which skills to isolate and which skills to synthesize at any given phase of the training is the essential consideration.

By providing a progressive series of practical, challenging, and hopefully eye-opening exercises this book, in many ways, intends to be for the director what Viola Spolin's *Improvisation for the Theatre* is for the actor. Spolin argues that if the environment permits it, anyone can learn to act,[3] and the same can be said for directing. Taking one creative step at a time, where complex and overlapping concepts are isolated into digestible tidbits, is the most productive and rewarding path for the beginning director. Only by deliberately narrowing the field of concentration is the

---

[1]Alexander Dean & Lawrence Carra, *Fundamentals of Play Directing*, (New York: Holt, Rinehart and Winston, Inc., 1974), p. 129.

[2]Ibid., p. 171.

[3]Viola Spolin, *Improvisation for the Theatre: A Handbook of Teaching and Directing Techniques*, (Evanston: Northwestern University Press, 1973), p. 3.

beginning director given a real chance to learn. No matter how basic or introductory, all the exercises are designed to be fulfilling creative experiences, but part of what makes them fulfilling is that they each limit the field to what is genuinely attainable at a particular phase of the training.

All this is not to suggest that the order of the exercises is sacrosanct. The workshop facilitator is free to put together the exercises in whatever order makes the most sense. Major considerations such as available time and the experience level of the group will undoubtedly influence the facilitator's choices of exercises. All of the exercises fall into the following five major divisions:

- Silent Scenes
- Justified Movement Scenes
- Ground Plan Scenes
- Open Scenes
- Closed Scenes

The sequential relationship between these major categories is explained as each is presented. Essentially the progression is from silence to sound, from the simple to the more complex. Even though the exercises in this book are designed as a cumulative charted experience, there is ample opportunity for the teacher to use the exercises diagnostically according to specific needs of the workshop. Just as the Spolin exercises can be used in a tremendous number of ways and contexts, so too can the exercises of this book. They may even be used outside of the workshop itself, in formal rehearsal situations. If the exercises do no more than inspire additional exercises (variations or totally new ones), then this book will have definitely served its purpose.

The exercises are written as calls to the imagination. Each exercise presents a definite challenge, similar to what Spolin calls "the point of concentration."[4] By focusing on a particular concept, each exercise hopes, above all else, to spark the student director's imagination. Sometimes igniting interest, as in the process of directing itself, requires a kind of cheerleading (you can do it) style, while at other times the writing is deliberately provocative, challenging the student director to think about every little important nook and cranny of the problem. Each exercise uses the format of: 1) Overview, 2) Discussion of pertinent topics, and 3) Suggested critique questions.

Go Team Go

From the very first exercise, the directors will need actors, and there are several ways of generating a pool of actors for the workshop. One is simply to bring in people from outside the workshop (friends, family, and any other willing warm bodies). In a college, university or conservatory setting it is often possible to have students from the Introduction to Theatre class receive extra credit for working with

---

[4]Viola Spolin, *Improvisation for the Theatre: A Handbook of Teaching and Directing Techniques*, (Evanston: Northwestern University Press, 1973), pp. 21-26.

student directors. If this kind of departmental cooperation is taken several steps further, then it might be possible to formally integrate the acting and directing students by bringing the classes periodically together. This obviously has the advantage of creating a pool of more committed, more motivated actors. It also has the fringe benefit of reducing the demand for rehearsal spaces, since the projects of two classes become combined, rather than competing activities.

If the directing workshop is large enough (eight or more), then an excellent way to generate actors is to create teams, where the workshop members when not actively directing take turns acting for each other. Dividing the workshop into teams of four (or however many are needed for a particular exercise) not only solves the problem of finding actors, but it creates a valuable perspective for the beginning director; teams allow the student to see through the eyes of both actor and director within the context of the same exercise. When acting, the student experiences first hand what it's like to *take* direction, and so when the tables are turned and the actor is now in the hot seat having to *give* direction, there is a definite opportunity to constructively avoid approaches which didn't seem to work and gravitate toward those that did.

Above all else, the team concept reinforces the all important fact that theatre is a team activity. Veteran filmmaker, Francis Ford Coppola is fond of saying that "collaboration is the sex of creativity...when you connect with another person and something magical happens, it's a sublime thrill."[5] Team work also has the benefit of demonstrating that a tight team, drawing on the particular strengths and skills of each member of the group, may be smarter and more effective than any individual member of that group. What one person lacks can be made up by another member of the team, and any member's brilliance is shared by all. Most of all, working in teams proves as no directing text can, that something made by several people can truly work, and that very often the whole is greater than the sum of its parts. Even for those in the workshop who never work in theatre again, it is worth remembering that much creative work later in life often requires problem solving as members of a team.

Great teams do not necessarily happen automatically. Often there is a need for the facilitator of the workshop (the director of the directors) strategically to group people together for the best possible "chemistry." For the formation of the first teams, when the workshop as a whole is still adjusting to each other, and insecurity is probably at its peak, it's probably best to let the group divide itself into teams. Later, when the group as a whole is more relaxed, and there is more interpersonal history to take into consideration, then the teacher can take a more active role in forming the teams; it's up to the discretion of the workshop director as to whether the reasons for the groupings are to be discussed publicly or privately, or whether the whole issue is better left unspoken. Along with who to pick for the teams, the facilitator has to also decide how often to change the teams; sometimes it is useful to change the team

[5]Francis Ford Coppola said this at a talk he recently gave at UCLA. A summary of his talk was reported on in: *Point of View* (Fall 1993), a newsletter published by the UCLA School of Theatre, Film, and Television.

members completely, whereas at other times it is better to keep at least half of the original team intact.

Physical and Psychological Space

With the exception of state-of-the-art pneumatic lift marvels, a large open space such as a simple black box theatre is probably the ideal. If the space is an actual theatre there is the advantage of at times being able to use light and sound facilities when needed, but generally just a large space is needed. Along with the space itself, an ample collection of stock black or gray rehearsal furniture is also needed. The amount of stock set pieces will depend on what's available, or what's affordable, along with what the space will comfortably allow.

Having the set pieces painted black or gray creates a neutrality and a uniformity that provides for the maximum versatility. The concept of using the same color set pieces puts a focus on line and mass and keeps distracting detail to a minimum. Gray or black may seem incredibly dull at first, but both lend themselves equally well to serious plays or comedies. When color is absolutely necessary for a particular effect, it can be easily created by a using a well-chosen set dressing such as a red table cloth.

There is a great latitude as to what is a workable number of set pieces for a workshop; a well-stocked workshop might include:

12	Small cubes	2	Rectangular tables
4	Platforms (4' x 8')	12	Folding chairs
2	Round tables (3' dia)	2	Wooden arm chairs
4	Round stools	6	Benches
2	Door units	2	Window units

Table and chairs can be as used, of course, as tables and chairs, but other items such as cubes and platforms can be used in a multitude of ways. Stacked cubes, for instance, can represents cabinets and bars, and even fireplaces. The door and window units need to be constructed so as to be free standing, and easily moved. Platform units of varying heights (or adjustable leg units) offer obvious advantages for working with level.

Along with stock set pieces, ideally stock costumes could also be put to great advantage. A simple costume rack with specially selected costume pieces to be pulled when needed could become a welcomed, permanent part of the workshop. Here also versatility is the ideal where neutral pieces (same color rehearsal skirts, jackets, etc.), or pieces that can be used in a variety of ways are the best choice. Since the workshop space is probably in great demand, used for both for the workshop itself and for rehearsals, it is imperative that the space be kept organized and clean. Establishing routine places for all tables, chairs, cubes, platforms, and the like will greatly reduce the frustration level of having to find a specific set piece when rehearsal time, as so often happens, is at a premium.

Just as it is ideal to have an openness for the physical space, it is every bit as important to have a psychological openness in the workshop as well. The workshop must foster an atmosphere in which there is genuine concern and compassion for each other's work. Compassion is what helps people work constructively together and to value someone's efforts even when their results fall short. Compassion on the individual level helps to lessen significantly the greatest creativity killer of all — self censorship, the inner voice of self blame and criticism in each of us that makes us afraid to try something, or fiendishly hounds us with doubt when we do. Creativity is synonymous with having the courage to take risks, and the self censor, above all else, is what discourages risk taking. Collective compassion creates an "openness" and a feeling of support that helps to quiet the self censor and makes it possible for each director to feel open enough to stretch his imagination and try truly new things.

Creating psychological openness is easier said than done, but there are several ways to stack the odds in favor of openness. Probably the most obvious is getting everyone to know each other. The best environment for creative work is the "one big happy family" atmosphere, and with this in mind, it is worth devoting the early part of the workshop to developing just this kind of feeling. An excellent source for these early exercises has already been mentioned — Spolin's *Improvisation for the Theatre*. Another is Augusto Boal's *Games for Actors and Non-Actors*.[6] Boal's blind exercises are especially valuable for orientation (getting to know you) type sessions because by taking away the dominant sense of sight, they force the players out of their comfortable ruts of perception and get them to explore in genuinely new ways.[7] The concept of getting everybody more comfortable with each other in these early exercises doesn't in any way mean that directorial principles and concepts can't be introduced with these exercises. For instance, Boal's statue exercises,[8] which are all variations of one partner literally molding another into a specific statue, are excellent ways to get the student to think visually. The statue exercises also let the student sense (through feel and sight) that directing is somewhat like sculpting in that both allow us to make something by manipulating something in space. It is a good idea to return periodically to these kinds of exercises in the training process, as both an effective way of introducing concepts and reinforcing a strong sense of ensemble.

The exercises in this book also are an effective means of fostering openness. The very fact that everybody is doing the same exercises at the same time means that everybody intimately knows what everyone else is doing, and this alone creates a common interest. In directing classes where everybody is asked to find scenes from

[6]Augusto Boal, *Games for Actors and Non-Actors*, translated by Adrian Jackson, (London and New York: Routledge, 1992).

[7]Ibid., pp. 106-115. He calls these exercises his "blind series."

[8]Ibid., pp. 127-130. He calls these exercises his "modeling sequence."

established texts, the snag is that the rest of the class is often unfamiliar with the material, all of which tends to work against a sense of ensemble. Yes, it's possible for the presenting director to introduce the basic situation of the scene, but the level of interest and comprehension often remains pretty superficial if the full text hasn't been read. The net effect of the separate scenes approach tends to be separate islands of distrust where the level of competition is unproductively high. Sometimes jealousies arise because one person's material is perceived to be infinitely superior or infinitely easier than someone else's. What is unfamiliar becomes ultimately threatening both to the workshop audience and the presenting director who is also bound to feel the very real gulf between himself and the group. In contrast, when everyone is working on the same exercise, and where everyone has a full understanding about what's going on, this common ground brings a sharper focus to the work, which thereby tends to bring the group together rather than apart.

Eventually separately done scenes can be brought to the workshop, but only much later in the training when a sense of trust and collective compassion have firmly been established. There are several excellent ways to introduce the workshop to formal scene work. One is to have students do the same scene from a particular play. Besides making sure that everyone is familiar with the material, this idea has the added advantage of letting the students see just how different the "same scene" can be, and just how important the signature of the director can be. Seeing the mark a director can make on exactly the same material is an eye-opening revelation for many of the students. And even those who were already aware of the impact a director can make, are still amazed because they have personally experienced it. A variation of this "same scene" approach is to have students pick any scene they want from the same play. This results in a variety of scenes, with a few perhaps doing exactly the same scene, but with everyone still knowing the play. A further advantage of either the same play or same scene approach is that it is fairly easy to schedule a meaningful script analysis session when there is but a single play to discuss. If script analysis is covered in a completely separate class, and if the workshop facilitator doesn't want students in relatively early work to spend a lot of time reading and analyzing, then an excellent choice to consider is doing complete plays that are five to ten minutes long. Granted there aren't a great many plays that fill this kind of a bill, but there are some such as:

- *24 Hours — A.M.*
  (12 very short plays, each based on the time of day, each written by a different playwright) Dramatists Play Service, 1983.
- *24 Hours — P.M.*
  (12 very short plays, each based on the time of day, each written by a different playwright) Dramatists Play Service, 1983.
- *Twenty-five Ten-Minute Plays from the Actor's Theatre of Louisville.*
  New York: Samuel French, Inc., 1989.

• Robert Mauro. *Two Character Plays for Student Actors*. Colorado Springs: Meriwether Publishing Ltd., 1988.

Each is no more than the typical five- to ten-minute scene, but the fact that they are complete plays means that even if the workshop hasn't read this material in advance, they will still be easily understood.

Working within a structure where everyone is familiar with the material, regardless of whether the exercises are from this book or from published plays, is also an obvious advantage in the critiquing process. Critiquing should take place after each scene where all members of the workshop as well as the facilitator enter into the discussion. To get the discussion started, it's a good idea to have a formal critiquer assigned before the scene begins; the assigned person begins, and the rest of the workshop members follow. The greatest let down for a director who has just presented a scene is to have no feedback. Silence will quite likely happen when all are working on separate scenes, but when the workshop is fully focused on the same work then there is automatically more willingness to contribute to the critiquing sessions. If the workshop is organized around teams, then there is not only a basic familiarity, but a familiarity formed from both having acted and directed the exercise.

A list of suggested critique questions is included with each exercise. The list is by no means designed to be slavishly followed; it is included simply as a conversation starter and source of ideas. Having a list of questions to fall back on is a way to bolster confidence in the critiquer, reinforcing the confidence already generated by having a solid understanding of the exercise. Some of the questions are completely objective, based on direct observation of what was presented, but there is no getting around the fact that subjectivity frequently enters into the critiquing process. Subjectivity should not be shied away from, but if anything exulted as that which makes theatre exciting. Many is the time when the very thing that one person loved is the very thing that another hated, but as long as the lover and the hater explain themselves as best they can, then the critiquing session will remain constructive and engaging. Critiquing is in and of itself an art form, and so when someone gives a particularly good critique it should be pointed out as such. One good critique has a way of begetting more, which is why the facilitator is advised to pick a particularly good critiquer at the start of the session. Inexperienced critiquers often tend to see everything as either all wonderful or all terrible, which is why one of the critique questions is always: What was your favorite moment, and what was your least favorite moment? Built into the phrasing of this question is an implicit balance, and a hint to the critiquer to do likewise whenever possible. Whenever someone says "I didn't really have a *least* favorite moment," this resistance is usually solved by simply asking the critiquer to think of himself as a film editor forced to cut twenty to thirty seconds, or by gently reminding the critiquer that the director wants to hear your real feelings, and that without this kind of openness less learning is the result.

The critiquing part of the workshop is an excellent way to gauge whether there is genuine openness amongst the group; if there is a consistent holding back, or a consistent wanting to play it safe with bland responses, then something needs to be done to create a more conducive workshop atmosphere. The more open the prevailing atmosphere of the group, the more that fear of judgments (one's own as well as those from others) will slowly dissipate. Regardless what is actually said in the critique, the through-line or subtext should be one of caring and wanting to help. Caring means being critical if the situation demands it, but it also means never losing sight of the need to nurture. When there is real openness, then it is possible to even go so far as asking a workshop member to "tamper" with a moment from another's work. Often tampering is prefaced with saying something such as, "the intent is not so much to make it better, but just to make it different." Tampering can be used to demonstrate a point from a variety of contexts, and it also is way of genuinely paying attention to another's work via a literal "hands on" approach. It takes openness and a sense of trust because it is a little like handing your baby over to another person. If someone is squeamish about tampering, either with respect to figuring out a specific moment to work with, or with exactly how to do it, side coach them not to think about the *best* way to change something, but rather to change something for no other reason than just for the sake of doing it. Once the self censor is relaxed, the student director will find tampering to be a highly communicative tool. In addition to tampering, replaying moments in general is a good idea, using the moments as a visual aid to clarify a particularly confusing point or interesting concept.

Maybe most significant of all is that a prevailing openness in the group will allow the student to do what he no doubt had in the back of his mind to begin with in joining the workshop — a desire to "open up" to the fascinating world of directing. Such an atmosphere will cultivate a capacity for joy where everything is done for the sheer pleasure of doing the work. When the world of the workshop really "works," a very contagious nothing without joy attitude permeates and fully fills the physical openness of the space.

Discovering the Darkness

Directing is a highly creative activity, and this book is centered around a series of challenging exercises that are designed, above all else, to cultivate creativity. All of the exercises are meant to be creative excursions into uncharted territories where new discoveries are the only possible pathways. In this sense, the exercises are genuine experiments, and a workshop centered around this work would become, to borrow Polish director Jerzy Grotowski's favorite term, a theatre "laboratory." With numerous experimental journeys ahead, it might be wise to ponder at least briefly what has to be the very heart and soul of this work — creativity.

In the four-part PBS television series, *The Creative Spirit*, an interesting parallel was made between creativity and darkness. Creativity is a willingness to play in the dark when the norm is to flutter about the light. Creative people are committed to delving into the darkness of the unknown. Everybody can see what's in the light, but the only true heroes are those who are willing to discover the new by facing the demons in the dark. Thinking about creativity in terms of light and dark imagery is reminiscent of the Sufi story about Nasrudin:

> "A man saw Nasrudin on his knees searching for something on the ground. 'What have you lost, Mulla?' he asked.
>
> " 'My key,' said Nasrudin.
>
> "So the man went down on his knees too and they both looked and looked for the key. After a time, the other man asked, 'Where exactly did you drop it?'
>
> " 'In my house,' answered Nasrudin.
>
> " 'Then why are you looking for it here?'
>
> " 'There's more light here than inside my house,' Nasrudin replied."[9]

Nasrudin teaches us that staying only in the light is a sure way never to find the key. Neglect the darkness and the key to creativity is forever lost. Not being afraid of the dark means a willingness to take risks so as to keep yourself open to new experiences of all kinds. Alan Alda puts it this way:

> The creative is the place where no one else has been. You have to leave the city of comfort and go into the wilderness of your intuition. You can't get there by bus, only by hard work, risking, and not quite knowing what you're doing. What you'll discover will be wonderful: yourself.[10]

Creativity cannot be separated from risk taking; creativity goes hand in hand with change, and there is often anxiety, fear, and disapproval associated with newness, but there is also the possibility for tremendous joy, excitement, and approval. Fear is a vital factor in any creative work, and Oscar Wilde, recognizing that anxiety is clearly the handmaiden of creativity, makes an important observation about this relationship between the two by saying, "The anxiety is unbearable. I only hope it lasts forever."[11]

Diving headlong into the dark pit of the unknown, no matter how creative the impulse, takes a substantial leap of faith and commitment. We love to keep our options as open as possible, but keep in mind that it's impossible to bungee jump by keeping one foot on the platform. Courage to commit to such a plunge, however, is

---

[9]Robert Ornstein, *The Psychology of Consciousness*, (New York: Viking Press, 1972), p. 187.

[10]Glen Van Ekeren, *Speaker's Sourcebook II*, (New Jersey: Prentice-Hall, 1994), p. 80.

[11]Daniel Goleman, et. al., *The Creative Spirit*, (New York: Penguin Books, 1992), p. 45.

largely predicated on the jumper's faith in the inherent safety of the elastic lifeline, albeit little more than a glorified rubber band. A workshop in directing should prod the student into taking a plunge into the fascinating depths of directing, but it should also be there to hold the director's hand in the dark, to reduce the anxiety of risk taking by assuring that the lifeline, give or take a little, is really there.

Each student's voyage of discovery is based on a single, fundamental principle: creativity increases as the director becomes more aware of his own creative acts. As the director develops the habit of paying attention to his own creativity, he will come to place greater trust in his creativity and instinctively turn to it when confronted with problems. As a way of maximizing this process, it is an excellent idea for the student director to keep a journal. Kept in a separate notebook, the journal becomes a way for the director to reflect and analyze his process. Writing about experiences of process increases the likelihood that the director will be able to recapture them. Paying more attention to the creative process is a way of letting it become a helpful habit, and letting what we know is truly within us start to become liberated.

Since anything we direct is inevitably a "direct" expression of who we are, the journal should reflect in a very personal way how our creativity can only happen when something within us is brought to life in something outside of us. Above all else the journal is a reminder to the student director that a premium needs to be placed on the process of the work, not simply the end product. Since empathy and under-standing of other people is vital to the workshop, and to the directing process in general, reflection about specific workshop members is also a worthy topic. In dis-cussing other people, the student director can also reflect on his own interpersonal intelligence and sensitivity — his ability to "read" other people, to speculate about what motivates them, and how to work effectively with them. Harvard develop-mental psychologist Howard Gardner reminds us that a sensitivity to others is indeed a type of intelligence, as he says:

> Traditional tests of intelligence ignore this knowledge of other persons, perhaps because the academics who designed these tests tended to be solitary thinkers. But if intelligence tests had been invented by politi-cians or business people, this form of intelligence would head the list. Even in some very young children, a special sensitivity to others is evident. They are the ones who observe other children with great care or who are able to influence others to behave in ways that are desirable to them.[12]

If teams are part of the workshop design, then there is an intense interpersonal interaction built into the system to begin with that will be further reinforced with journal entries focusing on workshop members — in other words, it has the advan-tage of keeping it, so to speak, all in the family. Student directors should be

---

[12]Daniel Goleman, et. al., *The Creative Spirit*, (New York: Penguin Books, 1992), p. 76-77.

encouraged to bring the journal to class, and form the habit of making entries during class such as after an exercise, or during a particular discussion. Specific entries might consist of:

- Responses to a specific exercise or scene.
- New insights, understanding, ideas, etc.
- Questions about an concept.
- Discussion about why a particular exercise was valuable or problematic.
- Reaction to other's work.
- Reactions to theatre experienced outside of the workshop.
- Reactions related to observing a rehearsal of an experienced director at work.

From the journal and the workshop exercises the student director is bound to learn a lot about theatre directing, but maybe even more valuable is what he will learn about his creative self. Well beyond the boundaries of theatre directing, creativity can be an asset in every part of life: family, work, and community. Creativity allows us to better our lot; it allows the subsistence farmer to dedicate less of life to sweating in the sun, just as it allows Tom Sawyer to better his lot by getting his aunt's fence painted without much effort. When we are creative, we draw on the passion, persistence, and willingness to take risks that make us feel alive.

What, then, is the essence of creativity? Creativity involves bringing something new to birth. Being creative, says Howard Gardner, "means that you do something which is first of all unusual."[13] Gardner is quick to add that it is not enough just to do something unusual, since standing on your head might be unusual, but not necessarily valued by others as creative. In other words, the unusual activity has to be valued in some way by a receptive and appropriate audience. Keeping an audience in mind is an obvious activity for theatre directors. The creative director is someone who gives other people, whether they be actors, designers, or the actual audience, a different way of looking at, or feeling about, the world. Theatre work drives home the point that creativity is not something that's entirely within the individual — it involves reaching other people. Creativity comes into existence during the process of interacting with others. A creative idea, therefore, has to be not only new, but valued by a receptive audience as well.

Creativity is like falling in love — it begins with an affinity for something. People who care passionately about what they are doing don't give up easily, which is what Thomas Edison had in mind when he said, "Sticking to it is the genius." We are more creative when we are engaged in a task that is inherently fun and challenging rather than a task that is merely work. Passion is the prime mover of creativity and it means wanting to do something for the sheer pleasure rather than for

[13]Daniel Goleman, et. al., *The Creative Spirit*, (New York: Penguin Books, 1992), p. 25.

12

any prize or competition. The best reward is simply the sheer delight and joy that can permeate an activity. Shakespeare perhaps put it best, "No profit grows where is no pleasure taken, in short, study what thou dost affect" (*The Taming of the Shrew*, Act I, Scene 1). As much as possible, let your creative activities be intrinsically, not extrinsically motivated.

The creative process involves a process of taking in new ideas, of being thrown into a disequilibrium and trying to reach a resolution with a new synthesis. Creativity involves combining and rearranging known elements in a new way — integrating parts into a coherent whole. This kind of integrating, says Dr. Teresa Amabile, a psychologist at Brandeis University whose research is on creativity often "includes the ability to turn things over in your mind, like trying to make the strange familiar and the familiar strange."[14] A perfect example of this is provided by Picasso, who one day was looking around his yard when he focused upon an old rusty bicycle resting against the porch, and he noticed that the handlebars reminded him of a bull. In his studio he transformed the familiar old bike into a wonderfully strange sculpture of a raging bull. Many of the exercises capitalize on the technique of taking things out of their ordinary context and creating a new pattern for them so that the familiar is made strange. Another skill useful to creativity, and one that is used in several of the exercises, is the ability to draw comparisons and analogies. Many breakthroughs are made by juxtaposing ideas that ordinarily do not go together, or detecting a hidden pattern of connections among things.

Breaking habitual ways of doing things is perhaps the best way of bringing about creative ideas. Heading into the unknown, old habits may not work because they tend to inhibit creativity and change. By breaking away from the habitual and the ordinary, in what is usually referred to as "breaking the set," there is the possibility of inventing a new pattern. The idea of breaking set is suddenly to fracture the routine consciousness that puts your powers of observation to sleep. Too often we go through life on automatic pilot where we become habitually fixed in our ways of seeing, and our expectation of how things are supposed to be replaces our seeing. All of the exercises in this class are designed to get the student director to look at things in a new ways. When habit is taken away, there is the possibility for even the ordinary to become potentially strange and exciting, just as it does when we are sightseeing in a completely new place.

A journey into uncharted, new terrain requires some precautions and practical considerations. What happens when we become fearful instead of fascinated with the darkness of the unknown? What happens when we become blocked and/or overly critical of our work? University of California psychologist Dean Simonton argues that when creative energies won't flow on one problem or project, it often helps to turn to a completely different one. As he says:

---

[14]Daniel Goleman, et. al., *The Creative Spirit*, (New York: Penguin Books, 1992), p. 30.

Most of history's great creators didn't just have their hands in one basket. They would have lots of things going on. If they ran into obstacles in one area, they put it aside for a while and moved on to something else. By having multiple projects, you're more likely to have a breakthrough somewhere...you're always moving along.[15]

It's easy to apply this thinking to the exercises in this book. There are plenty of scenes and projects to work on, and so an excellent suggestion to the student director is to look ahead at the upcoming work so that shifting from activity to activity, at least on the mental level, is possible. Each exercise begins with an "overview" of the work, making it very easy to quickly understand the basic requirements.

Another advantage of looking ahead to oncoming scene and project work is that there is frequently an incubation period for any creative work. A creative idea, as with any birth, requires a necessary gestation period. Oftentimes after struggling unsuccessfully with a problem, we find that when we come back to the problem after a night's rest, or a day's interruption, that a bright idea appears and we solve the problem easily. Most of us have had the experience of immersing ourselves in a problem, and then putting it aside for a while only to have the solution to the problem seemingly pop out of nowhere when we least expected it. Even though it seemed to have come "out of nowhere," chances are that it came from a chance observation that magnetically connected itself to the incubating problem. The incubation period is like a simmering stew, it is a comparatively passive phase when much of what goes on occurs outside of our focused awareness, in the mind's unconscious.

A creative project begins with the prospect of facing the darkness of the unknown, but the unconscious or incubatory part of the process becomes the very heart of the darkness. Mystery and darkness characterize the unconscious simply because it cannot be directly observed, and yet the unconscious is a vast storehouse of everything one knows, including those things that the mind can't readily call into awareness. Unconscious thinking is commonly referred to as "hunch," "incubation," "insight," or "intuition," and this is why many of our creative ideas seem to come from someplace other than the consciousness (the "aha" reaction). We often use the term intuition with respect to creativity, and here the idea is that intuition means relinquishing control of the thinking mind and trusting the vision of the unconscious. For the incubation process to happen at all, there has to be an initial struggle, and this preparatory phase should not by any means be taken lightly. Thomas Edison rightly reminds us that ninety-nine percent of genius is perspiration, not inspiration. Only with preparation, often accompanied by frustration and despair, will the simmering magic in the dark really have a chance to do the creative cookery.

Shame the teacher who reprimanded us with a "stop daydreaming and get to work" because it's moments of dreaming when we are most open to insights from the

[15]Daniel Goleman, et. al., *The Creative Spirit*, (New York: Penguin Books, 1992), p. 44.

unconscious mind. Daydreaming and relaxing are sensationally useful in the creative process. Modern life does its ever-loving best to keep us from daydreaming, but there will always be private moments when you can kick back and relax. Many people find that their most creative ideas occur while they are taking a shower or shaving, or driving to work. Creative ideas often come at a time when we are thinking about something else, or not really seemingly thinking at all.

Each exercise has very specific demands. Focusing on specific problems with specific goals is far more conducive to stimulating creativity than a more open-ended, free-for-all approach. Constraints (the rules) of the exercises are the very things which make creativity possible. Constraints map out a territory of possibilities for exploration and experimentation, all of which has the potential of opening doors to completely new places. To drop constraints from an exercise is to invite not creativity, but confusion.

The heartbeat of a healthy directing workshop is wonderfully expressed in three simple phrases:

> *Tell me and I will forget*
> *show me and I may not remember*
> *involve me and I will understand.*[16]

Above all else, this book advocates active learning. Directing is doing, and workshops for directors in training are worthless unless they are totally experiential.

Prepare for your journey by reading ahead about your itinerary, and then let there be darkness! Daydreams and discoveries await...bon voyage!

---

[16]Unknown author — clipping on the studio wall of Spokane artist, Harold Balazs. See Andrew Strickman, "Art's Renaissance," *The Pacific Northwest Inlander.* Vol. 2, #33, May 31, 1995, p. 11.

CHAPTER 2
THE SILENT SEVEN

Why begin with silence? Part of the answer is hinted at in our everyday vocabulary — we go to hear a concert, but we go to "see" a play. The philosophy behind "the silent seven" is simple: starting in silence — total silence — is the best way to learn the basics of directing because it obliterates what might be best described as the "talking heads" syndrome. Take away the words and the danger of too much telling (relying too much on words) and too little showing (strong visual communication) is not going to be a problem.

Emphasizing silence goes against two sacred views. One is the almost biblical belief that speech is the characterizing signature of humanity and the other is the theatrical reflection of this, which traditionally spouts that the dominant element of the theatre has to be dialogue. But sacred views aside, starting in silence in many ways mirrors what has been happening for the last twenty or so years in contemporary theatre. Audiences and artists have become increasingly distrustful of language, and often silence has been allowed to supersede speech as a way of communicating "unspoken experience beyond the limitations of human consciousness, such as fear, longing, and death, as well as the unspeakable experience beyond the comprehension of humanity such as the dehumanizing or bestial."[1]

Is there a specific reason for the desecration of speech in the theatre? Exactly why and when this trend in theatre started is worthy of a dissertation length debate, and is well beyond the scope of this book. Some see the seeds for this perceptual change happening in the shifting ground of the late nineteenth century, where the 100 year range from one *fin de siècle* to another has seen a benevolent technology bringing unprecedented improvements to our lives, but it has also seen a bestial technology bringing dehumanizing threats of global annihilation. Critic George Steiner argues that the dehumanizing disasters of world wars and the Nazi holocaust cannot be articulated in words; he says that "these unspeakable events quite literally exceed the boundaries of language because, inhuman, they defy verbal expression."[2] Drama critic Mike Steel attributes this perceptual revolution to the much more recent events of the last twenty-five years by suggesting that:

> The specter of politicians saying one thing while TV cameras off
> in Vietnam showed the opposite; the increasing deluge of hype, spin,

---

[1]Leslie Kane, *The Language of Silence: On the Unspoken and the Unspeakable in Modern Drama*, (London and Toronto: Associated University Press, 1984), p. 14.

[2]Ibid.

buzz words and ad-babble; the realization that language was constructed and controlled, giving rise to poststructuralism and the politicalization of words; television itself with its short sound bites and MTV images; the "post-literacy" of the technological age; the ever louder, more intense volume of the world from rock records to Broadway amplification; actors trained more to caress the microphone than to project into theatre spaces; breakthroughs in theatre technology from lighting to sound to projections, and so on, take your pick.[3]

Directors such as Peter Brook, Giorgio Strehler, Peter Stein and Robert Wilson have led the way in emphasizing the visual over the verbal. Their way of working with the visual isn't realistic; their "visual" is much more in keeping with the visual of modern art — "a visual filled with metaphor, with poetry, unexpected effects, [and] new ways of looking at the word."[4] Instead of letting the word dominate their theatre, they have found a way to make the word an equal partner. Led by the Absurdists, playwrights as well have increasingly intimated through disjunctive language and evocative silences that words do not adequately express feelings and communicate needs.

While the silent exercises of this chapter seem to be in simpatico with current artistic sensibilities, it is important to distinguish between a theatre aesthetic and a training approach. The similarity is more coincidence than anything else, and the intent of the silent training is not to advocate a certain type of theatre; taking away the words is simply a more efficient way for the beginning director to learn about the basics of staging — concepts which are totally visual to begin with. Silent work takes away the confusing variable of speaking and provides the beginning director with better "laboratory" conditions to "test" what is being learned. This approach is all the more necessary because, despite the recent trend, beginning directors still have more faith in the verbal than the visual. As any teacher of improvisation will tell you, put two actors together and they feel compelled to create contrived dialogue — they become way too text oriented. Beginning directors often fall into the same trap of worshiping only the word because they inadvertently adhere to the traditional idea that theatre is language and that, therefore, they must focus on the talk. Words are important, but leave it to a playwright to remind us that "in the theatre, everything must transform into the visible and sensible."[5] Many alternative approaches begin without any formal text at all, but even when there is a text, the text at best is limited. As Gaston Baty wrote:

---

[3]Mike Steel, "The Not So Empty Space," *American Theatre* 10, no. 10 (October 1993): 20. Mike Steel is the drama critic for the Minneapolis Star Tribune.

[4]Ibid.: 21.

[5]Fredrich Duerrenmatt, quoted by Randolph Goodman, *Drama on Stage*, (New York: Rinehart and Winston, 1961), p. 381.

A text cannot say everything. It can only go as far as all words go. Beyond them begins another zone, a zone of mystery, of silence, which one calls the atmosphere, the ambiance, the climate, as you wish. It is that which is the work of the director to express.[6]

Convincingly motivating the silence is the major challenge in each of the seven exercises. If the motivation is inadequate, the workshop audience will constantly be wondering why the characters don't talk. It's very possible that the beginning director has not thought too much about the ramifications of silence, but the task of directing often includes the fringe benefit of having to look at something in a completely new way. Thinking about the multidimensional facets of silence is a way of generating ideas and safeguarding against clichéd approaches.

Just a bit of reflection reveals that silence can be thought of as either positive or negative. Silence may be seen as positive when there is a chance for personal exploration, but negative when there is somehow a failure of language — an absence of communication. Silence can reflect the perfect equilibrium of body and spirit, or it can suggest the imbalance of solitary confinement. The Quakers stressed the seriousness of silence as opposed to the superficiality of talk, but there is also the Pentecostal speaking in tongues and public praying that clearly values noise over silence. The silence of a telephone is positive when the solitude brings about creative work, but the same silence is negative when someone is anxiously awaiting a particular call. Silence may be seen as positive even when it suggests the omission of something negative such as "if you can't say something nice, don't say anything." Likewise, silence may be seen as negative when it suggests the omission of something positive such as the omission of a greeting, which constitutes being snubbed. When two people know each other so well that they need to say less and less, silence is positive. But silence is negative when it suggests a wall of separation between two people. In an early scene of the film *Two for the Road*, Audrey Hepburn looks at an older couple at a nearby table in a restaurant and asks her lover Richard Harris, "What kind of people eat without talking to each other?" to which Harris responds with distaste, "Married people."

While silence is the common denominator for each of the seven exercises, the exercises are very different from one another because each exercise has a very distinctive:

- Situational requirement (and)

- Point of concentration (P.O.C.)

The "point of concentration" helps to isolate a particular concept or technique from complex overlapping factors. Even though factors such as body positions, stage

---

[6]Quoted by Helen Krich Chinoy, "The Emergence of the Director," in *Directing a Play*, Toby Cole and Helen Krich Chinoy, eds., (Indianapolis: The Bobbs-Merrill Co., 1953), p. 63.

areas, and right and left movement are inextricably connected, the point of concentration puts a spotlight on a single factor, and thereby keeps the student director from having to juggle too many theatrical balls at once. Point of Concentration is a term coined by Viola Spolin in her *Improvisation for the Theatre*. Spolin's book mostly speaks to student actors, but her discussion about point of concentration is every bit as applicable to student directors, and it is very much in keeping with the overall philosophy of the training exercises in this book; as she says:

> Presenting material in a segmented way frees a player for action at every stage of his development. It sorts theatre experience into such minute (simple and familiar) bits of itself that each detail is easily recognizable and does not overwhelm or frighten anyone away.[7]

In terms of situational requirements and point of view, the breakdown of the silent seven are:

SCENE	TITLE	SITUATION	P.O.C.
Scene 1	Silent Tension	The tension between characters is so strong that they are unable to speak.	Visual pauses
Scene 2	Sounds of Silence	The characters are so over-whelmed with emotion as to be bereft of speech.	Body positions
Scene 3	Silently Familiar, Silently Strange	The silence results in something familiar becoming something strange.	Right and left
Scene 4	Silent Journey	The silence centers around a literal or figurative journey.	Stage areas
Scene 5	Breaking Silent Boundaries	The silence centers around boundaries which are defined and broken.	Psychological areas
Scene 6	Silent Status Swapping	The sharply divided status between the two characters is somehow swapped or reversed in silence.	Level
Scene 7	Broken Silence Breakdown	The silence at some point is broken by one or both of the characters.	Visual progressions

Each scene description will detail the reasons specific items were paired together. We live in a world where the word has supremacy, and where traditionally the power of the spoken word has dominated the theatre, but with the "silent seven" the theatrical tables are very ready to be turned.

---

[7]Viola Spolin, *Improvisation for the Theatre*, (Evanston: Northwestern University Press, 1963), p. 22.

DIRECTIONS: SCENE 1
SILENT TENSION
(Experimenting With Visual Pauses)

Speech is silver,
silence is golden.

— **German Proverb**

OVERVIEW

Using *2 actors* from your team, create a 2-3 minute scene with clearly established characters, situation, and location (the who, the what, and the where) in which *the tension between characters is so strong that they are unable to speak*. In addition to communicating clearly the who, what, and where through the silence, plan on highlighting at least one important moment through the use of a *visual pause*.[8]

An example might be: *Where:* a bedroom, *Who:* two robbers, and *What:* looking for jewelry, but afraid of getting caught.

Create a workable ground plan by using available stock set pieces. Establish with the other workshop directors the specific set pieces that may be used, and even if other stock pieces are available, adhere only to the agreed upon units. A typical stock list might be:

• 4 chairs	• 4 cubes
• 1 small round table	• 1 sofa bench
• 1 single bed sized platform	• 2 benches

VISUAL PAUSES

In the fast moving, flamboyant theatre of Kabuki, the actors will upon occasion strike a *mie*, the traditional freeze which is held to allow the audience to appreciate fully the moment. The purpose of the pause is to draw attention to a key moment in the play. Film directors sometimes use freeze framing for much the same effect.

Visual pauses of this nature are blatantly presentational, but there is ample opportunity to make use of the visual pause in the representational, more realistic theatre, as well. It is a part of realistic theatre simply because it is a natural behavior of everyday life. Just a few of the possible reasons a character might stop moving might be due to:

---

[8]Minus the visual pause idea, credit for the basic concept of this exercise must be given to Viola Spolin. See her *Improvisation for the Theatre*, (Evanston: Northwestern University Press, 1963), p. 188.

- Thinking (lost in thought)   • Listening intently
- Suddenly getting an idea   • Resting
- Fear   • Disgust
- Shock   • Taking time to assimilate something

Visual pauses may involve a single character or a group of characters. In a sword fight, a visual pause might occur, for example, just after one of the fighters knocks the sword out of the opponent's hand — the pause being just enough time for both fighters to assess the situation. The "take" in comedy is a visual pause that has been "taken" to the extreme so as oftentimes to clue the audience into the joke, yet the impulse behind the take has its counterpart in real life as well.

Even though there are very down-to-earth behavioral reasons for the occurrence of visual pauses in realistic theatre, it's interesting that in performance the net effect is not that far removed from the *mie* of Kabuki theatre. The visual pause in realistic theatre, similarly to the *mie*, has the snapshot like effect of drawing our attention to the moment at hand. Just the fact that it provides a break in the visual rhythm is oftentimes enough to spotlight and, in some cases, suggest commentary on the emotional interplay. A director might choose to capitalize on a **single** visual pause, using it, perhaps, at the climax of the scene, or a director might decide to only bring into a play **multiple** visual pauses as a means of intensifying feeling or building tension. Imagine, for instance, the stalking killer making strategic pauses in his cat and mouse dance of death with the victim. A visual pause might reflect the calm before the storm, or any number of other possible outcomes, but the common denominator of all visual pauses is that it focuses attention on the fixed moment. Our first association with the word "pause" is probably the verbal pause, which offers tremendous possibilities. But the visual pause is every bit as valuable a technique to be taken into consideration by the director.

MOTIVATE THE SILENCE

The challenge of this exercise is to bring one or more visual pauses into play, and to create a situation that calls for silence. Make sure that the silence of the scene doesn't stretch our credibility, and that the silence is at all times well motivated.

Perhaps the ideal director for a silent scene might be the Taoist philosopher, Chuang-Tse who said: "Words exist only because of meaning. But where can I find a man who has forgotten words so that I may speak to him?"

Coach your actors to avoid **indicating**; indicating is caused by a fear that what is happening will not be communicated, and so the suspicious performer does much more than is necessary. Indicating is something always to guard against, but given the demands of silence in this exercise, the tendency toward indicating is especially likely to be a problem. Remind your actors that silence has the potential of creating a flow of energy and openness between performers. This scene is nonverbal, but not necessarily soundless: sighing, groaning, laughing, and even screaming are possible. Allowing this kind of release will help promote a more natural flow of energy in your performers.

A FIRST EXERCISE

Silent Tension has proved to be an effective first exercise for several reasons. Since the scene is silent, there is great dependency upon the visual, and yet the very basics of composition (body positions, stage area, level, focus, etc.) have yet to be discussed. The beginning student is forced to rely upon instincts and intuition as the only available means for getting the job done. While specific technique and principle have momentarily been ignored, the exercise with its specific problem solving demands is still a very real and valid directing experience. All directing involves problem solving, and even when the director is a seasoned professional backed with years of technical expertise, there will always be a prominent place for instinct and intuition in the work.

Having to integrate a visual pause into the work is, in itself, helpful in a first exercise. Visual pauses are all around us in everyday life, and yet few people give them much thought. As a concept it is easily understood once explained, but it is gen-erally not one that most beginning students have previously thought about. For this reason, the problem at hand is very new to most everyone, and regardless of the varying levels of experience, it will help everyone begin the journey on as equal a footing as possible. Anytime there is a new way of paying attention to something, the novelty alone will help in what psychologists call "breaking set," which refers to fracturing the routine consciousness that tends to put the mind to sleep. Breaking pat-terns of behavior, breaking our fixed ways of seeing, is a proven way to strengthen creativity. If after completing this exercise, the student is left craving specific tech-niques, so much the better; an exercise is perhaps most beneficial when it pushes us to want to do and learn more.

As a first exercise, I encourage students to preblock completely the scene on paper before working with their actors. Such a procedure is by no means the only way to work, but it is an excellent training aid for the beginning director. It reduces the element of chance, and allows the director to conceptualize the work fully. It also has the advantage of saving rehearsal time. Preblocking by no means prevents a director from changing things during a rehearsal, it simply provides the director with a detailed game plan to begin the work.

CRITIQUE

1. Was the situation (the **who**, the **what**, and the **where**) well communicated?

2. Did the players communicate through silence? Was there any indicating? If so, was it distracting?

3. Did the players seem to use inner dialogue?

4. Was the silence convincing, or was it, in part or in whole, too much of a stretch?

5. Was there more or less focus on a particular character?

6. Where were the visual pauses? What effect did they have, and what motivated their use? Was their placement in the scene effective?

7. Favorite moment? Least favorite moment?

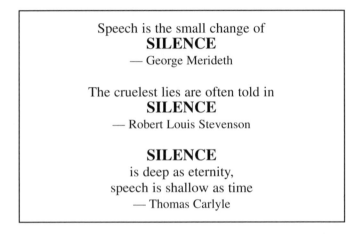

Speech is the small change of
SILENCE
— George Merideth

The cruelest lies are often told in
SILENCE
— Robert Louis Stevenson

SILENCE
is deep as eternity,
speech is shallow as time
— Thomas Carlyle

SOUNDS OF SILENCE
(Experimenting With Body Positions and Music)

Do you ever wonder what is music?
Who invented it and what for and all that?
And why hearing a certain song can make a whole entire time of your life
suddenly just rise up and stick in your brain?

— Lynda Barry
The Good Times Are Killing Me

OVERVIEW

Create a two-character silent scene that uses ***music*** to dramatize characters in a situation where they are ***so overwhelmed with emotion as to be bereft of speech***. As always, strive to make the who, what, and where as clear as possible, and strive for strong storytelling with a definite beginning, middle and end. In addition to using music as a means of tapping into the emotional core of the scene, plan also to use the communicative power of ***body positions*** fully to reinforce the "sounds of silence." In working with body positions, pay special attention to the nuances inherent in the relationship between ***head focus and body position***.

MUSIC AND SILENCE

Music and silence may at first appear to be opposites — one is fully with and one is fully without sound. Such thinking stems from the fact that we live in a world where the word has supremacy over silence. Language, not silence, is what makes us really human, and this supremacy of the word (and sound in general) leads to thinking of silence as simply that which happens when we stop talking or stop playing music. From this it is a simple step to interpret silence as not only an absence of sound, but an absence of communication. Since music is something heard, it shares with the spoken word a much higher status than silence.

But sound versus silence thinking fails to take into account the all-important bond of emotion between music and silence. Music is a direct tap to the emotions, and in this respect, silence is music's soul mate — not opposite. The most profound experiences of life tend to be wordless moments; the death of a loved one, the birth of a child, or the departure of a dear friend are emotionally loaded moments which often leave us speechless. To be struck speechless is not necessarily to be struck incommunicative. Silence in such situations may still be able successfully to express the awe, respect, reverence, joy, loss, or love that is demanded of the moment. Words

25

often fail with overwhelming emotions on account of their tendency to intellectualize and abstract, whereas music and silence are much more, as Duke in *Twelfth Night* puts it — "the food of love."

Film and television directors frequently spotlight a silent sequence with music. Such use may permit the film to slip into a more poetic or playful style or it may be used expressionistically to convey the inner feelings of one or more of the characters. In using silence and music in this way, modern films are really perpetuating a very long tradition. From the very beginning, the so-called silent films were never really silent since they were always accompanied by a local organist or pianist. In the back of Thomas Edison's mind was the idea of combining music and sound because he felt his "living pictures" invention would do for the eye what the phonograph could do for the ear, and in 1887 he "aimed at putting eyes into the phonograph."[9] Famous silent screen actress, Lillian Gish, in 1969 said: "many of our modern films seem to be returning to the purer form of telling a story in motion pictures, depending upon music and animation rather than words."[10] Film directors past and present sense the enormous potential of music instead of words to frame and enhance the story being told. In the theatre music is less of an ever-present convention, but the communicative potential is every bit as possible. All this discussion is not meant to advocate doing your scene in the style of a silent movie, since oftentimes there was an actual mouthing of the words which is very different from the fully justified silence asked of this exercise. The discussion is simply meant to highlight the all important emotional parallel between silence and music.

Even though the interplay of silence and music is basically pretty easy to accept and understand as a convention, it is relatively difficult to articulate fully why the two work so well together. The air waves and cables, what with all the commercials and MTV-type videos, are flooded with many moments of what we could consider fully justified silent scenes with music, but this does not make it any easier to "put into words" what is aesthetically taking place. A poetic approach is probably the only hope of explaining the mysterious bond between silence and music, and this is exactly what Max Picard does in his evocative *The World of Silence*. About music and silence he says:

> The sound of music is not, like the sound of words, opposed, but rather parallel to silence. It is as though the sounds of music were being driven over the surface of silence. Music is silence, which in dreaming begins to sound. Silence is never more audible than when the last sound of music has died away. Music is far ranging, and could occupy the whole of space. This does not in fact happen, for music occupies space very slowly, shyly, rhythmically, always returning to the same basic

[9]Charles Hofmann, *Sounds for the Silents*, (New York: Drama Book Specialists, 1970), p. 2.
[10]Ibid., Forword.

melodies so that it might seem that the sounds of music never moved away at all, that music were everywhere and yet always in a definite limited place. In music the distance and nearness of space, the limitless and the limited are all together in one gentle unity that is a comfort and a benefaction to the soul. For however far the soul may range in music it is everywhere protected and brought home safely again. This is why music has such a calming effect on nervous people: it brings a wideness to the soul in which the soul can be without fear.[11]

Maybe the most radical view of relationship between music and silence is brought to mind by avant-garde composer John Cage. Silence as both a subject and a form of expression is used by Cage in a musical composition he wrote for piano called *4'33*. His musical composition for supposedly piano subsists solely of silence — no music is ever played. Cage's intent is for both the performer and instrument to remain completely silent so that the audience can focus all of its attention on the random sounds that happen to filter into the area. Cage, in using silence as the main fabric of the piece, is highlighting the nonabsoluteness of silence. Silence to Cage is a fiction because there are always nonintended sounds and noises that can be elevated to the status of music.[12] His composition was inspired by looking at the blank canvases of Rauschenberg and discovering that absolute silence did not exist. The absurdity of silence fully hit home to Cage when he was taken into a sound-proof room, called an anechoic chamber, in the physics laboratory at Harvard. In the chamber he antici-pated total silence, but in point of fact he heard two sounds — one high and one low. In coming out of the chamber he was told that the high sound was his nervous system, and the low one was his blood circulating.[13] From this point on he never looked upon silence in the same way.

As with many aesthetic topics, words (and even John Cage) will only take us so far, and yet the world abounds with ideas for practical applications. Artistic choices that should be considered in this exercise concerning music are:

- ***The source of the music.*** It can be used *realistically*, coming from a natural source, such as when Joe from William Saroyan's *The Time of Your Life* plays the jukebox, or when the Jewish orchestra plays in Chekhov's *The Cherry Orchard*. Or it can be used more *expressionisti-cally*, such as when Blanche from Tennessee Williams' *A Streetcar Named Desire* is haunted by memories of her dead lover.

- ***The duration of the music.*** There can be music throughout the entire scene, or it might be used intermittently. Keep in mind Max Picard's

---

[11]Max Picard, *The World of Silence*, (Chicago: Henry Regnery Co., 1952), p. 27

[12]Adam Jaworski, *The Power of Silence*, (London: Sage Publications, 1993), p. 161-162.

[13]Ibid.

point that "silence is never more audible than when the last sound of music has died away." The moments when the music is brought in or out can be every bit as important as the musical selection itself. If the music is not constant, then there needs to be some kind of justification for its coming in or out. Whether the music fades in or out, or more directly cuts on or off is also an important factor.

- *The selection of music.* Any kind of music (classical, pop, jazz, rock, etc.) with or without lyrics is fair game. A single selection is fine, or several selections are possible. If you have the means and the inclination, even multitrack, sound on sound mixes are not out of the question. There also is the possibility that the choice of music is deliberately playing against the prevailing mood of the scene for a particular effect.

- *In sync with the silent action.* The music must be carefully integrated with the action. The music might provide a *general* frame to enhance the action, or it might provide an extremely *specific*, beat-by-beat syncopation with the staging. Or maybe it begins as a general frame, but ends as a very specific one. There are several valid variations to consider along these lines. The characters may be aware of the music or oblivious to it (as in most films). Maybe the music is used to anticipate an important moment, or maybe the music is used to create a lag effect where it holds onto the mood long after the specific moment has passed. Maybe the music is deliberately out of sync completely with the given action and/or mood in order to create a specific effect.

- *The volume of the music.* Obviously there is not the usual problem with underscoring of having to balance the level of the music with the spoken dialogue, but volume is still an important factor. Maybe the intent is for the music to be almost subliminal, or maybe it is in and of itself a force meant to be very definitely noticed.

- *The direction of the music.* It may not make any difference where the music emanates, or it may make a considerable difference.

Maybe the most important point of all is to keep in mind that the interplay of music and silence has potential for directors far beyond the dimensions of this exercise. With actual texts, the playwright sometimes provides valuable ideas for music. Tennessee Williams, for instance, has Tom in *The Glass Menagerie* tell us that "The play is a memory…In memory everything seems to happen to music."[14] More often than not, however, it is up to the director to interrelate music and silence imaginatively. For instance, in William Ball's production of *Tiny Alice* at the American Conservatory Theatre, a silent moment with music was created when Julian made his

---

[14]Tennessee Williams, *The Glass Menagerie*, (New York: New Directions Books, 1970), p. 23.

28

final, futile escape to the cataclysmic sounds of "Dies Irae" in Verdi's *Requiem*.[15] As Julian fell down the giant stairway he was trying to climb, the fanfares climaxed as red banners streamed from the doorway he was unable to open. As with any tool music may be overused, but when used carefully it can be pure magic. With all of its very useful variations, music and/or silence should definitely be a valued possession in any director's tool kit.

BODY POSITIONS

Just as music is so well suited to expressing the nuances of variably shifting moods, there is strong communicative potential in the "musical plasticity" of body positions. Variety in body positions adds a great deal of visual interest to a scene, and is a very powerful communicative tool. As the diagram indicates, generally the more open an actor is to the audience, the stronger the position. It's no surprise that full front is the strongest position, with the quarter and profile positions ranking second and third, but it may not be immediately obvious as to why full back is stronger than the three-quarter position. Full back demands more focus than three-quarter because of the tension created by not being able to see the actor's face and the larger body mass.

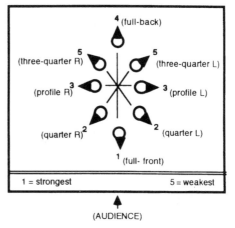

This hierarchy of strength is based on body positions in relation to the audience, but just as important is body position in relation to other characters. In a two-character scene, the actors may ***share*** the scene (equal focus), or one actor may ***give*** the scene to the other. Changing body positions is an excellent way to help shift focus from one character to another. Body positions can also be used to focus on a specific stage or off-stage area. Planning specifically where you want the audience to watch at any given moment is a vital part of the blocking process, and the skillful handling of body positions is an excellent tool with which to accomplish this.

Besides focus concerns, there is the all-important factor of ***body language*** inherent in the body positions. For instance, in the everyday world, when two people are in simpatico, they will stand the same way, or mirror each other with harmonious spatial relationships. Turning toward or away from another character has numerous interpretive possibilities, as do more subtle physical shifts between two people. Protecting personal space, extroverted or introverted impulses, are just a few of the

---

[15]Robert Cohen & John Harrop, *Creative Play Direction*, (New Jersey: Prentice-Hall, Inc., 1984), p. 163.

many psychological ramifications that can be effectively expressed through body positions. Beat changes or changes in a character's tactic are often reflected in the body language of positioning.

Keep in mind that body positions can be strengthened or weakened by the ***direction the head is turned***. For instance, a full-front position can be weakened by turning the head profile, just as a three-quarter position can be strengthened by turning the head profile. Interrelating head turns with body position offers a wealth of possibilities for creating communicative body language, as well as greatly increasing the variety of approaches possible for creating a visual progression. Think of the potential for visual progression in a scene in which the head positions were always at odds with the body positions, and what an impact there could be when body and head angles become aligned for the first time during the climax.

MOTIVATE THE SILENCE

The judicious use of music and body positions is all secondary to the primary objective of motivating the silence. The challenge of the exercise is to find the kind of silence that is able to supersede the spoken word in emotionally charged situations. The silence may be partially motivated by using conventional places of silence such as churches, courtrooms, schools, libraries, hospitals, funeral homes, battle sites, and the like, but the primary motivation must stem from overwhelming emotion. There are a great many possibilities as to why someone might be struck speechless, and given that there are two characters in this situation where the terrain for this kind of silence is vast indeed. Important questions to ask might be:

- Do both characters relate equally to the silence?
- Does one or the other of the characters seem to "own" the silence?
- Does the silence of the scene help to bind or sever the relationship?
- Does the silence seem to reveal or hide emotions?
- Does the silence come across as positive or negative presence?

CRITIQUE

1. Was the situation (the ***who***, ***what***, and ***where***) of the scene clearly communicated? Was there a definite beginning, middle, and end?
2. Was the music in any way distracting, or did it enhance the scene? Would someone unfamiliar with the demands of this exercise be consciously aware of the music? Was the music ***generally*** or ***closely*** in sync with the action?
3. Was the silence fully justified?

4. Was there variety in the use of body positions? Did the choice of body positions help shift the focus between the two characters? Were the choices in body positions justified psychologically? Was there effective interplay of body position and head focus?

5. Was there any indicating or did the players communicate through silence?

6. Were there any effective visual pauses?

7. Favorite moment? Least favorite moment?

SILENTLY FAMILIAR, SILENTLY STRANGE

(Experimenting With Right and Left)

The world, dear Agnes, is a strange affair.

— Molière
L' Ecole des Femmes (1662)
Act II, Scene 6

OVERVIEW

Create a two-character silent scene in which *something familiar becomes something strange*. Justify the situation and the silence by strategically bringing into play the dynamic differences between right and left. Both the ground plan and the staging should be carefully designed with the vectors of right and left in mind. As a means of further highlighting the differences between the right and the left, the scene will be presented two ways:

• First, as originally staged.

• Second, as a mirror-imaged staging of the scene where everything is identical except for the fact that right and left with both the setting and staging is reversed.

By reversing the directions of right and left in a mirror-image staging of the scene, there are oftentimes astonishing differences in the overall effect. In some cases, the difference parallels the situational requirements of the scene in that what was familiar has now become very strange.

MAKING IT STRANGE

Ask any small child whose bedroom lights have just been turned out how easy it is for the familiar to become strange, since monsters under the bed, goblins in the closet, and shadows of real-live skeletons dancing on the ceiling are definitely strange. We have all, perhaps, whistled in the dark after reading one too many a novel by Stephen King where ordinary dogs, clowns, closets, and even cars are transformed into beastly unfamiliar terrors that love to go bump in the night. We may be able to leave quietly the horror genre, but we can't escape the strange, since virtually everyone has had the experience of having the ordinary become very strange and exciting when

33

sightseeing in a brand new place. And just the commonplace activity of looking in your side view mirror can cause a surreal flush of confusion when you see:

Objects in mirror
may be closer
than they appear

Transforming the familiar into the strange is done twice in this exercise; once in conjuring up the basic situation, and again when the scene is viewed as its mirror image. One is artistically manipulated for such an effect, whereas the other is essentially automatic. Both are based on breaking apart habitual ways of looking at something as a means of gaining a fresh viewpoint. The eye-opening potential of this technique is undoubtedly why it is so popular with writers, artists, and directors. Rod Serling's *The Twilight Zone* and David Lynch's *Twin Peaks* clearly capitalize on the concept of making the familiar strange. Both these artists have the ability to get us to see the seemingly ordinary in new, unusual ways. William James was fond of saying that "genius, in truth, means little more than the faculty of perceiving in an unhabitual way."[16]

The basic idea of making the familiar strange is a technique borrowed from creativity researcher W. J. J. Gordon, who since 1944 has sought to uncover the basic psychological mechanisms of creative activity. The title of both his Cambridge based company and his now classic book is *Synectics* — a term derived from the Greek meaning "the joining together of different and apparently irrelevant elements."[17] Gordon argues that making the familiar strange through distortion, inversion, or the like, is fundamental to the creative process. Since we are incredibly prone to wrap our world in comfortable familiarity, the way to shake us out of our customary ruts of perception is to intentionally turn our secure and familiar world into a very unfamiliar place. He stresses that this pursuit of strangeness is not just for the novelty and shock effect, but rather in order "to achieve a new look at the same old world, people, ideas, feelings, and things."[18] The same child who will tell you about the instant transformation of his bedroom when the lights are turned out may very well be telling you this as he bends over at the waist and looks at you from between his legs. The everyday world is always right side up, but the imaginative child peering through his legs knows how wonderfully strange it all looks when turned upside down. If by chance you choose to bend over with the child, you'll notice, perhaps, how startling a conversation from this perspective can be — the lower lip not only has a way of taking the place of the upper one, but it appears to be oh so strangely mobile. Still bent over, with your habitual associations diminished, you may also notice that colors

---

[16]Quoted in Sidney J. Parnes, et. al., *Guide to Creative Action*, (New York: Charles Scribner's Sons, 1977), p. 100.

[17]William J. J. Gordon, *Synectics: The Development of Creative Capacity,* (New York: Harper and Brothers, 1961), p. 3.

[18]Ibid., p. 34.

seem more vivid as do contrasts of light and dark. And if you dare bend over so far that you're forced to gaze upon clouds in the sky, what wonders await! Play the topsy-turvey kid's game of "backwards land" where you can eat dinner for breakfast and wear your shoes on the wrong feet or maybe even on your arms, and you'll be making W. J. J. Gordon and his Synectics company very happy. An adult version of backwards land might be to imagine your house with the colors switched around, or with the floors on the ceilings, or as a bizarre mixture of all the houses you ever lived in. Most of what we look at is not necessarily new, but the challenge in this exercise is to view the ordinary in a new way.

Apart from the needs of this particular exercise, the transformation of the familiar to the strange is an excellent tactic to keep in mind for creative work of all kinds. And in the case of where the world of the play is strange to begin with, consider the equally useful synectic tactic of *making the strange familiar*. When faced with something strange, the process of analysis and reduction into categories is a direct attempt to make the strange familiar by fitting it into accepted, known patterns. Regardless of whether the strange is made familiar or the familiar is made strange, the fundamental point of both approaches is to foster creative seeing.

RUMINATING ON THE RIGHT AND LEFT

Take an ordinary photographic slide and flip it around, and you'll instantly see that all is not the same. Even though the rational part of our mind thinks such activity is pretty silly, it is "transparently" clear that all is not equal when it comes to looking at the right and left. Before creating your ground plan and staging your scene, consider the following specifics about the differences between the right and the left.

Stage Right Looks *Stronger*

Alexander Dean, in his legendary *Fundamentals of Directing* text, argues that in general *stage right is stronger than stage left*. As he says:

> Why this is so is an unsettled fact in the psychology of aesthetics. Years of tests in the classroom have shown it to be a fact but have given no satisfactory reason. The obvious reason is that we are naturally inclined to look from left to right in reading and that we carry this inclination to all phases of observation. In looking at a painting the first glance is in the left direction; and in the theatre, as the curtain rises at the beginning of the act, the audience can be seen to look to their left first in taking in the immediate impression of the stage setting.[19]

Dean's reasoning, as he himself mentions, is supported by the Chinese theatre.

---

[19]Alexander Dean & Lawrence Carra, *Fundamentals of Play Directing*, (New York: Holt, Rinehart and Winston, Inc., 1974), p. 103-104.

Orientals read from right to left and, interestingly enough, in their theatre the more important position is stage left. For example, stage left in the Chinese Theatre is where chairs are placed for the royalty and other important people. In a scene between a hero and villain, the Chinese convention is to always have the hero on the right, and the villain on the left.

If a picture (stage or otherwise) is read in our culture from left to right, pictorial movement toward the right (stage left) is perceived as being easier, requiring less effort because it seems to go *with the flow*. On the other hand, if someone crosses from right to left (stage left to stage right) the mover is, in effect, going *against the flow* and seems to be encountering more resistance and requires more effort. All of this corresponds to the findings of psychologist H. C. Van der Meer who noticed that *spontaneous movements of the head are executed more quickly from left to the right than in the opposite direction* and that when subjects were asked to compare the identical speeds of trains going from right to left, and the other from left to right, the *movement to the left was seen as faster*.[20] Stage directors can apply this thinking to their work by thinking of movement stage left to stage right as overcoming stronger resistance; it pushes against the current instead of drifting with it.

Rudolf Arnheim in his fascinating study of *Art and Visual Perception*, makes several interesting points about right and left. He begins by mentioning that certain biological theorists believe that:

> ...a symmetrical response is biologically advantageous so long as nervous systems are focused on movement and orientation in a world in which attack or reward are equally likely from either side.[21]

He disagrees with this theory because as soon as humans began to use tools that felt better in one hand versus another, the *asymmetrical* rather than the symmetrical became important. Arnheim then takes the same position as Alexander Dean in arguing that the asymmetrical became even more pronounced when man learned to read since reading meant that one lateral direction came to dominate the other. All this is interesting, anthropologically perhaps, but it doesn't take us any further than Alexander Dean's reflections about the impact of reading.

Stage Left Looks *Heavier*

Arnheim's second point about right and left, however, is definitely of value in theatre directing; he makes the observation that the right side of a picture (equivalent to stage left) tends to *look heavier*. He uses the inverted figure of Sixtus in Raphael's *Sistine Madonna* to support his point, as shown in Figure 1:

---

[20]Rudolph Arnheim, *Art and Visual Perception: A Psychology of the Creative Eye*, (Los Angeles: University of California Press, 1974), p. 35.

[21]Ibid., p. 33.

The composition becomes so heavy that the whole composition seems to topple. The aesthetic principle is that when two equal objects are shown in the left and right halves of the visual field, the one on the right looks larger.

But why do objects on the right (stage left) look larger? The popular thinking about the distinction between Right and Left Brain may have something to do with it. Art theorist Mercedes Gaffron speculates that the focus on the left, despite the fact that objects appear heavier on the right, is related to the dominance of the left brain — that part of the brain involved with speech, writing, and reading.[22] His reasoning is as follows:

1. The Left Brain (i.e., the left cerebral cortex) corresponds to the left visual field, whereas the Right Brain corresponds to the right visual field.

2. The dominance of the Left Brain, which is associated with the functions of reading, writing, and speech, is why we have heightened attentiveness to objects to the left of us.

3. Yet vision to the right, perceived by the right brain, is more articulated because this part of the brain is more visually oriented. The more articulated right side is why objects on the right appear heavier and more conspicuous.

4. So while the right side is more visually conspicuous, the left side by virtue of the importance we place upon reading, writing, and speaking, appears more central, more important, and more emphasized by the viewer's identification with it.

5. Because the center of attention is initially on the left, the "lever effect" adds to the weight of the objects on the right.

If this last theory is slightly confusing, fear not, since it's, at best, just a theory. Part of the fun of all art is its inherent mystery. The truth of the matter is that we really don't know for sure why there is a distinction between the left and the right.

[22]Rudolph Arnheim, *Art and Visual Perception: A Psychology of the Creative Eye*, (Los Angeles: University of California Press, 1974), p. 35.

Even psychologists (demystifying head shrinkers, to some) offer little help in this regard. Researchers, for instance, have been able to find very little hard evidence related to whether we are naturally right or left handed. Psychologist Van der Meer claims that education seems to play a definite part in it; she discovered that persons of limited education are less inclined than university students to perceive a distinction between the right and left. But before rushing to the explanation that it's all related to our behavior of reading, consider that in the same study she also discovered that sensitivity to left-right vectors appears rather suddenly at the age of fifteen, surprisingly late if the causal factors are supposed to be related to reading and writing.[23] "Ah, sweet mystery of Life."

CRITIQUE

1. Were the vectors of right and left used well in designing the ground plan and staging the scene?

2. What happened when right and left were reversed in the mirror image staging of the scene? Which of the two scenes was the most effective (sometimes, the workshop audience has been known to like the mirror image version better, or maybe moments of the mirror scene better)? What was the overall difference in effect between the two scenes?

3. Was the silence justified, or was it, in part or in whole, a stretch?

4. Was the familiar made strange, and was it theatrically exciting?

5. Were there any effective visual pauses?

6. Were body positions worked with effectively?

7. Favorite moment? Least favorite moment?

> The world is full of fools, and he who would not see it
> should live alone and *smash his mirror*.
> — Discours Satiriques, 1686
> attributed to Claude Le Petit

---

[23]Rudolph Arnheim, *Art and Visual Perception: A Psychology of the Creative Eye*, (Los Angeles: University of California Press, 1974), p. 36.

DIRECTIONS: SCENE 4
SILENT JOURNEY
(Experimenting With Stage Areas)

The longest journey
Is the journey inwards
Of him who has chosen his destiny,
Who has started upon his quest
For the source of his being
(Is there a source?).

— Dag Hammarskjöld

OVERVIEW

Create a two-character silent scene centered around a *literal or figurative* journey. Since a journey is almost always associated with a passage through space (traveling), it is appropriate that this particular motif is paired in this exercise with the judicious use of stage areas. As always, convincingly justify the silence while clearly communicating the who, what, and where of the situation. Even if the journey is strictly metaphorical, use the creative interplay of movement in association with stage areas, to reinforce the theme of traveling visually.

THE JOURNEY

If the choice is *literal*, the possibilities for a journey could range from the extraordinary to the commonplace. Perhaps it's about the trip of a lifetime, or maybe it's about traveling through your house madly searching for your keys as you're trying to get to work. The journey can be focused around either the arrival or departure — or both. Viola Spolin in her *Improvisation for the Theatre* has devised a series of "What's Beyond" acting exercises where the point of concentration for a single character is to show "what room he has come from, and what room he is going to."[24] Depending on the exercise, there is the choice to concentrate on what went on in the place the player has just left, or what is about to happen when the player gets to where he's going. This kind of literal journey is certainly fair game, and since there are two characters instead of one, even more possibilities open up. For instance, one of the characters might in some way be associated with the place just left, whereas the other might be tied to the destination. Perhaps the journey brings about a personality conflict, or maybe it resolves one. Robert Benchley reminds us that there are two classes of travel: first class, and with children.

[24]Viola Spolin, *Improvisation for the Theatre*, (Evanston: Northwestern University Press, 1963), pp. 102-103.

If the choice is *figurative*, the dramatized "journey" will very likely be related in some way to discovery or change. Bestseller writer Gail Sheehy in both *Passages* and her sequel *Pathfinders* visualizes the stages of life as a journey, as does the title of Eugene O'Neill's *Long Day's Journey into Night*. To seek, to study, to create is metaphorically traveling; Jung reminds us that heroes are always travelers in that they are restless and that traveling "is an image of aspiration, of an unsatisfied longing that never finds its goal, seek where it may."[25] Regardless of whether the journey is approached with acquiesence or a wish to escape, the heart and soul of a journey is evolution which is why so many creation myths and initiation rituals take the form of symbolic journeys "representing a quest that starts in the darkness of the profane world (or of the unconscious — the mother) and gropes toward the light."[26] Christianity implies a journey as does the Hindu belief that once an individual frees himself from the shackles of the everyday world, the spirit follows a route which is the inverse of that path which he took when entering it.

As with the literal approaches discussed above, the traveling may range from the cosmic to the commonplace, and the emphasis may be on the arrival and/or departure. Keep in mind also that sometimes a journey can be *both* literal and figurative as dramatized so well in Eric Overmyer's *On the Verge* and in the arrival and departure plays of Chekhov. Whether literal or figurative, the spotlight on the journey inspires many questions such as:

- Will both characters undertake the journey?

- Will the journey impact each of the characters equally?

- Will the journey abate or exacerbate the conflict between the two characters?

STAGE AREAS

The challenge of this exercise is to discover an effective way to stage a journey. Implicit or explicit in any journey is a passage through space, and similarly the director has to find an imaginative way to dramatize the journey in actual space. Proscenium stage space is divided into

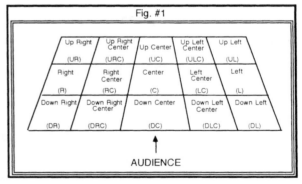

[25]Quoted from J. E. Cirlot, *A Dictionary of Symbols*, (New York: Philosophical Library, Inc., 1962), p. 157.
[26]Ibid.

fifteen separate areas (see Figure 1), and for the director to use space effectively in any capacity (from creating a functional ground plan to actual blocking), it is essential to have a firm grasp of the nuances and dynamics inherent in each of the stage areas.

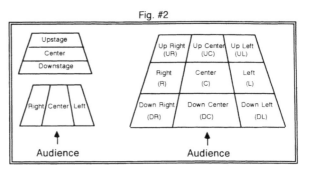

Fig. #2

All space is not perceived as equal. Stage space is conventionally divided three ways horizontally (upstage, center, and downstage) and three ways vertically (right, left, and center). Intersecting the horizontal rows with the vertical columns, as shown in Figure 2, creates nine separate areas. In practice, six additional "in between" areas are used by directors to fully define the space as diagrammed in Figure 1. As important as it is for directors to be able to use these terms fluently when speaking to actors, it is even more crucial for directors to understand the dynamic differences in strength between the major areas.

Just as differences in body positions are distinguished by relative strengths, so too are stage areas. Three interrelating factors affect the strength of the stage areas:

- *Stage right is stronger than stage left* (as was experimented with in Scene Two: Sounds of Silence, pp. 25-31).

- *Downstage is stronger than upstage* (because of the proximity to the audience).

- *The center of a framed area is stronger than any of the peripheral parts.*

Putting all these factors together, and for the moment discounting such details as the ground plan, movement, levels, costume, lighting, and the like, the relative strengths of the nine basic areas are delineated in Figure 3. Of debate is whether DR shouldn't be #2 instead of #3, since DR has the power of being both farther downstage plus the extreme power of the stage right.

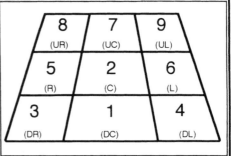

Fig. #3

Stage center has slightly more strength, however, because it is "framed" by the peripheral areas. The fact that Western audiences read from left to right is the reason most often cited as to why the stage right areas are stronger than the stage left areas, although this is not the only possible explanation.[27]

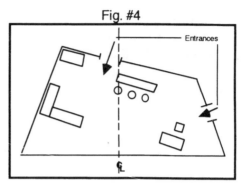

Fig. #4

Entrances

All it takes, of course, is a single set piece to shatter this clarity of relative strengths. Normally DR is a fairly strong area, but notice, for example, in the ground plan of Figure 4 that it is virtually nonexistent. In this particular plan, DL is the strongest area, surpassing even DC, since all the lines of the set draw our attention to this area. Set pieces, levels, and certainly lighting are monumental factors affecting the relative strengths of the stage areas, but if there is a solid understanding of the basic principles, then it is fairly easy to adapt them to specific circumstances.

In the process of conceptualizing your scene, assess the specific strengths of your working ground plan and then strategically use this information to put your journey into stage space. Even though your scene is about a special journey of some sort, it is worth remembering that in the broadest possible context, every scene needs to "go somewhere," so with many spatial regards, enjoy the trip.

CRITIQUE

1. Were the relative strengths of the stage areas strategically used to tell us about the silent journey? Was the handling of these areas as a communicative tool well done, or was it too subtle or heavy-handed? Was the staging effective in putting the journey into space?

2. Did specific areas tend to become associated with a specific character and/or idea or mood?

3. Was the situation (the *who*, *what* and *where*) well communicated?

4. Was the silence convincing, or was it, in part or in whole, too much of a stretch?

5. Outside of a workshop exercise, would this scene stand up on its own? Would it keep our interest?

6. Were there any visual pauses?

7. Favorite moment? Least favorite moment?

---

[27]See pp. 35-38 for the discussion of the dynamics of right and left (Ruminating on the Right and Left).

BREAKING SILENT BOUNDARIES
(Experimenting With Psychological Areas)

Any idiot can face a crisis —
it's this day–to–day living
that wears you out.

— Anton Chekhov

OVERVIEW

Create a two-character silent scene in which the boundaries are defined and broken. Whether implicit or explicit, a scene about invading territory will inevitably require putting to use *psychological areas*, the featured directorial technique of this exercise. In creating a situation that fully justifies both the silence and some sort of literal or figurative "space invasion," plan on using one or more well-defined psychological areas.

PSYCHOLOGICAL AREAS

Every bit as important as the relative strengths of the stage areas, are the psychological areas that evolve in the staging of a scene or play. As a play is staged, a certain area and/or set piece may take on a special meaning through its repeated association with a character and/or idea or mood, and these special places are, perhaps, best termed *psychological areas*. A single psychological area becomes, in effect, a spatial motif that the audience learns to associate with specific characters, ideas, or moods. The psychological area may be associated with a single character only, or it might be associated with several, and in any given play there may be several different psychological areas put to use. When more than a single character is associated with an area, oftentimes the variation in feeling or perception about the area becomes the dramatic point. For instance, the various characters in Chekhov's *The Cherry Orchard* have radically different feelings about the orchard, and a director might choose to highlight these differences by showing us the different ways in which the characters approach a specific window that looks upon the orchard. As with any aesthetic value, there is a danger in using psychological areas too blatantly, but when handled well they have enormous dramatic potential.

Sometimes the playwright provides ideas for psychological areas. Ibsen has Hedda Gabler hovering around her stove, which some have interpreted as a compensation for her inner coldness. When she uses the stove to burn Løvborg's manuscript she is symbolically warmed by an act of destruction. Hedda takes her life in the more private back room very near the portrait of her father, a psychological area which dramatizes that her successful suicide of the present is very much tied to her past relationship with her father. Chekhov has Løvborg and her brother Gaev in *The Cherry Orchard* comically wax eloquent about their favorite bookcase. Laura is drawn to her special collection in Tennessee Williams' *The Glass Menagerie*, and a kooky character from Michael Weller's *Moonchildren* spends most of her time under a table.

Psychological areas are just as possible in less realistic theatre as well. Even when empty space becomes the issue, where the void becomes a visual symbol for the spiritual emptiness of the human condition, there is ample opportunity for the use of psychological areas. Samuel Beckett's minimalist settings (a single tree, a rocking chair, or tape recorder) do not, by any means, preclude the use of psychological areas. Even in the void of Beckett's *Waiting for Godot*, there is the potential for specific areas within the wasteland landscape; perhaps a psychological area could be created, for example, when the youthful messenger announces at the end of each of the two acts: "Mr. Godot told me to tell you he won't come this evening but surely tomorrow." If this line were delivered in exactly the same area, the verbal repetition would be visually reinforced as well.

While entire settings provided by the playwright can take on psychological and symbolic dimensions, more often than not it will be the director who creates specific psychological areas. Space speaks volumes when psychological areas are carefully put into play. Simple activities such as picking up a photograph on a mantel, looking out the window, or rocking in a specific chair typify the kinds of stage business that could very well be used to create psychological areas. Oftentimes psychological areas evolve as the director gradually trains the audience to associate a character and/or an idea with a specific set piece or stage area. At other times, when the first association is striking enough, the birth of a psychological area may be instantaneous. A sofa, for instance, would become an immediate psychological area if it was used for either an on-stage or off-stage rape.

BOUNDARIES

The challenge of this exercise is to use one or more psychological areas within a context of breaking boundaries. Since a psychological area relates to a real space, there have to be literal borders, but that doesn't necessarily mean that a particular character is always conscious of the boundaries. Breaking literal or figurative boundaries relates to territoriality. There is such a natural connection between psychological areas and breaking boundaries that it might lead to the thinking that with one there has to be the other, such as when the "Meathead" of *All in the Family* sits in Archie's chair. But psychological spaces may or may not become territorial, and may or may not become invaded depending upon the basic situation.

Cultural anthropologists remind us that territoriality has to do with the way territory is defined and defended by everything from fish to modern man, and that the delicate ecological balance of life has much to do with the use of space. Territoriality is all around us — animal life abounds with examples. Carnivorous animals stake out well-defined territories where they hunt, just as birds and bees have recognizable territories where they feed and nest. Dolphins and whales return to the same breeding grounds, just as "individual seals have been known to come back to the same rock year after year."[28] Even bulls groomed for fighting will try to establish safe territories in the ring, making it very difficult for the matador to prod them into action.[29]

People are by no means immune from the activity of creating boundaries. Wars alone dramatize the insatiable need to wrestle space from interlopers. Technology has in one sense greatly extended our territorial boundaries but in another sense it has boxed us in with the threat of annihilation. Prostitutes who work their own sides of the street, salesmen who sell in specific territories, and beggars who have their own beats all exemplify human territoriality. Teachers notice that even by the second day of class, students tend to sit in exactly the same seats. Everyday expressions metaphorically stress the importance of territoriality:

• Moving in on someone	• Crossing the line
• Stepping on too many toes	• When push comes to shove
• Breathing down my back	• Nosy or pushy
• Horn in on (butt into)	• Have a finger in the pie
• Press on	• Stick one's nose into
• Foist one's self upon	• Get out of my face
• Refuse to budge an inch	• Brushing someone aside

Sometimes spatial metaphors suggest a successful merging of territories, as in the phrases "meeting halfway," "finding common ground," or even "coming together." Just how easy it is for the metaphor to slip into reality has been noticed by many a parent who has had to deal with "the line" between two or more children in the back seat of a car.

The use of space is inevitably linked with status. Chickens have a pecking order just as horses have a "kick bite" order. At formal occasions, the distance one sits from the head of the table oftentimes spotlights the "pecking order" of importance. At home, there are also the heads of the table, who more often than not are also the occupants of the "master bedroom." Exclusivity of space is exemplified with the executive washroom, reserved parking spaces, and faculty lounges. Status is symbolized spatially through factors such as exclusiveness, quantity, or proximity, but

---

[28]Edward T. Hall, *The Silent Language*, (Greenwich: Fawcett Publications, 1959), p. 147.
[29]Ibid., p. 51.

symbolism aside, the boundaries are very real.

The specific manner in which a territory is defended can reveal a great deal about a character. In *The Silent Language*, cultural anthropologist Edward T. Hall provides a familiar, domestic example:

> How many people have had the experience of coming into a room, seeing a big comfortable chair and heading for it, only to pull themselves short, or pause and turn to the man and say, "Oh, was I about to sit in your chair?" The reply, of course, is usually polite. Imagine the effect if the host were to give vent to his true feelings and say, "Hell, yes, you're sitting in my chair, and I don't like anybody sitting in my chair!" For some unknown reason our culture has tended to play down or cause us to repress and dissociate the feeling we have about space. We relegate it to the informal and are likely to feel guilty whenever we find ourselves getting angry because someone has taken our place.[30]

Territorial feelings of women toward their kitchens are nightmares for today's feminists, but a fifties sitcom might very well have depicted that even a mother can't wash her daughter's dishes without annoying her. In Hall's anthropological study, an actual woman bemoans: "I have three older sisters and a mother, and every time they come to town they march right into the kitchen and take over. I want to tell them to stay out of my kitchen, that they have their own kitchens and this is my kitchen, but I always thought I was having unkind thoughts about my mother and sisters, thoughts I wasn't supposed to have."[31] Territories change with the times, some fading away while others fall into place, but territories there will always be.

PERSONAL SPACE

In addition to actual rooms, set pieces, and possessions, boundaries can also include ***personal space***. Normal conversational distance is dependent upon the need to maintain personal space; if this space is in any way encroached upon, there is an immediate sense of discomfort. When two people are talking and one gets too close, the other will almost immediately back up. The amount of personal space needed is dependent upon both the individual and the culture. There are certainly times when people, regardless of the culture, are pushy or distant in their use of space; due to these kinds of individual differences in personal space, people often interact with foreigners by mistakenly associating them with the similar type behavior they have experienced on the home front. For instance, what is a perfectly natural speaking distance for the Latin American would evoke either sexual or hostile feelings in the North American. Put representative people from these two cultures together, and

---

[30]Edward T. Hall, *The Silent Language*, (Greenwich: Fawcett Publications, 1959), p. 147.
[31]Ibid., p. 148.

typically the North American will back away from what he perceives to be an invasive conversation, whereas the Latino will perceive the North American as unfriendly, cold, and distant.

Distance can also directly affect the subject matter of a conversation; there are certain topics difficult or impossible to broach when one feels they are not in the proper conversational zone. Distance provides hints about possible subject matter as well as hints about the relationship in general. Among other things, distance between people causes shifts in the voice, and cultural anthropologist Edward T. Hall has observed the following divisions of distance with Americans:[32]

1.	Very close (3 in. to 6 in.)	Soft whisper; top secret
2.	Close (8 in. to 12 in.)	Audible whisper; very confidential
3.	Near (12 in. to 20 in.)	Indoors, soft voice; Outdoors, full voice; confidential
4.	Neutral (20 in. to 36 in.)	Soft voice, low volume, personal subject matter
5.	Neutral (4 ½ ft. to 5 ft.	Full voice; information of nonpersonal matter
6.	Public distance (5 ½ ft. to 8 ft.)	Full voice with slight overloudness; public information for others to hear
7.	Across the room (8 ft. to 20 ft.)	Loud voice; talking to a group
8.	Stretching the limits of distance (20 ft. to 24 ft. indoors up to 100 ft. outdoors)	Hailing distance; departures

Within a culture, there is ample opportunity for personal space to be violated, but obviously cultural differences further increase the possibilities. Hall uses the following anecdote to bring into focus cultural differences concerning personal space:

> I had the good fortune to be visited by a very distinguished and learned man who had been for many years a top-ranking diplomat representing a foreign country. After meeting him several times, I had become impressed with his extraordinary sensitivity to the small details of behavior that are so significant in the interaction process. Dr. X was interested in some work several of us were doing at the time and asked permission to attend my lectures. He came to the front of the class at the end of the lecture to talk over a number of points made in the preceding hour. While talking he became quite involved in the implications of the lecture as well as what he was saying. We started out facing each other

[32]Edward T. Hall, *The Silent Language*, (Greenwich: Fawcett Publications, 1959), pp. 164-165.

and as he talked I became dimly aware that he was standing a little too close and that I was beginning to back up. Fortunately I was able to suppress my first impulse and remain stationary because there was nothing to communicate aggression in his behavior except the conversational distance. His voice was eager, his manner intent, the set of his body communicated only interest and eagerness to talk. It also came in a flash that someone who had been so successful in the old school of diplomacy could not possibly let himself communicate something offensive to the other person except outside of his highly trained awareness.

By experimenting I was able to observe that as I moved away slightly, there was an associated shift in the pattern of interaction. He had more trouble expressing himself. If I shifted to where I felt comfortable (about twenty-one inches), he looked somewhat puzzled and hurt, almost as though he were saying: "Why is he acting that way?...Having ascertained that distance had a direct effect on his conversation, I stood my ground, letting him set the distance.[33]

The breaking of boundaries in your scene can be very subtle or obvious. As long as the psychological area is brought into play, the boundaries themselves can be literal or figurative, overt or covert. Part of what may help you to justify the silence of the scene is to remember that our manners and behavior often speak more plainly than words. Nonverbal communication is a silent but enormously revealing language.

CRITIQUE

1. Was there at least one distinct psychological area? Was the psychological area related to a character, idea, or mood, or a combination of these things?

2. Was a boundary clearly established, and did the breaking of the boundary make sense and create interest? Was the boundary related to, or separate from, a particular psychological area? Was the boundary:
    • Subtle or obvious (overt or covert)?
    • Literal or figurative?

3. Were the dynamics of **stage areas** and **body positions** strategically used to establish boundary or psychological area?

4. Were the dynamics of **right and left** strategically used to establish boundary or psychological area?

5. Were there any effective visual pauses?

6. Was the silence justified?

7. Favorite moment? Least favorite moment?

[33]Edward T. Hall, *The Silent Language*, (Greenwich: Fawcett Publications, 1959), pp. 161-162.

SILENT STATUS SWAPPING
(Experimenting With Level)

*He that is greatest among you
shall be your servant.*

— Matthew 23:11

OVERVIEW

Create a silent scene in which the ***sharply divided status between the two characters is somehow "swapped" or reversed*** by the end of scene. Silence is to be used by one or both characters as a deliberate control tactic — i.e. a *strategy for power*. Highly appropriate for "power plays" of all types is the *dynamic use of levels*, which is the featured technique of this exercise. Judiciously use levels to dramatize the shifting status between the two characters.

STATUS STRIVING

Sociologist T.H. Marshall defines status as "the way a man is treated by his fellows and reciprocally, the way he treats them."[34] Vance Packard in *The Status Seekers* argues that even though class boundaries are contrary to the American dream, the United States is no exception to the fact that every society of any complexity has very definite patterns of social stratification. Packard defines class as "any group of people within a population who have a common status or origin that tends to set them apart — and who develop a style of life that emphasizes the apartness.[35] Status is revealed in the car you drive, the clothes you wear, the church and schools you attend, the house or apartment you live in, your sexual behavior and even your choice of words. Status symbols are a means of identification — a king needs his crown in order for others to see him as king just as the executive needs his own washroom, private secretary, and parking space. Presidents are given their own airplanes and private barbers, and teachers are given faculty lounges where they can talk about the "status quo" of merit raises and tenure. People need symbols in proportion to their status. Status symbols, says Packard, are more than just luxury items because:

> ...if we aspire to rise in the world, but fail to take on the coloration
> of the group we aspire to — by failing to discard our old status symbols,

---

[34]August B. Hollingshead and Frederick C. Redlich, *Social Class and Mental Illness*, (New York: John Wiley & Sons, Inc., 1958), p. 162.

[35]Vance Packard, *The Status Seekers*, (New York: Simon and Schuster, Inc., 1966), p. 39.

friends, club memberships, values, behavior patterns, and acquiring new ones esteemed by the higher group — our chances of success are diminished. Sociologists have found that our home address, our friends, our clubs, and even our church affiliations can prove to be "barriers" if we fail to change them with every attempted move up the ladder. This is a most disheartening situation to find in the nation that poses as the model for the democratic world.[36]

Status is evident in all socioeconomic "levels." Prostitutes may be lumped together into a single group by the country club set of suburbia, but as with many occupational groups, there is a fairly rigid hierarchy of status. Call girls at the so-called top of their profession shun the common streetwalkers; status among prostitutes is largely based on the fee they command, and a $75-a-trick girl wouldn't dream of swapping telephone numbers of prospects with a $50-a trick girl. In the hallowed halls of higher education, people may see only the simple division of administration, faculty, and students, but there are very rigid hierarchies for each. There is, for instance, the ranking system of professors ranging from full professor to instructor and, as with prostitutes, the difference in status is reflected in the salary scales.

Attaining status can be as simple as being the first to do something — the first kid on your block to own a two-wheeled bike, the first of your friends to "score" on a date, or the first in your family to go to college or graduate school. Shifts in status may be suitably advanced subject matter for sociologists, but they can also be as simple as beating out your best friend, the uncontested campus champ, at Super Nintendo. The clique in the greenroom, or the fellowship of a fraternity are designed to be obstacle courses for outsiders. According to Vance Packard, the four criteria most commonly used by Americans to determine whether or not fellow citizens are sufficiently different from themselves to form a wall are:

- By recency of arrival in the locality.
- By national background.
- By religion.
- By pigmentation.[37]

Whether in the microcosm of the playground, or the macrocosm of world war, the net result of status seeking is wall building. The upgrading urge of status is a persistent thread running through the theatre; for instance, Arthur Miller in his *Death of a Salesman* describes, just in the name alone, the status trap of the central character — Willie Loman. Ibsen's *A Doll's House* and *Hedda Gabler*, to name just a few of his plays, focus on the contrasting status of husband and wife. And with August

---

[36]Vance Packard, *The Status Seekers*, (New York: Simon and Schuster, Inc., 1966), p. 5.

[37]Ibid., p. 42-45. For each of these categories, Packard provides many interesting examples.

Strindberg's *Miss Julie*, think of how the contrasting dreams of Julie and Jean symbolize the lethal limits of status seeking. Jean dreams of rising out of the filth of his servile past, whereas Julie fantasizes of falling into the filth. Strindberg also in his one-act *The Stronger* interrelates the concepts of status and silence by having one of the two characters fight for dominance by never saying a single word. Typical characters of film, theatre, and literature are those "who rise too fast, find themselves in unfamiliar patterns, and are penalized for their unfamiliarity."[38]

Spatial metaphors remind us that status is often associated with space. An arrogant person "tramples over people" or "brushes people aside." Such metaphors are excellent hints for creating blocking or motivating an actor to create movement. Clive Barker in his *Theatre Games* provides an excellent discussion about personal space bringing up the point that "master/slave relationships presume that the master has complete right of access to the space of the slave, who has no privacy."[39] The master has an expansive free rein over space, whereas the slave tends to remain withdrawn within his own tight space. Subservience says Barker "can be expressed as having no clearly defined center but standing on the perimeter of someone else's space and relating directly to their [*sic*] space."[40]

Keith Johnstone devotes an entire chapter to the idea of using status as an acting tool in his *Impro: Improvisation and the Theatre*. His thesis is that status is a pivotal part of our behavior because "we are pecking order animals and that this affects the tiniest details of our behavior."[41] He makes the all-important point that playing "high" and "low" status (his terminology) is not necessarily dependent upon actual class, since high and low status can be played in any situation. In a working-class community, for instance, there will inevitably be high and low status transactions. Within any socioeconomic group there can be status transactions between two people where (1) both lower status, (2) both raise status, (3) one rais status while the other lowers, and (4) the status is reversed by the end of the transaction. The dance of dominance and submissiveness (high and low status) is often revealed, says Johnstone, via eye contact. Holding eye contact is an act of aggressiveness, and a way of attaining high status power. Breaking eye contact can also be high status, provided that the "breaker" doesn't look back for even a split second; ignoring someone is a way of raising status, but the high status will immediately be lowered if the "breaker" feels compelled to look back again. Besides eye contact, high and low status tends to be revealed, says Johnstone, in the amount of space used. This paragraph hardly does justice to Johnstone's fine chapter which should definitely be recommended reading for anyone thinking seriously about the theatricality of status.

---

[38]Edward T. Hall, *The Silent Language*, (Greenwich: Fawcett Publications, 1959), p. 116.

[39]Clive Barker, *Theatre Games*, (New York: Drama Book Specialists, 1977), p. 138.

[40]Ibid., p. 138.

[41]Keith Johnstone, *Impro: Improvisation and the Theatre*, (London & Boston: Faber and Faber, 1979), p. 74. The entire chapter is full of perceptive observations and practical suggestions.

SILENT STRATEGIES

Status is very much played out in silence. The way we speak hints at our status, but, status "talks" without the use words as well. Status is often lurking in the background when silence is used as tactic or strategy for power. Silence, for example, may be used between strangers in a public place, such as seatmates on a bus, train, or plane to maintain privacy. A correlation between silence and status is suggested by Apostle Paul of the Bible who bespoke in favor of the patriarchy by preaching: "Let a woman learn silence with all submissiveness. I will permit no woman to teach or to have authority over man; she is to keep silent."[42] Silence may be used as a tactic to question, promise, deny, warn, threaten, insult, request, or command. All in all, silence tends to be a concept unusually pregnant with meaning.

Silence may often speak louder than words, but by its very nature, it is often open to interpretation. For instance, using the right to remain silent of the fifth amendment may include several tactics. As a tactic, it might support (1) the right not to say what one *does not* believe, (2) the right to say what one *does* believe (3) the right not to say what one has knowledge of.[43] When two people are silent together, there is also ample room for interpretation. Even though two people together are both, logically speaking, equally responsible for the silence, there is often a sense that one of them "owns" the silence. Jane Fonda seemed to feel that her father owned the silence with her admission, "I can remember long car rides where not a word would be spoken. I would be so nervous that my palms would be sweaty from riding in absolute silence with my own father."[44] Somebody else besides his daughter might have interpreted Henry Fonda's behavior more positively, perhaps perceiving him as the strong, silent type.

Silent tactics can be used either positively or negatively. Through a positive lens silence can be seen as a useful strategy in managing a difficult situation. Silence can establish a needed distance between highly emotional people. Silence may be the best preventative medicine in keeping people from wounding each other. Silence, as with status, can form a wall of protection as is often needed, for instance, in a crowded city where talking to people can at times be very dangerous. Before distrust and suspicion are broken down, a relationship is often marked by much silence, which gradually decreases as they get to know each other better, and ultimately, as good friends they may very likely return to using more and more silence. Lovers will spend hours of silence happily together, each feeling understood, and each in perfect communication. Silence in this respect reflects a special bond — a strategy for togetherness.

---

[42]I Timothy 2:11,12.

[43]For a complete discussion of this see George Rice, "The Right to Be Silent," *Quarterly Journal of Speech* 47, 1961:349-54.

[44]Deborah Tannen & Muriel Savelle-Troike, eds., *Perspectives on Silence*, (New Jersey, Ablex Publishing Corporation, 1985), p. 100.

Through a negative lens, silence can definitely wound. Think of pain caused by "the silent treatment." An ultra negative view of silence is given to us by Thomas Mann who tells us that "Speech is civilization itself. The word, even the most contradictious word, preserves contact — it is silence which isolates."[45] Because it is so open to interpretation, silence may permit each person involved to exaggerate the wrong committed by the other person. Depending upon the strategies, silence in relationships can sever or bind, heal or wound, reveal or hide emotions. Likewise, it can be used to communicate assent or dissent, favor or disfavor, sinfulness or saintliness. Whether or not you tend to view silence positively or negatively may be partially revealed by the way you react to the following poetic description of silence by Hammarskjöld: "Silence shatters to pieces the mind's armor, leaving it naked before autumn's clear eye."[46]

LEVELS

The challenge of this exercise is to creatively connect status with the use of levels. All things being equal, ***the actor on the highest level will command the most attention***. Obviously factors such as body position, stage area, movement, costuming, and lighting have the potential of intensifying or counterbalancing the use of level. There is also the factor of contrast; any time an actor is in contrast to the rest of the group, the actor in the generally weaker position will in this case take focus. Position a group of actors on a platform, and place a single actor at stage level, and the lowly actor will be the center of attention. In addition to level, ***emphasis through contrast*** can also be used with area, body positions, and plane. Figure 1 shows that three standing actors are superseded by a single sitting actor.

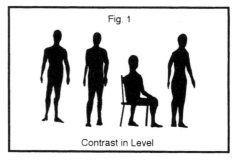

Fig. 1

Contrast in Level

Like it or not, we associate height with superiority. The fact that the tallest person in a room will stand out from all the rest is significant enough, but add to this the cosmic impact of a very high heaven and a very low hell for a hint of the magnitude that height has upon our thinking. God hovers over us all, and it's no coincidence that kings and judges are typically seated above all others. Also, it is not very hard to understand why divas of the past loved to make grand entrances by sweeping down a flight of stairs, only to remain strategically perched upon the second to the last step from the bottom.

Everyday expressions attest to the status associated with height:

---

[45]Thomas Mann, *The Magic Mountain*, trans. H. T. Lowe-Porter, (New York: The Modern Library, 1927), p. 518.

[46]Dag Hammarsjöld, *Markings*, trans. Leif Sjoberg & W. H. Auden, (New York: Alfred A. Knopf, 1964), p. 167.

- Head and shoulders above
- Upward mobility
- Upgrading and upscale
- On the up and up
- The upper crust
- Sitting on top of the world
- Measuring up
- It's uptown

- Work your way up to the top
- Top dog/under dog
- Social climbing and yuppies
- Get the upper hand
- Shoot for the moon
- Climb the ladder of success
- Cut above
- Make it to the top of the heap

It's "thumbs up" for height, but before doing your "level best" to use every platform in sight, consider that *variety in level can easily be attained without any platforms at all*. Stairs and platforms are obvious aids in working with level, but there are innumerable other possibilities. Something as subtle as one actor sitting on the raised arm of a sofa talking to a slightly lower actor on the sofa itself, is an example of level effectively put to use without the use of actual platforms. Sitting, kneeling, lying on the floor are all very viable possibilities, as shown in Figure 2. It's even quite possible to have a variety of level with two actors lying on the floor. Obviously, standing is stronger than sitting, and sitting is stronger than lying down. Level may be a way of creating focus by isolating an actor from the rest of the group or by creating vertical emphasis.

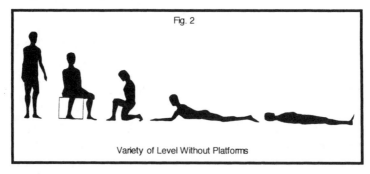

Fig. 2

Variety of Level Without Platforms

CRITIQUE

1. Was the silence justified and was it used effectively as a strategy for power? Was the silence equally associated with both characters, or did one character in particular seem to "own" the silence?

2. Was there a clear division of status between the two characters?

3. Was the status between the two characters convincingly reversed by the end of the scene?

4. Did the use of levels create a convincing shift of status, or was the change accomplished in other ways?

5. Were there any effective visual pauses?

6. Was the use of body positions, stage areas, and movement well integrated with the use of level?

7. Favorite moment? Least favorite moment?

BROKEN SILENCE BREAKDOWN
(Experimenting With Visual Progressions)

For everything there is a season,
and a time for every purpose under heaven...
a time to keep silent, and a time to speak.

— Ecclesiastes 3:1,7

OVERVIEW

Create a two-character silent scene which **builds** **steadily** *to some sort of breakdown*. Interpret the breakdown as the climax of something that has been literally or figuratively "breaking," such as:

• Broken Dreams	• Broken Bones	• Broken Promises
• Broken People	• Broken Hearts	• Broken Nerves

As yet a further play on the word breaking, *let the silence itself at some point,* **for a single moment only** *be broken by one or both of the characters*. Think of this scene as an opportunity to synthesize skills which have previously only been focused upon individually. Bring into play:

• Body Positions	• Stage Areas	• Psychological Areas
• Right & Left Moves	• Visual Pauses	• Level

Combine all of the above skills by creating a very definite *visual progression* that fully reinforces the required build of the scene.

MOTIVATE THE SILENCE AND THE SPEECH

This is a highly appropriate exercise to culminate the silent work because the moment of broken silence provides a perfect transition to the "talkies" ahead. At some point in the scene the silence is broken by one or both of the characters. What motivates this silence? Is there so much tension in the silence that a verbal outburst is the only possible outcome? Or is there a lapse of concentration which causes the verbal moment? Maybe, instead, the moment is somehow very controlled and planned. Is the end of the scene the only effective place to break the silence, or is a return to silence for the ending an exciting dramatic possibility? Obviously there are many effective strategies for breaking the silence — the only essential requirement is to justify not just the silence convincingly, but the speech as well.

Max Picard in *The World of Silence* poetically describes the relationship between silence and language:

> Speech came out of silence, out of the fullness of silence. The fullness of silence would have exploded if it had not been able to flow out into speech.
>
> The speech that comes out of silence is, as it were, justified by the silence that precedes it. It is the spirit that legitimizes speech, but the silence that precedes speech is the pregnant mother who is delivered of speech by the creative activity of the spirit. The sign of this creative activity of the spirit is the silence that precedes speech.
>
> Whenever a man begins to speak, the word comes from silence at each new beginning.[47]

Speech as the resonance of silence, as something bursting from the depths of silence, may be a positive or negative experience depending upon your point of view. There is the belief in certain cultures that as soon as an experience is put into words, its real essence vaporizes. In Japan there is the belief that when parents die, when a son passes an entrance examination to a university, or when looking at something incredibly beautiful, there should only be silence.[48] Similar to this is the poem that starts out with the words, "Oh, Matsushima," (the name of an island in Japan) but becomes interrupted because the poet was so overwhelmed with its beauty.[49] Speech is also thought of as a very negative experience for Ashanti children who are taught at an early age to be silent at meals for fear that speaking will cause the father to die.[50]

Silence in these kinds of situations is more revered than speech, as suggested also by the pop poster slogan, "If you do not understand my silence you will not understand my words." Silence may be more valued, but behind each of these examples is the implication that words still have power. In virtually all cultures, a careless word may cause a fire which is difficult to extinguish. Yet silence as well can be the cause of the wound, and can be as difficult to heal as any wound caused by words. A silent "cooling off" period between enemies is possible, but just as possible is for the cooling off to coalesce into the freezing of an out and out cold war. Just as silence may be interpreted positively or negatively, so also with speech. In any case, many are the possibilities for justifying both the silence and speech of your scene. Whether your burst of inspiration for this scene comes to you in silence or speech, may very well provide a hint about which of the two you generally tend to favor.

[47]Max Picard, *The World of Silence*, (Chicago: Henry Regnery Co., 1952), p. 24.

[48]Deborah Tannen & Muriel Savelle-Troike, eds., *Perspectives on Silence*, (New Jersey: Ablex Publishing Corporation, 1985), p. 8.

[49]Ibid., p. 8.

[50]Ibid., p. 12.

VISUAL PROGRESSIONS

You are asked to create not just a steady build in general, but specifically to reinforce the build with a visual progression. Just as beginning directors tend to be initially much more aware of verbal, rather than visual pauses, there seems to be a similar tunnel vision with **verbal versus visual progressions**. Asked to "build" a scene, most beginning directors will very readily consider a verbal progression by resorting to one or more of the following techniques:

> • Increasing the volume.
>
> • Lessening the amount of pausing.
>
> • Overlapping the lines (and the overlapping itself may become progressively more pronounced).
>
> • Increasing the rate of speaking.
>
> • Increasing the frequency of speaking.
>
> • Changing the pitch.

Even when a beginning director instinctively resorts to using a visual progression, chances are that the director is unconscious of doing so until it is pointed out. The term visual progression refers to the idea of **building a scene visually**, which may be accomplished by doing one or more of the following:

> • Gravitating to stronger stage areas.
>
> • Using increasingly more open body positions.
>
> • Making crosses go increasingly "against the flow" instead of "with the flow," (i.e. going increasingly stage left).
>
> • Working increasingly from upstage to downstage.
>
> • Working from a higher to lower level, or vice versa.
>
> • Working with increasingly more, or increasingly less visual pauses.

Obviously, many combinations and variations of these approaches are possible. The art of blocking in general depends on creatively combining these variables. There are also many nuances inherent in the above listing. For instance, with body positions there is the all important factor of head focus; an actor could conceivably be in a three-quarter position but he might be looking profile. Imagine the possibility of creating a visual progression by having the head positions always at odds with the body positions up until the climax when for the first time, the body and head angles become perfectly aligned.

In a given scene there may be several visual progressions, or only one. In your scene, where a *steady* build is called for, chances are that there will be only a single visual progression. The best way to determine if there is a visual progression is to completely divorce the movement from its subject matter, and then analyze whether the movement in the abstract increasingly happens to keep our attention. In a series of say twenty moves, not every single movement will necessarily be "stronger" than the previous one, but certainly the overall progression should be from the weaker to the stronger. And, there may be a special circumstance when a director deliberately might want to make a visual *regression* instead of a visual *progression*. Both verbal and visual progressions are tremendously useful, but altogether too often visual progressions are not given careful consideration.

SAMPLE VISUAL PROGRESSION

Scene: Morning; a writer is anxiously awaiting a phone call from his agent. Even though he has had success after success with his current agent, he fears that the silent phone is a sure sign that his agent hates his play. Just like every other time, he is going to have to break down and call his agent, but he has not yet got up enough nerve to pick up the phone. His roommate, who has been through this with his friend several times before, enters and calmly goes about the morning ritual of preparing breakfast.

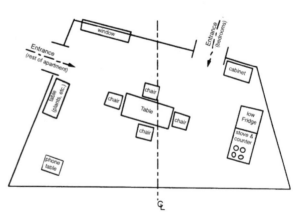

Title: *To Call or Not to Call*

INTRO. POSITIONS

W = the writer........................ **W:** looking out window (full back)
R = the roommate.................. **R:** ready to enter from UL

---

1. **W**: Turn and face phone, sip coffee eyeing phone, X toward phone (DR) a few steps, sip coffee; X quickly to stove, pour more coffee; X back to UR area as shown.

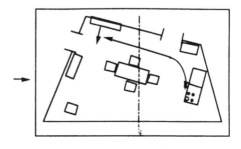

2. **R**: Enter from UL, just awakened, X one or two steps in, look

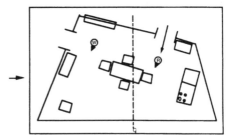

3. **R**: Shake head, turn and X to get cup of coffee at stove. Turn and face **W**.

   W: Exits quickly UR, upset. **R**: sip coffee, then X to cabinet, getting cereal box and bowls, and spoons.

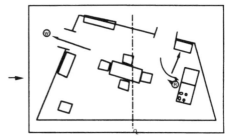

4. **R**: X back to sink area with bowls and cereal, set down items. Then get milk out of refrigerator. Fix cereal.

   W: Re-enter, look at phone (DR), turn quickly to face window, turn and face phone, then X a few steps toward phone.

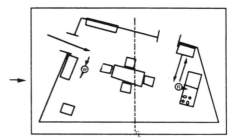

5. **R**: X with bowls of cereal to center table. Set bowls on table (right and left table settings), sit in (L) chair. Start eating cereal.

W: X to window, X back to plant table, eyeing phone all the time. Nervously pull a leaf on one of the plants, then throw it on floor. Look at roommate, who nods, "yes." **W** finally gets his nerve to cross and pick up the phone. He dials his agent and says, "Max? Max? Did you get a chance to read it?"

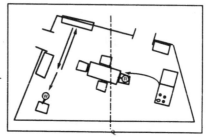

Even though this scene is probably considerably shorter than the one you will create, it still demonstrates a ***visual progression***. Again, it is important to point out that in a visual progression, the general progression is from weaker to stronger movements, but that ***not*** every move necessarily needs to be stronger than the previous one. Two examples of weaker movements in this scene were:

- For instance, in step 3 when the writer crosses to the cabinet to get the cereal, this is definitely a weaker move than the previous one. This weaker move, however, helps to shift the focus back to the writer, whose next move is definitely stronger.

- In step 5, the upstage cross to the window is weaker than the previous one (because it is going upstage), but due to the fact it is part of the all important "telephone-window axis," the cross is so full of tension that it takes on a "psychological strength" that fully maintains our interest.

With the exception of these weaker movements, the overall progression is from the upstage to the window to the telephone. From the very beginning of the scene, the axis running from the window to the telephone is clearly established as the most important axis of the ground plan.

CRITIQUE

1. Was the silence and the break in silence justified?

2. What motivated the breakdown? Was the breakdown effective?

3. Was the moment of speech (the breaking of the silence) effectively placed?

4. What exactly was the relationship between silence and speech? Was the silence looked upon as positive or negative? How about the speech — positive or negative? Even if both silence and speech were viewed the same (both positive or both negative), did one seem to have more impact than the other?

5. Was there a visual progression? What elements (body position, stage areas, level, right and left movements, and level) were most responsible for bringing about the progression?

6. Were there any distinct psychological areas? Were the areas related to character, idea, or mood?

7. Favorite moment? Least favorite moment?

CHAPTER 3
JUSTIFYING MOVEMENT

Something is missing! The exercises in this chapter all provide detailed movement along with a detailed ground plan, but that's all they supply. What's missing, of course, is the text — the dialogue. The challenge with each is to create a situation, characters, and accompanying lines that *justify* the given movement.

Blocking, but no text — why? Why go against the nature of "normal" directing by beginning with blocking first instead of text? Why not weave blocking from the available textual threads, instead of reversing the process? The answer is in the silence. Words are wonderfully communicative, but if relied upon too much, they can become major obstacles for the beginning director. With the previous chapter (Scenes 1-7) we experienced the communicative power of silence. These Justified Movement Exercises are the perfect follow-up work for the very reason that they too begin in silence. To some extent, working with justifying exercises is similar to watching someone else's silent scene and attempting to make sense out of the staging.

With justifying the movement exercises, there is no alternative but to ponder each and every move carefully — to become more sensitized to the nonverbal, visual feast at hand. Soon the beginning silence becomes transformed into a thundering roar of would-be words for consideration. Creating dialogue within the context of a meaningful situation requires the student director to distinguish between strong and weak movements, and in general, to become more sensitive to the moment by moment communicative potential of composition and movement. Gradually these kind of exercises bring a fully felt understanding that movement in and of itself is tremendously communicative.

Besides spotlighting the communicative power of movement, justify exercises also explore the interrelationship between movement and lines. Blocking a given text also does this, but an advantage with justifying exercises is that it puts the *initial* focus on the visual dimension of the scene. Even though there is dialogue eventually, the priority given to the visual makes these exercises a natural extension of the silent work. A secondary advantage of the justify exercises is that they automatically take away (at least for the duration of the exercises) two destructive, counterproductive attitudes, which are:

- Taking blocking for granted — an overly confident attitude arising from the assumption that blocking will automatically take care of itself, and/or that it really isn't that important.

• Taking blocking *too* seriously — a lack of confidence brought about from the feeling that it is tremendously important, and/or that it is tremendously complicated.

While clearly opposite, both can become very nasty snake pits for the beginning director. The potential harm from each of these attitudes is circumvented via the justifying movement exercises, plus by the time all of these exercises are completed, the student will likely have a far more positive attitude toward the blocking process. The "take it for granted" director will have a new respect for the power of composition and movement, whereas the "fearful" director will have had studied enough models to generate confidence. Both types of directors will probably be champing at the bit to create their own blocking, and blocking coming out of a need, instead of ignorance and fear, is the only positive path to take.

The therapeutic value of justifying work is definitely there, yet even the best "medicine" is prone to unwanted side effects. At first I had beginning students jump into the deep end of the justifying pool by doing Scene 13 (or its equivalent) right away. While some were exhilarated with the challenge, others were thrown off by its complexity — a seemingly insurmountable puzzle which, to say the least, becomes very bad workshop "medicine." Powerful medicine which initially cures the destructive disease of attitude, but ultimately kills the patient's confidence is hardly worth taking. Through the inevitable trial and error process of this early justifying work, it became obvious that other exercises were needed, that missing steps needed to be found, in order to make the "medicine" easier to take. The progression of exercises in this chapter is from greater to lesser freedom, meaning that in the earlier exercises there is considerably more latitude for making up additional movements to fit into the given movement, making the justifying process much easier (i.e. instead of beginning with the equivalent of a 500-piece puzzle, a 50-piece puzzle seems a much better place to start). After being gradually weaned from this freedom, by the time the student gets to the final justifying exercises, they become a relatively easy puzzle to solve and the "medicine" works in the way it was designed.

The need for neutral, stock rehearsal furniture painted the same color becomes especially obvious with justifying movement exercises. With neutral set pieces, the given ground plans are easily interpreted in many ways. A cube can become a chair, a television, an end table, a present, a bomb, etc., whereas an actual chair is much less conducive to multiple interpretations. The student director needs to be reminded that there are many solutions to these exercises, and that the goal should be to create a "signature" scene that is unmistakably the director's own work. Even though the basic blocking in the advanced exercises (Scene 13 and 14) remains the same, it is fascinating to witness the unbelievable number of very valid interpretations from the very same staging. Part of the reason why these advanced exercises are so interesting to watch is because the exact same blocking and ground plan are interpreted so radically differently by each director. Even in this very early work, and specifically because of the initial sameness, the beginning director becomes aware of just how important the role the director happens to be, and just how distinctive his work happens to be from everybody else's.

A word of caution: ***These exercises are not playwriting exercises.*** Directors should strive to create simple lines which can be easily memorized by the actors. The specific progression of exercises are as follows:

SCENE	TITLE	DESCRIPTION
Scene 8	Serial Starters	Introductory work in justifying variations in level, plane, and body position.
Scene 9	Pick up Six	Two characters. Six separate movements are drawn from a stack of cards. They can be arranged in any order, and extra movements can be added as transitions when needed.
Scene 10	Justified Patterns	Two characters. Work with a specific pattern, and move on the "tracks" provided by the pattern. A variation is to use a different pattern for each character.
Scene 11	Fixed 'N Freed	Two characters. One character has fully *fixed* movements, whereas the other is *free* to move as needed. The *fixed* movements may be interrelated with the *free* movements in whatever configurations seem interesting.
Scene 12	Mosaic Movement	Two characters. Both characters are given a specific set of movements, but the movements between the two characters can be interrelated in a number of ways.
Scene 13	Fully Fixed	Three characters. Exact movements in exact order shown in the blocking diagrams must be followed.
Scene 14	Movement Swap	Three characters. Two directors each create a scene and then swap movements with each other. Both the "original" and justified version are performed.

These exercises, as with most of the exercises in this book, capitalize on a ***spatial intelligence***. Unfortunately, for the most part, our formal education has done little to foster this kind of intelligence. As Ann Lewin, Director of the Capital Children's Museum in Washington, D.C. argues:

> Spatial intelligence is virtually left out of formal education. In kindergarten we give the children blocks and sand with which to build. Then we take these things away for the next twelve years of their education and expect kids to become architects and engineers.[1]

[1]Daniel Goleman, et. al., *The Creative Spirit,* (New York: Penguin Books, 1993), p. 93.

There is a need in these exercises, as with all creative activity, to get lost in the work — to ferret out the countless possibilities from the many visual clues. As with spatial intelligence, "getting lost in the work" is also something that you may have experienced more fully as a child. Watch children, and it becomes obvious that children have a much better capacity to get lost in what they are doing than do most adults. If you learn nothing other than how to awaken this forgotten ability for total absorption, you will have learned a great deal that is easily applicable to life activities far beyond the boundaries of beginning directing.

Another excellent reason for reversing the conventional (text first, please!) directing process is simply because creativity often comes from turning things upside down and seeing something in a new way, with new eyes. In general, creative solutions often come from turning the problem over and looking at it from the other side — discovering that which was previously hidden. It's not until you turn a beautiful tapestry upside down that you are able to discover not the lovely surface images, but the beauty of the interconnecting threads. Likewise, by turning the directing process upside down you will better be able to discover the connecting threads of movement and text — also a beautiful tapestry.

Creative breakthroughs often come from topsy-turvy mind games such as trying *to make the strange familiar and the familiar strange*.[2] Many who watch a play take blocking for granted as a familiar part of the theatre. Here the familiar is deliberately made strange (blocking by itself is strange!), and the challenge is to make the "strange" once again familiar by justifying the movement with meaningful text. Helen Keller perhaps provides the best advice for approaching these exercises; when a friend of hers returned from a long walk in the woods, Helen was shocked that her friend had noticed nothing in particular:

> I wondered how it was possible to walk for an hour in the woods and see nothing of note. I who cannot see find hundreds of things: the delicate symmetry of a leaf, the smooth skin of a silver birch, the rough, shaggy bark of pine. I who am blind can give one hint to those who see: *use your eyes as if tomorrow you will have been stricken blind*.[3]

---

[2]Making the strange familiar was the creative catalyst for *Scene 3: Silently Familiar, Silently Strange*, see pp. 33-38.

[3]Daniel Goleman, et. al., *The Creative Spirit*, (New York: Penguin Books, 1993), p. 174.

SERIAL STARTERS
(Beginning Justified Movement Exercises)

God is in the details.

— Mies Van Der Rohe

OVERVIEW

Working with three actors and the provided ground plan, create four different short scenes with a definite beginning, middle, and end based on the following:

- *Scene A:* Justify the fact that at all times, every stage picture has to include a *standing*, *kneeling*, and *sitting* character. This means that if a kneeling character decides to stand up, one of the other two characters must fill the void and assume some sort of kneeling position.

- *Scene B:* Justify the fact that at all times, every stage picture has to have a character in the *upstage*, *midstage*, and *downstage* planes. Should one of them move out of the plane he or she is in, then one of the other two must shift to the unoccupied plane.

- *Scene C:* Justify the fact that at all times, each stage picture has to have a character in a *quarter*, *profile*, and *three-quarter* body position. When one character switches to a different body position then one of the other two must compensate for the change.

- *Scene D:* Adhere to *all* the conditions specified in Scenes A, B and C at the same time in a single scene.

The challenge is to transform each of these four artificial structures into fully justified, totally convincing scenes.

NOTES AND VARIATIONS

If it is felt that Scene D is too difficult, try working up to it gradually by bringing together the demands from just two, instead of three scenes. Working with a single given ground plan is at first helpful because it limits the choices, and keeps the work from becoming a ground plan exercise. Also the provided ground plan puts workshop directors literally on a common ground, and seeing how different directors solve the justifying problems in exactly the same space also brings an excitement to the workshop. Later, having the workshop directors create their own ground plans instead of relying on the one provided can become a valuable ground plan training aid. Further reason to repeat these exercises later in the training is that they can also be easily used to integrate various staging concepts. For instance, these same exercises could challenge a director's agility in working with direct, indirect focus and counter focus compositions; is the director able to convincingly justify the basic demands plus effectively integrate other staging concepts? Regardless of whatever else is brought to these basic exercises, the overall intent has to remain the same: all must be fully justified within a realistic context.

THE GROUND PLAN

Use the following ground plan to create situations for each of the four scenes. As the ground plan to the right indicates, there is considerable leeway in interpreting the various set pieces.

Set pieces may be moved during the course of the action, but the scene needs to begin in its given configuration. Attempt as much as possible to bring all of the set pieces into use. Do not add any other major set pieces; props and set dressing may be included as necessary.

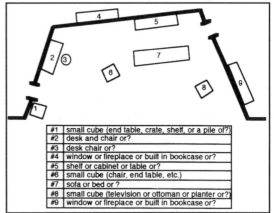

#1	small cube (end table, crate, shelf, or a pile of?)
#2	desk and chair or?
#3	desk chair or?
#4	window or fireplace or built in bookcase or?
#5	shelf or cabinet or table or?
#6	small cube (chair, end table, etc.)
#7	sofa or bed or ?
#8	small cube (television or ottoman or planter or?)
#9	window or fireplace or built in bookcase or?

CRITIQUE

1. Was the situation (the **who**, the **what**, and the **where**) well communicated?

2. (To the director) Which of the four scenes was the hardest to motivate?

3. Was everything fully justified, or were there some motivational problems and/or stretches?

4. Was there a balance between the verbal and visual elements of the scene? Or did one tend to dominate the other?

5. Favorite moment? Least favorite moment?

PICK UP SIX

(Separate Movements — Justified Movement Exercise)

Whenever you fall, pick up something.

— Oswald Theodore Avery
(Canadian bacteriologist, 1877-1955)

OVERVIEW

Teams of three — one director and two actors. A bag of "cards" is prepared from the blocking diagrams provided on pages 73-77. These diagrams can be copied and then individually cut out, or the directors can simply draw numbers which refer to the numbered diagrams. *Each* actor draws *six* cards (i.e. a total of twelve cards will be used).[4] The challenge is to create characters and a situation that fully integrate the selected movements. Two important ground rules are: 1. Each character must do *all* of the selected movements, exactly as depicted, but *they may be done in any order*, and 2. If needed, up to six transitional movements per actor may be created.

SUGGESTIONS

- Run through the movements, searching for movements that flow together with other movements. One or more of these links may provide the "seed" for your basic situation. With the situation in mind, it will be fairly easy to create whatever transitional movements are needed to connect all the movements fully.

- Another approach is to create the specific order of movements before deciding upon a situation. Begin by finding all the possible links, and creating whatever transitory movements are needed in order to use *all* of the selected movements. Then run through the movements several times until someone gets an interesting idea to try. If the idea seems to "catch," continue to refine it, improvising dialogue suitable for the situation.

- Remember, this is not a playwriting exercise. Strive to create simple lines which can easily be memorized by your actors.

---

[4]This number has proven to work well in our workshops, but obviously other possibilities are fine, depending on the time and needs of the group.

THE GROUND PLAN

The setting is an interior with two entrances. The logic of the space and the specific designation of the set pieces depend upon your situation. For instance, #10 can either be a sofa, desk, a trunk, a shelf, or something else. Possibilities for each of the given set pieces are offered below — feel free to make up your own.

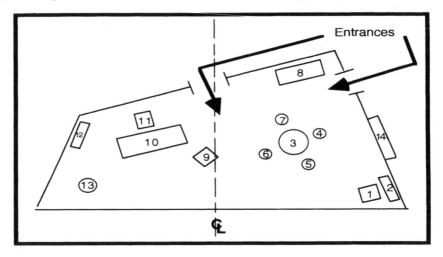

SET PIECE #	DESCRIPTION
1 & 2	Maybe a small chair and desk, or a stool and shelf, or ?
3-7	Table with four chairs or an exercise trampoline with four pillows, or ?
8	Rectangular set piece (maybe a cabinet, bar, gun case, trunk), or ?
9	Cube or chair (maybe a television, swivel chair, bed table), or ?
10	Large platform (maybe a bed, desk, trunk, low table, rowing machine), or ?
11	Small cube or chair (maybe an end table, a wastebasket, a CD player stand), or ?
12	Vertical unit (maybe a cabinet, gun case, large screen TV), or ?
13	Circular stand (maybe a pedestal for a statue, plant, bottled water), or ?
14	Vertical unit (maybe a fireplace, window, cabinet, closet), or ?

THE CARDS

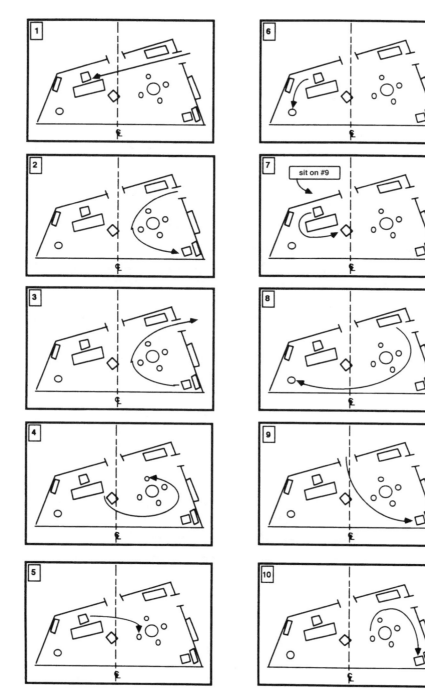

THE CARDS *(Continued)*

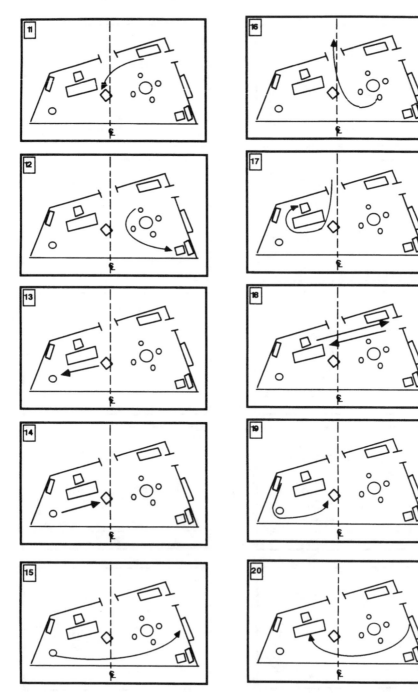

THE CARDS *(Continued)*

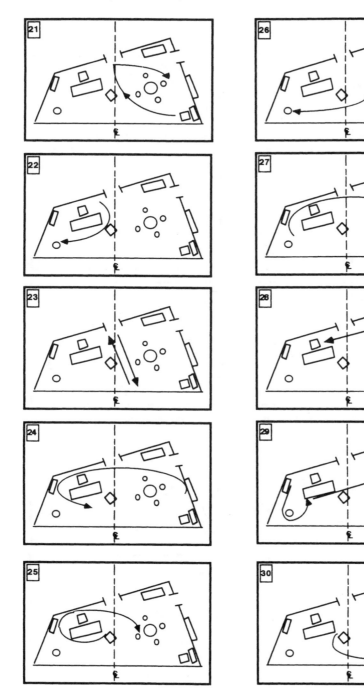

THE CARDS *(Continued)*

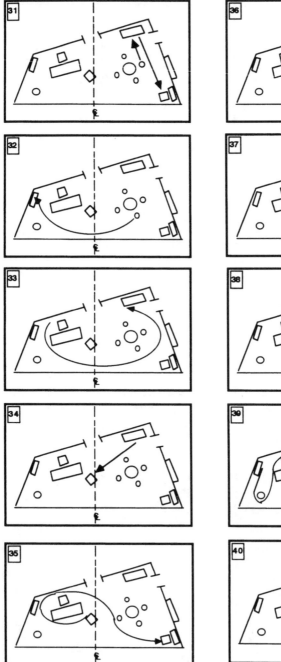
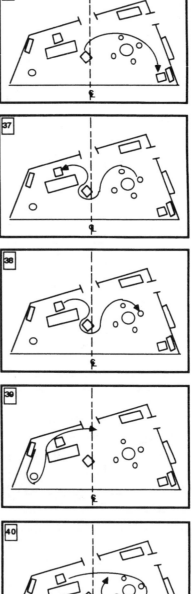

THE CARDS *(Continued)*

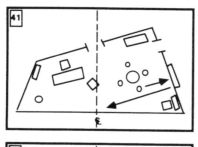

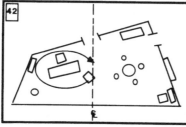

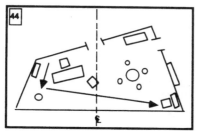

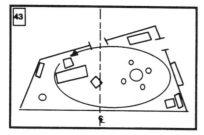

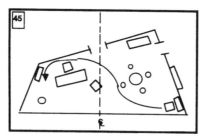

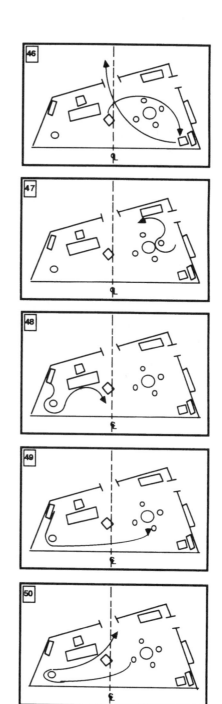

CRITIQUE

To the director

1. Did you end up creating the flow of movements first, and then figuring out the situation, or did a particular movement provide the inspiration for the idea? In other words, what was the major stimulus in bringing about the idea for the scene? Did it come from a specific movement, or from a discovered "link" between two movements? Or did the idea come after the series of movements was completed?

2. Were there any specific movements that were especially difficult to motivate? Did you ultimately overcome the difficulty?

3. How helpful were the team members in solving this exercise?

To the rest of the workshop

1. Was the *who*, *what*, and *where* clearly established?

2. Were there any interesting *psychological* areas created?

3. Was the overall situation interesting? Would the scene stand on its own, meaning if someone didn't know the exercise, would this still be considered effective theatre? Was there a definite beginning, middle, and end?

4. Were there any effective visual pauses?

5. Did the dialogue seem to fit the movement? Were there any moments that didn't seem motivated? What moments worked especially well?

6. Were there times when the dialogue completely took over, and the storytelling was more verbal than visual? In general, did the director rely more on the visual or verbal elements of the scene to communicate the story, or was there a pretty good balance?

7. Favorite moment? Least favorite moment?

DIRECTIONS: SCENE #10
JUSTIFIED PATTERNS
(Pattern-Generated Movement)

Art is the imposing of a pattern on experience,
and our aesthetic enjoyment in recognition of the pattern.

— **Alfred North Whitehead (1861-1947)**

OVERVIEW

Teams of three — two actors and a director. Using stock rehearsal furniture, create *two* scenes as follows:

Scene 1

Select a *single* pattern from those provided on page 81. Think of the lines of the pattern as potential movement *tracks* for each of your actors. An actor may go in any direction whatsoever (backward, forwards, etc.) as long as there is no deviation from the given "track." Any type of movement and stage business is possible as long as it is justified, and the actors stay on the provided "tracks" of the pattern. As with all justified movement exercises, the overall objective is to create a situation, characters and accompanying lines that fully justify the given circumstances. Strive to make the scene build, and support this rising tension with a *visual progression*.

Scene 2

Similar to Scene 1, except that a different situation is played, and this time a pattern for *each* actor is selected.

DISCUSSION

The ground plan doesn't need to look like the chosen pattern, but it does need to be the *stimulus that brings about the pattern*. A good ground plan will always encourage a pattern of movement, and so linking a particular pattern to a ground plan is not all that unusual. While our focus at this point is not on ground plans, it's pretty obvious that this is just as much a ground plan exercise as it is justifying exercise.[5] It's possible to begin first with a situation, and then pick a pattern that seems to best

---

[5]In fact, the very same concept of this exercise is repeated as formal ground plan exercises (see Scene 18 and 19, pp. 135-147).

fit the intended storyline. But it's equally as possible to begin first with the pattern, or the ground plan generated from the pattern, and let either or both of these inspire the situation. Figuring out what to start with is equivalent to pondering whether the proverbial chicken or the egg comes first.

There are countless ways of moving within a given pattern. The lines of the pattern are potential movement "tracks," and there are multiple possibilities of moving within the same pattern. Two characters in the same pattern would very likely use the "tracks" of the pattern differently from each other. A character might become attached to a particular part of the pattern, or maybe as the scene progresses a character for some reason begins to use increasingly more space or less space. If, for instance, one of the characters "own" the space, and the other character is a guest, then the use of the pattern would be presumably very different. Invading space and psychological areas such as was experimented with in Scene 5 are a certainly a possibility.[6]

Some of the available patterns are actually two patterns superimposed on each other. This is certainly the case with #3 and #6 and #7. In the case of #3, for instance, maybe one character is associated with the rectangle, while the other is associated with the diamond. But then again maybe the a director of #3 doesn't choose to emphasize the diamond, but instead decides to stress the two triangles 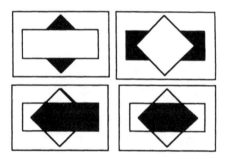 that are also made by the intersecting lines. The four variations of diagram #3 above are just a few of the many "interpretations" of this single pattern. What first seems like a simple overlay of a rectangle and a diamond becomes a potentially rich series of patterns within patterns. Needless to say, that in the second scene, when a pattern for each character is used, there is a multitude of pattern within pattern possibilities.

Sometimes the director only wants the individual movements to be important, and whether or not the audience perceives the overall pattern is insignificant. But at other times, the director wants to emphasize how the movements add up — i.e. the overall shape of the pattern. Staging a representational (realistic) scene in this exercise is probably more challenging than working with a more presentational, abstract scene, so plan on having at least one of the two scenes be a "slice of life" type approach. Beware of the most serious trap of all, which is not motivating a movement. Just because there are given "tracks" to be followed doesn't mean that there isn't a need to motivate each movement. Justifying each movement is the primary objective of the entire exercise. As always, the exercise should be able to stand on its own; in other words, if someone was completely oblivious of the constraints of the exercise, he should be fully able to appreciate the scene as effective theatre.

[6]See *Scene 5: Breaking Silent Boundaries*, p.43.

POSSIBLE PATTERNS

1.

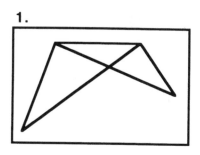

2.

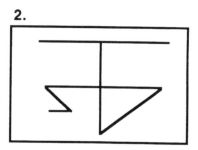

3.

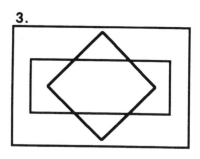

4.

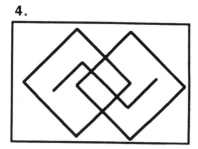

5.

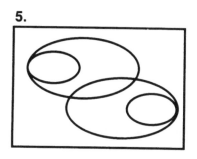

6.

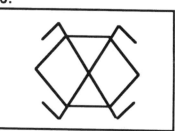

7.

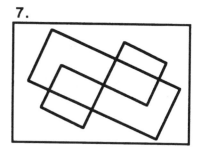

8.

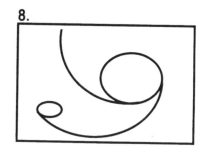

VARIATIONS

- No lines are used — the objective is to create a "silent scene."

- A pattern is used by one actor, but the other actor is "free" to move as needed.

- Used as a rehearsal exercise for either an actual scene, or for an improvised situation stemming from the world of the play.

CRITIQUE

To the director

1. What was the catalyst for creating the scene — the situation, ground plan or pattern?

2. Were there any parts of the pattern that were especially difficult to motivate? Did you ultimately overcome the difficulty?

To the rest of the workshop

1. Was the situation (the *who*, *what*, and *where*) clearly established? And was there an effective *visual progression*?

2. Were there any interesting *psychological* areas created? How were the characters related to the pattern or patterns?

3. Did the dialogue seem to fit the movement? Were there any moments that didn't seem motivated? What moments worked especially well?

4. In general, did the director rely more on the visual or verbal elements of the scene to communicate the story, or was there a pretty good balance?

5. Was the pattern itself stressed? In other words, by the end of the scene, was the overall shape of the pattern evident to the audience? Or were just the individual moves, rather than the pattern, emphasized?

6. Was the overall situation interesting? Would the scene stand on its own, meaning if someone didn't know the exercise, would this still be considered effective theatre? Was there a definite beginning, middle, and end?

7. Favorite moment? Least favorite moment?

FREE 'N FIXED
(Half Free Form — Half Fixed Movements)

Freedom's just another word
for nothing left to lose.

— **Kris Kristofferson** (Actor & folk musician)
Me and Bobby McGee

OVERVIEW

Teams of three — one director and two actors.

Character A has a *fixed* set of fourteen movements (see pages 85-87) which must be followed exactly as given, whereas Character B is *free* to move as needed. Character B's "free" movements may be interrelated with Character A's movements in whatever ways seem effective. The challenge is to create a two-character scene in which the situation, characters, and lines fully justify and integrate the movements of both players.

SUGGESTIONS

1. Run through all the movements for Character A at least twice. Ask both the actor playing this character and the other actor what their impressions of the movements were.

2. If there is time, experiment with different rhythms and tempos, since these changes can also affect the meaning of the movements. Keep in mind that a **contrast in the character rhythms** can be dramatically exciting, although identical character rhythms can also be very interesting depending upon the situation.

3. Brainstorm with your team possible situations and characters which might work. **Remember that you have a completely free rein in devising movement for Character B**.

4. In most cases the body position at the end of a particular cross is left unspecified; it is up to the discretion of the director to figure out what will work best. Also, as long as the basic movements are executed as diagrammed, additional stage business and props can be added to the given blocking.

5. Remember that Character B's free movements can be woven in whatever way seems effective with the "fixed" movements of Character A.

6. Run through the selected situation enough times so that the dialogue is "set."

THE GROUND PLAN

The setting is an interior with two entrances. The logic of the space, and the specific designation of the set pieces depend on your situation. For instance, #4 can either be a drafting table and lamp, or a chair and end table, or two art objects. Additional possibilities are listed below, but use these as springboards for your own ideas.

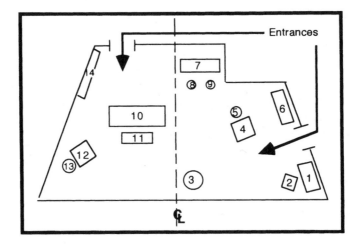

SET PIECE #	DESCRIPTION
1 & 2	Maybe a small chair and desk, or a stool and shelf, or two trunks, or ?
3	Maybe an ottoman, a television, a fireplace, a fish tank, or ?
4 & 5	Maybe a chair and lamp, a stool and drafting table, art objects, or ?
6	Maybe a table, trunk, bar cart, curio cabinet, or ?
7-9	Maybe a bar and stools, workbench, sofa with two small coffee tables, or ?
10 & 11	Maybe a sofa and coffee table, a bed, a tanning bed, an exercise mat, or ?
12 & 13	Maybe a chair and end table, a CD player and lamp, or ?
14	Maybe a window, fireplace, cabinet, closet, or ?

MOVEMENTS FOR CHARACTER "A"

Intro. Position:

A: Seated at #8.

1. **A:** Rise from #8, and X to #1, end in ¼ L.

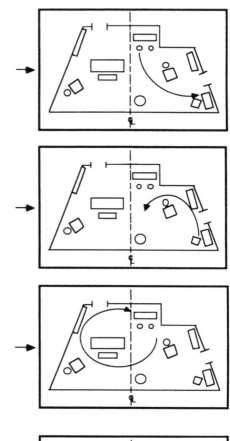

2. **A:** Glance at UR entrance, then arc X to ULC as shown.

3. **A:** X to #8, then X to URC entrance, X downstage as show, faces #1.

4. **A:** X to #7 (profile R), then X to #12 (¾ L).

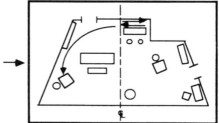

MOVEMENT FOR CHARACTER A *(Continued)*

5. **A**: Arc X to #3, sit on #3, (end in ¾ R).

6. **A**: Exit Left, then re-enter and X to D.C. by #3, look back at L exit, then focus someplace else.

7. **A**: Arc X to #5, end in ¼ R

8. **A**: X to DL, by #1 and #2, pick up an object.

9. **A**: X to #8, and sit.

MOVEMENT FOR CHARACTER A *(Continued)*

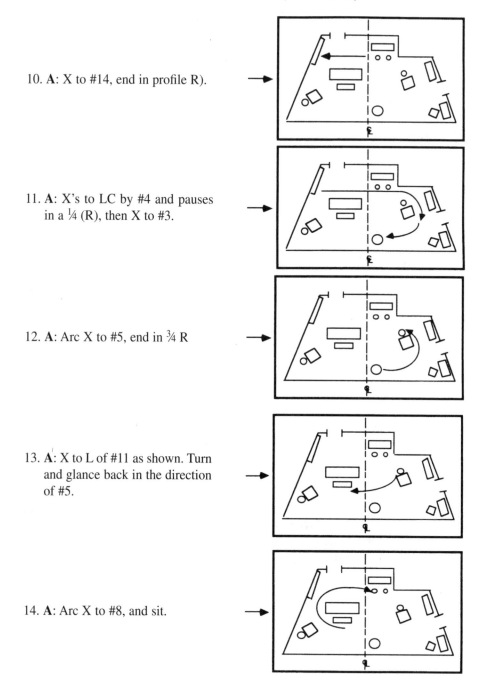

10. **A**: X to #14, end in profile R).

11. **A**: X's to LC by #4 and pauses in a ¼ (R), then X to #3.

12. **A**: Arc X to #5, end in ¾ R

13. **A**: X to L of #11 as shown. Turn and glance back in the direction of #5.

14. **A**: Arc X to #8, and sit.

VARIATIONS

- No lines are used — the objective is to create a "silent scene."

- Three actors are used — one with fixed movement, and two with free movement.

- Used as a rehearsal exercise: improvising a situation stemming from the world of the play.

CRITIQUE

To the director

1. Did the built-in flexibility of the exercise, where you were totally in control of creating movement for Character B, make it easier or harder?

2. Was the ground plan more important than the specific movements in bringing about the basic situation?

To the rest of the workshop

1. Was the situation (the *who*, *what*, and *where*) clearly established?

2. Were there any interesting *psychological* areas created? Were any boundaries broken?

3. Was focus shared between the two characters, or did one tend to dominate? Did Character B's movements seem convincingly integrated with Character A's? Did the focal shifts between the two characters make sense, or were there moments when an important line was thrown away because the focus was on the other character?

4. Did the dialogue seem to fit the movement? Were there any moments that didn't seem motivated? What moments worked especially well?

5. In general, did the director rely more on the visual or verbal elements of the scene to communicate the story, or was there a pretty good balance? Any effective visual pauses?

6. Was the overall situation interesting? Would the scene stand on its own, meaning if someone didn't know the exercise, would this still be considered effective theatre? Was there a definite beginning, middle, and end?

7. Favorite moment? Least favorite moment?

MOSAIC MOVEMENT
(Interrelating Two Fixed Tracks)

Mosaic: a pattern or picture
made by placing together small pieces of
glass or stone, etc. of different colors.

— *Oxford American Dictionary*

OVERVIEW

Both characters (A and B) are given a very specific set of movements. The intent is to create specific characters in a specific situation, and the accompanying lines that fully justify the given movement.

The word "mosaic" in the title of this particular justified movement exercise is based on the idea that A and B's movements are ***deliberately separated***, challenging you to create a "mosaic of movement" by determining the specific interaction or sequence of movements. For instance, all of A's movements have to be followed as written, but maybe you decide to do the first three movements as notated before B does anything, or maybe B does two movements first, followed by three of A's. Or maybe there are interesting sequences where the movement becomes simultaneous — the possibilities are virtually endless. As always, the all important intent is ***to fully justify every action*** in an integrated context.

SUGGESTIONS

1. Run through all the movements for Character A at least twice. Ask the actor playing this character what his impressions of the movements were.

2. Do exactly the same thing with Character B's movements.

3. Brainstorm with your team possible situations and characters which might work. If there is time, experiment with a couple of these possibilities, letting the actors improvise their lines each time.

4. As a group make a final decision, and run through the selected situation enough times so that the dialogue is, for the most part, "set."

5. Remember you can add objects and create business as needed, as long as you adhere to the given notation.

6. Keep in mind that even though you have to follow each of the movements in exact order for Character A and B, there is total flexibility as

89

to the specific interaction of movements between them. Also, keep an eye open for *simultaneous movement possibilities*.

THE GROUND PLAN

The setting is an interior with two entrances. The logic of the space and the specific designation of the set pieces depend on your situation. For instance, #2 can either be a bed, a sofa, a trunk, or something else. The descriptions below describe only the actual objects; what you make of them is totally up to you.

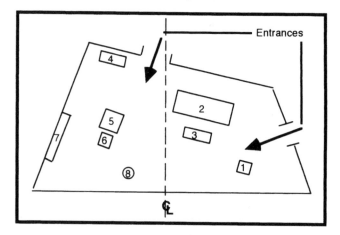

SET PIECE #	DESCRIPTION
1	Small cube (maybe a TV, chair, fish tank, plant, art object, toy box), or ?
2	Platform (maybe a sofa, bed, bathtub, coffin, trampoline), or ?
3	Low platform (maybe a coffee table, trunk, keg in crate, wagon), or ?
4	Rectangular set piece (maybe a cabinet, counter, gun case), or ?
5	Large cube (maybe an arm chair, low table, bar unit, exercise machine), or ?
6	Small cube (maybe an end table, a wastebasket, a CD player stand), or ?
7	Vertical unit (maybe a fireplace, window, cabinet, closet), or ?
8	Circular stand (maybe a pedestal for a statue, plant, bottled water), or ?

MOVEMENTS FOR CHARACTER A

Intro. Position:

A: Ready to enter from URC.

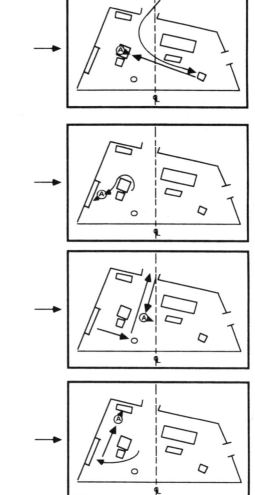

1. **A**: Enters and X's to #1, kneels, then rises and X's to #5. Sits on #5, facing #1 as shown.

2. **A**: Rise and arc X to #7, end in ¼ R.

3. **A**: X to #8, then X to URC entrance, X downstage as show, faces #1.

4. **A**: X to #7 (profile R), then X to #4 (¾ L).

MOVEMENT FOR CHARACTER A *(Continued)*

5. **A**: Turn and face #7, then exit URC. Enter and X to downstage as shown, focus on #1.

6. **A**: X to #1, then X back to #5, end in ¼ L, focusing on #1.

7. **A**: Glance at #7, then X a few steps downstage to #8, end in ¼ R.

8. **A**: X to #7, then arc X above #2 to LC as shown, end ¼ R.

9. **A**: Exit L as shown.

MOVEMENTS FOR CHARACTER B

Intro. Position:

B: At #4 (facing upstage)

1. **B**: Turn and face DR, turn back upstage, and then once again face downstage. Then arc X to (UL) end of #2 as shown (end in ¼ R).

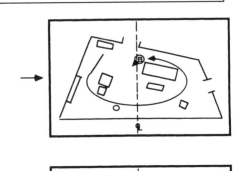

2. **B**: Turn, face URC entrance, then X to #1, end in ¼ L).

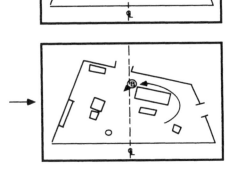

3. **B**: X back to UL end of #2 as before, end in ¼ R.

4. **B**: Glance at #1, then glance at URC entrance. X to #8, then arc X to #4, end facing upstage.

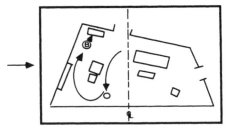

93

MOVEMENT FOR CHARACTER B *(Continued)*

5. **B**: X and sit on L end of #2, end in a ¼ L.

6. **B**: Exit URC, then enter and X above #2, and arc over to #7, end in profile R.

7. **B**: X to #4, then back downstage and arc around to URC exit. Then X toward #8, making a large arc X back to UL end of #2 (end in ¼ R).

8. **B**: Glance at URC exit, then arc X to #1 and kneel, facing #1.

9. **B**: Rise and arc X to #2, sit on #2, end in ¼ L.

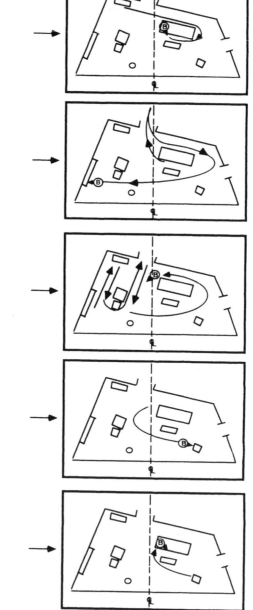

DISCOVERING RHYTHM

Mosaic movement is a transitional exercise between the intermediate *Free 'N Fixed* (Scene 11) and the advanced *Fully Fixed* (Scene 13). More than any other justified exercise, *Mosaic Movement* offers unique opportunity for the student to discover that blocking is intimately related to rhythm. Faced with the task of integrating two separate tracks of fixed movement, the director of this exercise is somewhat like a film editor. In cutting from shot to shot or scene to scene, a film editor has to be very sensitive to rhythm, and so does the director of this exercise. Fast cuts in a film create a staccato rhythm. Similarly "cutting" from move to move, where one actor's moves are countered move for move by another's, can also create a staccato effect. Maybe there is a contrast of rhythms between the two characters, where one moves fairly slowly and infrequently, contrasted with the other character who moves quickly and often. Or maybe there is a reversal of character rhythms — the hyper character ends mellow, and the mellow one ends hyper. Or maybe the director is interested in creating a rhythmic progression. Three possibilities for rhythmic progression are:

- A progression of intervals. Maybe the scene begins where Character A tends to do about five moves before Character B does anything, but as the scene progresses the number of Character A's moves becomes increasingly less.

- A progression of impact. Maybe the movements of one character have increasingly more impact upon the movements of the other character.

- A progression of spatial separation. Maybe one character gets progressively closer to the other character.

JOURNAL SUGGESTIONS

Below are potential topics to discuss in your journal:

- Did the fact that both tracks were "fixed" make it easier or harder than the previous (*Free 'N Fixed*) exercise? In the process of integrating the two tracks, were you able to create interesting **rhythms**?

- In terms of easiest to hardest, do you agree or disagree with the order of justified exercises up and through this exercise? Why?

- Was there any specific movement/s that were especially difficult to motivate? Did you ultimately overcome the difficulty?

- What was the major stimulus in bringing about the idea for the scene? Did the team contribute valuable ideas in coming up with a specific situation? And once the basic situation was settled, did the team continue to creatively help each other?

CRITIQUE

To the director

1. Did one track tend to function more as a catalyst than the other in bringing about the basic situation, or was it the combination of tracks that inspired the scene?

2. Was it difficult to keep the focus where you wanted it? Was there sometimes a problem with a speaking actor not having effective focus?

To the rest of the workshop

1. Was the situation (*who*, *what*, and *where*) clearly established?

2. Were there interesting rhythms created in the intercutting between the two tracks? Was there any kind of rhythmic progression?

3. Was focus shared between the two characters, or did one tend to dominate? Did Character B's movements seem convincingly integrated with Character A's? Did the focal shifts between the two characters make sense, or were there moments when an important line was thrown away because the focus was on the other character?

4. Did the dialogue seem to fit the movement? Were there any moments that didn't seem motivated? What moments worked especially well?

5. In general, did the director rely more on the visual or verbal elements of the scene to communicate the story, or was there a pretty good balance? Any effective visual pauses?

6. Was the overall situation interesting? Would the scene stand on its own, meaning if someone didn't know the exercise, would this still be considered effective theatre? Was there a definite beginning, middle, and end?

7. Favorite moment? Least favorite moment?

FULLY FIXED

(Three-Character, Completely Fixed Movement)

Between us and you there is a great gulf fixed.

— Luke 16:26

OVERVIEW

You are provided a ground plan and detailed blocking, ***but no lines***, for a three-person scene. Casting from your team, create a situation, characters, and accompanying lines that justify the given movement. Most of the blocking notes are very specific, but where details such as body positions and head focus are unspecified, the director is free to do as desired. Strive to create a dynamic, fully stage-worthy scene. All stage business, movement, and dialogue should, as usual, be ***fully memorized***.

AN ADVANCED EXERCISE

This and the following exercise (*Movement Swap*) are the advanced justifying exercises. This exercise in particular is an advanced exercise for three reasons.

- One reason is suggested by the title of the exercise — *Fully Fixed*. This is the first of the justifying exercises where the blocking is "fully fixed." Up to this point there has been a dance between the fixed and the free form, but in this exercise the dance is over and the blocking is completely set.

- A second reason is simply because there is an additional actor. Keeping the focus where you want it with three characters is definitely more challenging than with two. There will be even more danger than before of having an actor throw away an important line due to the fact that the focus is wrong. From this point on, most of the exercises will require three actors, so this exercise functions as an important turning point.

- A third reason is due to the fact that this is the first of the justified ground plans to use platforms. The set forces the director to think vertically as well as horizontally.[7] The visualizing leap from ground plan to three dimensional space is harder when levels are involved.

---

[7]See pp. 53-54 for a discussion about the dynamics of level.

INTERPRETIVE STRATEGIES

Although the given blocking is open to a great many interpretations, this does not by any means suggest that it is neutral or irrelevant movement. As with all justify exercises, there are definite structures or designs built into blocking. With the previous justify exercises, the free form part of the work kept open the possibility of downplaying the built-in structures. With this exercise, however, where there is no slack whatsoever, it is especially important to become aware of the given structures.

A good place to start is to look for any possible visual progressions. Does the scene begin and end the same way, or if not exactly the same, is there a similarity? Or is there an incredible difference that can't be ignored? Looking closely at the beginning and the ending helps to highlight the "frame" of the scene. The frame functions as the special window for the director as a Peeping Tom to look through. The frame is like a filter that leaves a trace of itself on every single particle that passes through it. Find the frame, and the situation will very likely fall into view.

Examining the specific movements in terms of strength and weakness is another excellent way to analyze the given blocking. Level in this particular ground plan plays an important role. Height is equated with strength, but this doesn't mean that every time an actor is on a platform he will take focus. Body position, head focus, and the positions of other actors all affect whether a character on a platform will dominate others. Also keep in mind the principle of contrast; if everyone is on a platform, it is very possible that the single actor who is not on the platform will command our attention. Strength and weakness is also inherent in upstage and downstage moves, as well as right and left moves. All things being equal, moving downstage is stronger than moving upstage, just as moving stage left to stage right is stronger than moving from stage right to stage left.[8]

Another excellent source of clues to consider is whether a particular character tends to become associated with a particular area or set piece. If a character keeps coming back to the same place, there has to be a reason. Audiences are very adept at remembering and associating a particular character with a particular set piece or area, and these "psychological areas" have the potential of creating continuity and coherence in the dramatic structure of the scene.[9] The psychological areas are not hard to find, but to ignore them is to go against the built-in design of the blocking; the hard part is not so much finding them, but figuring out how these psychological "pieces" relate to the overall puzzle. Related to psychological areas is the possibility of "space invasion" or breaking boundaries.[10] People, as with a great many other animals, are very territorial and if space is invaded it may very well be a highly significant event.

---

[8]See pp. 35-38 (*Ruminating on the Right and Left*) for a discussion about the strengths and weaknesses inherent in right-left movements.

[9]See pp. 43-44 for a discussion about psychological areas.

[10]See pp. 44-48 for a discussion relating to breaking boundaries.

Such boundary breaking can be very obvious or very subtle. Even an action as subtle as a turn of the head can become an invasion, but whether subtle or not, it is always a good idea to keep an eye open for this kind of behavior. By first analyzing the blocking objectively, ideas for situations will readily surface.

THE GROUND PLAN

Use the following ground plan for your scene. Each platform and set piece has been given a number, which is used for clarity in the blocking notation. Since levels are used, a perspective sketch has been provided below to help visualize what the actual space will look like. As usual, interpret each set piece and the plan as a whole as desired; with this particular plan, it is purposefully ambiguous as to whether the space is an interior or exterior.

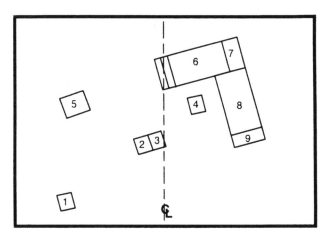

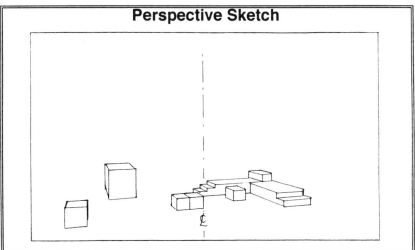

Drawing by Richard Slabaugh

99

DETAILED BLOCKING NOTATION

$$\left\{ \; = \; \begin{array}{l} \text{simultaneous} \\ \text{movement} \end{array} \right.$$

Intro. Positions

- **A**: Sitting on cube #1 — facing downstage (d.s.).
- **B**: Sitting center of cubes #2-3 — facing upstage (u.s.).
- **C**: Sitting on #7 — profile R.

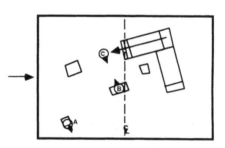

1. **C**: Rises and X's R and down steps to URC area facing B.
2. **B**: Rises.

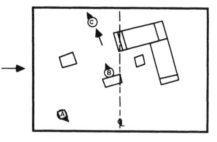

3. **C**: X's u.s — faces u.s.

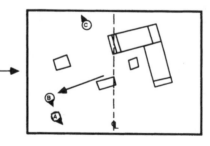

4. **B**: X's DR (faces ¼ L).

5. **A**: Rises and X's DC (faces ¼ L).

6. **B**: X to cube #4 and sit (facing R) as shown.

7. **A**: X's u.s. to just below cubes #2-3, kneels, facing u.s.

8. **C**: turn and face A.

9. **C**: X's 2 or 3 steps toward (*not to*) A.

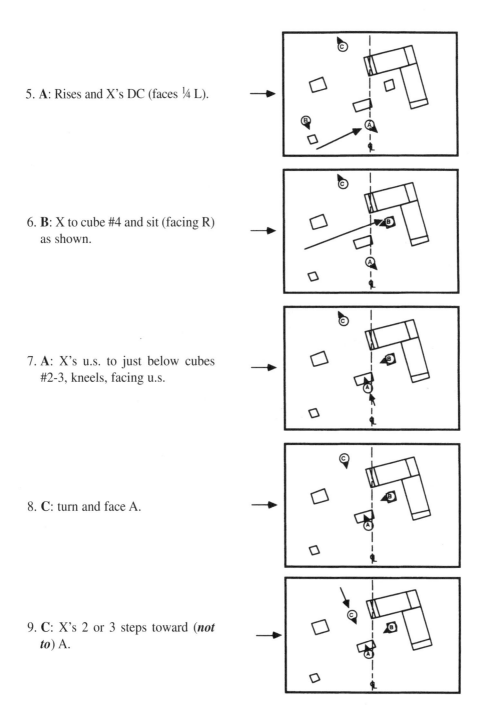

10. **A**: Rise and *back* one or two steps downstage.

11. **B**: Rise.

12. **A**: X back to cubes #2-3 and once again kneel.

13. **C**: Arc X to #5 as shown and pick up object, then X back to center area (using the same arcing pattern to return to center).

14. **C**: Turn in to a profile L (make eye contact with B) then X R to RC area — end in ¼ R.

15. **C**: X back to center — face A.

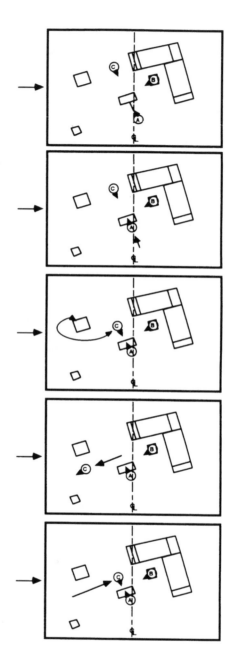

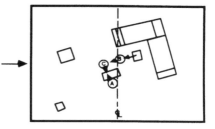

16. **B**: Rise and X to character C, taking object from C.

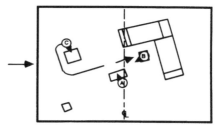

17. **B**: Returns and sits as before on cube #4.

    C: Arc X to #5 (URC area) as before.

18. **C**: Start arc X back to center, pause, then X quickly to DL (just below #9).

    A: Backs step or two downstage, then makes break to DL going up #9 and onto #8 but tripping and falling onto #8.

    B: Rise from #4 and X up steps to #6 (focusing on A).

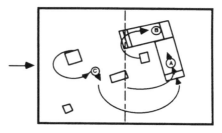

19. **A**: Rise — turn and face character C, back up a step or two, turn and focuses on B.

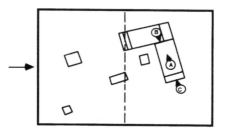

20. **B**: X's toward A, end DL, having just stepped off #9 (end ¾ R).

    A: X's to UL corner of cube #3 (end ¾ R).

    C: Arc to UL corner of #5 area (end ¼ L).

21. **B**: X and sit on #4 as shown.

    A: X and kneel by cube #2-3 (same position as before).

    C: X L a few steps.

22. **C**: X onto #6 (focusing on A).

    B: Rise (standing by #4).

    A: Rise and X R a step or two (end ¼

23. **A**: X to L of #5 (end ¾ R).

    B & C: Focus on A.

24. **A**: Turn out to ¼ R slamming fist on #5, then X to DRC (end ¼ R).

25. **C**: X to downstage edge of #8 (focusing on A).

   B: X up steps to #6 (focus on C).

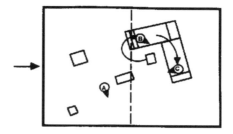

26. **A**: X (L) and kneel as shown.

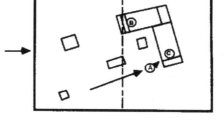

27. **A**: Rise and arc around to #2-3, sitting on #2-3 (facing upstage).

   B: X and sit on #7 (focusing on #5).

   C: X and sit on #1, facing downstage.

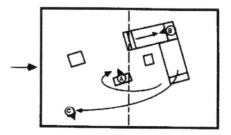

End Positions

- **C**: Sitting on cube #1, facing downstage.

- **A**: Sitting center of cubes #2-3 — facing upstage.

- **B**: Sitting on #7 — profile R.

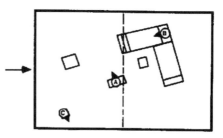

CRITIQUE

To the director

1. What was the primary catalyst that brought about the idea for the scene?

2. Was it difficult to keep the focus where you wanted it? Was there sometimes a problem with a speaking actor not having effective focus?

To the rest of the workshop

1. Was the situation (the *who*, *what*, and *where*) clearly established?

2. Was the blocking accurately executed?

3. Did the director emphasize the frame of the scene? Was focus shared between the three characters, or did one tend to dominate? Did the focal shifts between the two characters make sense, or were there moments when an important line was thrown away because the focus was on the other character?

4. Did the dialogue seem to fit the movement? Were there any moments that didn't seem motivated? What moments worked especially well?

5. In general, did the director rely more on the visual or verbal elements of the scene to communicate the story, or was there a pretty good balance? Any effective visual pauses?

6. Was the overall situation interesting? Would the scene stand on its own, meaning if someone didn't know the exercise, would this still be considered effective theatre? Was there a definite beginning, middle, and end?

7. Favorite moment? Least favorite moment?

MOVEMENT SWAP
(Swapping Movement With Another Director)

It is not best to swap horses
while crossing the river.

— Abraham Lincoln

OVERVIEW

Working with a pre-established ground plan, each member of the workshop will create the blocking notation for a *three*-character scene. Following the format provided in Scene 13 (see pages 100-105) the recorded blocking notes should have a total of twenty separate moves, and the notation should provide only the movements — *not the lines*. When this has been completed, members of the workshop will *swap* their movement plans with each other. Each director will be perform *two distinct scenes*:

- *Scene A:* The scene based upon the movement that the director was given. This scene is the director's interpretation of the twenty moves he was given by another director.

- *Scene B:* The original scene that was created on paper to give to another director. This scene is what the director had in mind when he created the twenty moves.

After Scene A is presented to the workshop, the "original" scene from whence it came will then be performed by the director who first created the moves.

A TRANSITIONAL EXERCISE

Most directors in conjuring up a situation for Scene A will rely upon the given ground plan for inspiration. It's theoretically possible to create the twenty moves oblivious of the situation, which of course would have the effect of creating a self-made justified movement exercise. But most directors will key off the ground plan, since this is the only tangible given item. In the previous justify exercises, more likely than not, it was something about the movement more so than the ground plan that sparked the idea for the scene. Here the ground plan is spotlighted from the start, and this makes *Movement Swap* an excellent bridge to the ground plan exercises ahead. Focusing on the ground plan will very likely bring about the discovery that a ground plan generates specific movements. A good ground plan encourages specific patterns of movement, and this fact will inevitably become obvious after watching scene after scene using the same ground plan. With each director in the workshop doing two scenes each, part of the fun is savoring the differences, but among these inevitable differences there will also be a definite opportunity to pick out the patterns of similarity brought about by the same ground plan.

In trying to justify the given blocking of the previous scenes, there was very likely some curiosity as to what the originator of the blocking had in mind. Here that curiosity is ultimately gratified since after performing each scene, the workshop then gets to watch the original. The comparison between the original and the "copy" can be fascinating; it would be an interesting experiment to bring in people from outside of the workshop to see whether or not they would happen to notice the hidden similarity between the two scenes. Other than the focus on the ground plan and gratification of getting to view the original, the justifying work is virtually the same as that of Scene 13.

SUGGESTIONS

1. After brainstorming a series of ideas with the given ground plan, settle upon a favorite.

2. Generate and notate *twenty* separate moves within the ground plan. Use the blocking notation of Scene 13 (pp.100-105) as a format guide. Since another director will be reading your notes, strive for neatness, completeness, and specificity. The suggested format uses both blocking diagrams and phrase descriptions as means of attaining maximum clarity. Make sure it is very definite as to which diagram goes with which phrase. Remember to:

   - Include movements only, and *not the lines*.

   - *Not refer to specific objects and set pieces*, since they would probably give away the basic situation.

   - Include the introductory positions.

   - Use brackets to indicate simultaneous movement.

3. Swap with another director. Study the blocking early enough so that if there is something you don't understand, you have time to consult the creator before beginning rehearsals.

4. Rehearse both scenes. Generate scripts for your actors as early as possible. Remember that these are not playwriting exercises — keep the dialogue as economical as possible so that it is relatively easy for your actors to memorize the lines.

5. When you are working with your given blocking, you may add stage business and properties as needed, however, you must stick *exactly* to the given blocking. Do not add or subtract any given movements or body positions. Where body position is not specified, you have free rein to create something that is appropriate to the given characters.

THE GROUND PLAN

The setting can be either an interior or exterior. Since the set pieces are stock rehearsal items, each of them may represent many different things. The arrows indicate some of the possible entrances, but certainly consider others as well. There are many possibilities for seating areas, but even when a set piece is only seat height consider using imaginary vertical space when needed. For instance, a cube could represent something as high as a grandfather clock, a floor lamp, or even a tree. If there is any guiding principle at all, let it be to work with, not against, the given design. The logic of the space, and the specific designation of the set pieces completely depend upon your situation.

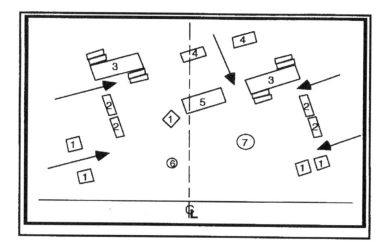

SET PIECE #	DESCRIPTION
1	(1) Small cubes
2	(4) Benches
3	(2) Platforms with step units
4	(2) Rectangular set pieces
5	(1) Single bed or sofa-sized unit
6	(1) Small circular unit (low footstool height)
7	(1) Larger circular unit (seat height)

109

CRITIQUE

To the creator of the movement

1. Was the blocking accurately executed?

2. Did the dialogue fit the movement? Were there any moments that didn't seem motivated, or seemed forced?

3. Were there any moments that seemed similar (in mood and/or inner monologue) to your own? Any moments that were very different from your own?

4. What surprised you most about the use of your movement?

5. Was there a definite beginning, middle, and end to the scene?

6. Could the scene stand on its own?

7. Favorite moment? Least favorite moment?

To the rest of the workshop

1. Was the situation (the **who**, **what**, and **where**) clearly established?

2. What did the movement encourage the director to do?

3. Did the focal shifts between the three characters make sense, or were there moments when an important line was thrown away because the focus was on the other character?

4. Did the dialogue seem to fit the movement? Were there any moments that didn't seem motivated? What moments worked especially well?

5. In general, did the director rely more on the visual or verbal elements of the scene to communicate the story, or was there a pretty good balance? Any effective visual pauses?

6. Was the overall situation interesting? Would the scene stand on its own, meaning if someone didn't know the exercise, would this still be considered effective theatre? Was there a definite beginning, middle, and end?

7. Favorite moment? Least favorite moment?

CHAPTER 4
GROUND PLAN EXERCISES

Thirteen exercises later, and now the focus is finally on ground plans. Why not begin this all-important work much earlier? Given that a ground plan is literally the creative foundation of the directing process, wouldn't it make sense to start our training exercises from, so to speak, the ground floor up? As logical as this may seem, it is impractical simply because at the beginning the basics such as the dynamics of right and left movement, stage area, level, psychological area, etc. have not been assimilated, and designing ground plans undeniably has to take these basics into account. A good ground plan crystallizes a concept into a single space, which is why these exercises come at the perfect time — a time when there is finally the means to synthesize the many disparate skills.

There are many facets to consider in creating ground plans. Think of the impact just a single concept, such as psychological area[1], can have on an effective ground plan. Just trying to determine who owns the space, or who controls certain aspects of it can provide significant clues as to what the space should be like. Not only should a ground plan be able to accommodate a variety of acting areas, but there should be ample possibilities for creating psychological areas as well. Along with characters being associated with a particular set piece or stage area (psychological areas), there is also the interesting idea that playing different moments in the same area will consciously or unconsciously invite a comparison between them. Related to psychological areas is the idea that certain elements in the setting are more important than others. Just as a director may want to put focus on a particular character in a stage full of people, the director will probably want certain set pieces or areas of the stage to stand out more than others. A ground plan creates focus even when there are no actors on stage. And to add to all this, a good ground plan should foster effective visual progressions. All these are interrelated pivotal concerns for creating a ground plan — concerns which would be meaningless to most students at the beginning of their training. As necessary as it is at any phase of the training process, conceptualizing ground plans is definitely not beginning work.

Some beginning directors question the need to worry about ground plans at all. After all, thinks the student, the director is usually given a set designer to work with, and so ultimately the responsibility for creating an effective ground plan is with the designer. In the professional situation, directors are often forced to design their ground plans before the designer has been hired, making the initial director-designer meeting a discussion of the director's plan. By no means is this meant to imply that

---

[1]For a discussion about psychological areas, see pp. 43-44.

this is ideal — a more collaborative arrangement where the director and designers work together to discover the ground plan, is a far better situation, but too often this doesn't happen. Moreover, even under ideal conditions, the director needs to be fully knowledgeable about ground plans in order to be a good collaborator. As a training tactic, the best way to learn is simply to assume the full responsibility of having to come up with a dynamic ground plan.

The neon slogan that needs to flash throughout all of the exercises of this chapter is a great big one that says: *A well-designed ground plan will almost stage the play for you, whereas a poorly designed one will drive you forever crazy!* Create a good ground plan and there will likely be smooth sailing ahead; create a bad one and even the most brilliant director in the world will end up shipwrecked. A ground plan is a bird's eye view of the setting and as such it functions as a map of the intended usage of the stage space. A good map will help take you where you want to go, but a poor one will get you forever lost. The ground plan is at the very heart of the directing process because it generates picturization and determines the visual shape of the play.

Since several of the previous exercises have given students functional ground plans to work with, there is good reason to believe that some practical learning about effective ground plans has unwittingly transpired already. This "osmotic" process — learning by unconsciously doing — is the way we learn about a lot of things and in this case, it provides an excellent foundation — a more effective "ground floor up" kind of learning. Supplying models to osmotically learn from is also applicable to learning blocking, which is why the justifying exercises came before the more formal blocking work. In analyzing and following the blocking diagrams in the various justify exercises, the students were provided "osmotic" models, the benefit of which is not felt until considerably later. Art students copy paintings as a training aid in capturing a particular style or technique, and this same kind of learning can happen with directing students when they are allowed to get a feel for the space by being given a specific ground plan to work with.

The trap of not breaking something down into comprehensible steps is especially true with ground plan work. Read the ground plan chapter, read a play, and simply put the two together by creating a floor plan is the approach often followed. Reading plays is wonderful, but in the helter-skelter of student life, the limited time is better put to use with the actual ground plan work. Time taken for play reading is time taken away from rehearsing scenes with experimental ground plans. Staging may not seem absolutely essential to learning about ground plans, since scene design courses seem to do fine studying ground plans without ever having to take the work into performance. Even design students would greatly benefit from a drafting board to performance approach, and it's usually pragmatic considerations rather than teaching philosophy that prevent this from happening. Performance is the best way to test whether a ground plan is workable, and for this reason, the seven exercises in this chapter all require performance as well as paper work. The exercises, progressing from general to more specific challenges, are as follows:

SCENE	TITLE	DESCRIPTION
Scene 15	Pick a Plan	With a specific three-person situation in mind, a ground plan is picked from several available choices that best suit the storyline. The scene is staged and the director is asked to discuss the pros and cons of the plan.
Scene 16	Power Planning	Restricted to only a table, six chairs, and a bottle, the challenge is to create a ground plan in which one chair becomes the most powerful object in relation to the other chairs, the table, and the bottle. The ground plan is used to stage a short scene about power.
Scene 17	Gestalt Ground Plans	A dynamic ground plan based on either: proximity, similarity, line of direction, or contrast is created, and then the plan is used to stage a three-person scene.
Scene 18	Pattern Play	A given pattern is used as a catalyst in designing a ground plan for a two-person scene.
Scene 19	Pattern Plan Swap	A specific ground plan based on a specific pattern is created and then exchanged with another director. Each director directs two scenes — one based on his pattern-generated plan, and the other based on a ground plan provided by another director.
Scene 20	Time to Let Go	A specific situation with complete script and subtext provided. The challenge is to create a ground plan that best brings across the subtextual demands of the script.
Scene 21	Subtext Swap	Two directors create their own three-character scenes, and then swap just the subtext, but not their ground plan with each other. Both the "original" and interpreted version are performed.

As a natural extension of this "osmotic" approach mentioned above, the beginning exercise — *Scene 15: Pick a Plan* — provides the student with a given ground plan. In this first exercise, even though the student is asked to think intently about ground "planning," the pressure is temporarily off actually creating one. After this introductory exercise, the student creates ground plans on his own, but the work remains nonthreatening because the steps are small enough to be taken comfortably one at a time. A significant part of the learning process, as is true with a great many of the exercises in this book, is seeing how other members of the workshop handle exactly the same material. For instance, in *Scene 16: Power Planning*, everybody creates a ground plan out of exactly the same set pieces. Learning how to create effective ground plans ultimately necessitates script analysis, which is why the final two advanced exercises are centered around miniature scripts. The brevity of the scripts keeps them from becoming play reading assignments, plus the analytical work is greatly reduced because all of the pertinent subtext is provided. By providing the necessary detail, the given subtext narrows the creative field enough to keep the focus on ground plans rather than script analysis.

CREATING DYNAMIC GROUND PLANS

Before launching directly into the work, it will be beneficial to outline basic concepts and terminology applicable to all of the exercises. Perhaps the best "ground rule" to consider first is to remember a stage setting is not a real place, but a symbol of a real place. Verisimilitude of setting is often less important than theatrical concerns. For example, if a survey was taken of most living rooms, it would probably be found that sofas were positioned against a wall, whereas a similar survey with sofas in stage designs (even "realistic" settings) would show them away from the walls. In other words, a sofa surrounded by space becomes a more useful "symbol" for a living room even though it is counter to the conventional arrangement.

Part of the reason symbol wins over verisimilitude is because a good ground plan needs to function primarily as an ***obstacle course***.[2] Plays are studies in tension and conflict, and actors can play tension much more effectively with a physical obstacle between them. It is much more difficult for actors to play tension when they are in an empty space with no obstacles. Classic chase scenes in films are exciting because of the twists and turns taken to avoid collisions — a chase down an unobstructed straightaway would be pretty dull. In a play, two characters playing a figurative chase in pursuing their contrasting objectives, are in just as much need of an obstacle course as the careening cars in films. To return to the living room, this is why a sofa against a wall isn't a very effective obstacle. By putting obstacles in the paths of actors, there is a much better chance to effectively dramatize conflict and tension. A ground plan is the all-important foundation for effective blocking because it is essentially an obstacle course. An effective ground plan has a variety of acting areas. The definition of an acting area, as succinctly defined by Francis Hodge in his chapter on ground plans is: two sit-down positions which are at least six or more feet apart.[3] A good ***rule of thumb*** to follow in creating a ground plan is to:

> Make Sure Your Plan Has At Least:
>
> **5** Acting Areas.

[2]For an excellent discussion relating to ground plans as "obstacle courses," see Francis Hodge, *Play Directing: Analysis, Communication, and Style*, (Englewood Cliffs: Prentice-Hall, 1988), pp. 79-91.

[3]Francis Hodge, *Play Directing: Analysis, Communication, and Style*, (Englewood Cliffs: Prentice-Hall, 1988), pp. 84.

Obviously, the length of the play, and the style of the play are qualifying factors that may very well prompt the director to deviate from this rule of thumb, but the basic intent is to create a space that keeps the staging visually interesting. See Figures #1 and #2 for examples.

Fig. #1

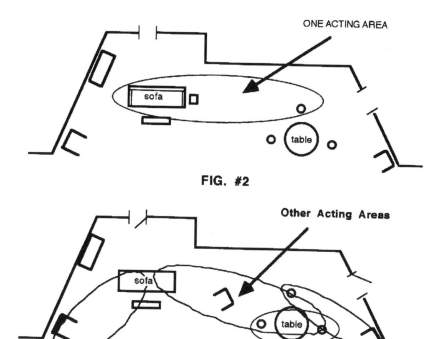

ONE ACTING AREA

FIG. #2

Other Acting Areas

The best way to create an effective obstacle course is to place the primary objects in space *free of the walls*. It's true that in many rooms the furniture tends to be placed against the walls, but on stage when the biggest wall is often upstage, the net effect is that the characters look as if they are playing in front of their furniture rather than within it. The room tends to look as if had been prepared for a party. And when inevitable sitting does occur, it forces all the action upstage. An opposite extreme is to place the majority of the set pieces downstage. This doesn't work very well either, because the furniture literally becomes a barrier between actors and audience. By placing the primary objects free of the walls, and keeping set pieces in the downstage areas fairly low, the flaws from either of these two extremes are avoided. Set pieces free from walls allow actors to move easily around them (see Figure #3). Objects placed against the walls merely create standing pieces with *no obstacle course possibilities*. They will provide a certain amount of verisimilitude (likeness to real life), but they will not normally provide possibilities for conflict.

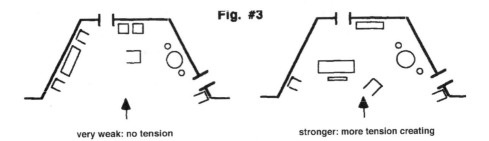

Fig. #3

very weak: no tension   stronger: more tension creating

Diagonals can be very effective because they create more tension than objects parallel to the proscenium line (note the direction of the arrows in Figure 4). In general, pay close attention to the *axes* (shown by the arrows) of a ground plan because they greatly affect your overall blocking patterns. Placing objects in contrasting positions creates tension by their oppositional force. As also shown in Figure #4, the position of the entrances can also create dynamic diagonals. In general, use a variety of entrances (upstage, downstage, etc.), and carefully plan their location.

Fig. #4

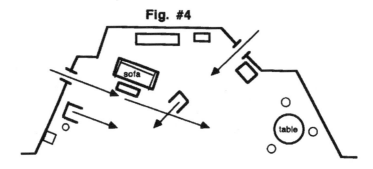

Several factors need to be taken into consideration in determining the location of entrances. If an entrance is to be emphatic, then it needs to be positioned in a dominant area. A blinded Oedipus entering from up center will probably be a better choice than having him enter from either the right or the left. Not only would the emerging king be automatically put in a strong, full front position, but the entrance itself is in full view of the audience, allowing tension to build with the anticipation of his entrance. Determining whether a door or a direction is to be used more as an entrance or an exit is also a factor; a downstage exit can be effective because the character will be moving toward the audience and remaining relatively open, but the same exit is not as an effective entrance because the entering actor is in a profile or weaker position. Well-positioned entrances and exits can create effective "flow" of movement, and help promote fluid, visually interesting, groupings.

In a proscenium setting the side walls of a typical box set are raked (slanted) so that even the upstage corners of the setting remain in full view.

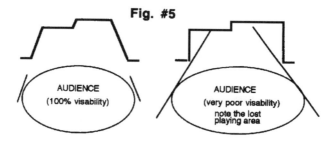

Fig. #5

AUDIENCE
(100% visability)

AUDIENCE
(very poor visability)
note the lost
playing area

Successful staging to a large extent means that the audience will focus upon what it's supposed to focus upon at any given moment. No matter what its other virtues might be, a ground plan that doesn't allow actors to stay open and visible to the audience isn't worth very much. In order to let the actors face the audience as naturally as possible, the primary set pieces need to be as open to the audience as possible. The general rule is that all much-used furniture pieces be placed as far downstage and as near center as possible, as illustrated in Figure #6.

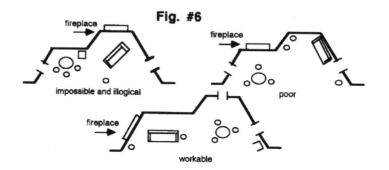

Fig. #6

fireplace

fireplace

impossible and illogical

poor

fireplace

workable

When working in a proscenium space, a ground plan can be greatly improved by figuring out a creative way to pin the downstage corners to the rest of the plan. With interiors, downstage set pieces will help create the effect of a walled enclosure, as well as increasing the illusion of depth to the room. With exteriors, the depth created by downstage objects can also be very effective. By placing chairs and other objects in the downstage corners, you will create more acting areas, and motivate your actors to take more advantage of the available space.

This arrangement will provide a downstage foreground to contrast with the midground and background, thus unifying (holding together) the ground plan as well as creating a three-dimensional quality to the staging. This rule is important because such set pieces will help *frame* the actors in all the positions they take on stage (see Figure #7). Moreover, without such downstage objects, actors will tend to avoid using the downstage corners, which will result in only a partial use of the total acting area.

Fig. #7

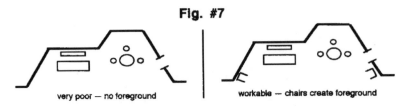

very poor — no foreground   workable — chairs create foreground

Raking the set can mean elevating the upstage areas or placing the set at an angle rather than parallel to the curtain line. Both changes can improve playing areas and the strength of door positions. Since a raked set emphasizes diagonals, this kind of a plan, in general, conveys more tension than does a full-front design, as shown in Figure 8. Even more so than the imaginary center line, the proscenium line is an incredibly strong visual presence, and deciding whether to play with it or against it is a very important decision.

Fig. #8

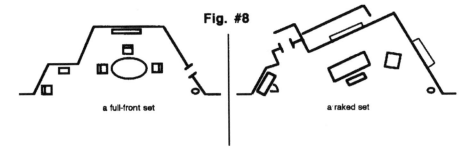

a full-front set   a raked set

While most of this discussion has centered around proscenium staging, the basic concepts are easily adapted to any space. For instance, theatre in the round or thrust staging can simply be thought of as spaces with more than one proscenium. All of the following exercises can be played in whatever spatial arrangement seems best.

PICK A PLAN
(Experimenting With Given Ground Plans)

The best way to have a good idea
is to have lots of them.

— Linus Pauling

OVERVIEW

Pick a ground plan from the three available selections. Without changing any aspect of the selected ground plan, create dialogue and a very specific location that adheres to one of the following scenarios:

- Characters A and B are already on stage when Character C enters. In the course of the scene, Characters A and B discover where C has been without C ever having told them.

- Characters A, B, and C are on stage. It's never openly discussed, but either they have done something before they entered, or they are soon going to do something when they leave.

With either scenario, the intent should be to utilize the given ground plan to its maximum potential. Make sure that as a group, the characters make contact with *each* of the set pieces; in other words, all of the set pieces should be used by someone at least once during the scene.

DISCUSSION

Here the intent is to deliberately defer having to create an actual ground plan. Conceptually this exercise is very similar to the justified movement exercises. Just as the justified work focused on interpreting rather than creating blocking, *Pick a Plan* is designed to interpret, not create, a ground plan. When there isn't pressure to actually make a ground plan, more time can be devoted to finding creative ways to use it. With the justified movement exercises, both ground plan and specific movements were provided; now only the ground plan is provided. But this is a relatively superficial difference, because even though the given ground plan doesn't come with specific movements, the major discovery awaiting the director in this exercise is that a ground plan encourages specific patterns of movement. The major challenge is to discover what kinds of built-in movement patterns the ground plan is designed to elicit.

The inspiration for picking a plan could be one of the scenarios, but it could just as easily be one of the ground plans that brings about the idea. One way to get inspiration for a situation is to trace the possible movement patterns in a particular plan without worrying at first about the significance of the particular moves. Try to determine interesting patterns by asking: What kinds of movement does the ground plan want me to make? What is unique about this space, and what blocking patterns can come from it? If this process is followed, the exercise becomes a very close relative to the justified movement exercises.

VARIATIONS

1. Create two contrasting scenes, using a *different plan* and a *different scenario* for each.

2. Create two contrasting scenes, using the *same plan* but *different scenarios*.

3. Create two contrasting scenes, using the *same plan* and the *same scenario*.

SUGGESTIONS

1. Both scenarios are based on unspoken communication or discoveries. Make sure that this information is for the most part shown rather than told.

2. Do not alter the ground plan in any way. Chairs at a table can be shifted slightly as needed, but for the most part stick to what is given. If platforms are unavailable, use tape to indicate the boundaries.

3. Use props as needed, but avoid set dressing. As with the set pieces, whatever props are on stage should be used.

4. In some way, make sure all the set pieces are put to use. Remember that the overall intent of the exercise is to maximize the use of the ground plan.

5. Keep the overall focus on what happened or is about to happen off stage.

6. As usual, be as economical as possible with dialogue. Avoid turning a ground plan exercise into a playwriting exercise — your actors will be grateful.

7. Strive to create a visual progression, and make sure there is a definite beginning, middle, and end to the scene.

POSSIBLE GROUND PLANS

Select *one* plan from the following three selections, and then connect it with one of the two available scenarios mentioned on page 119.

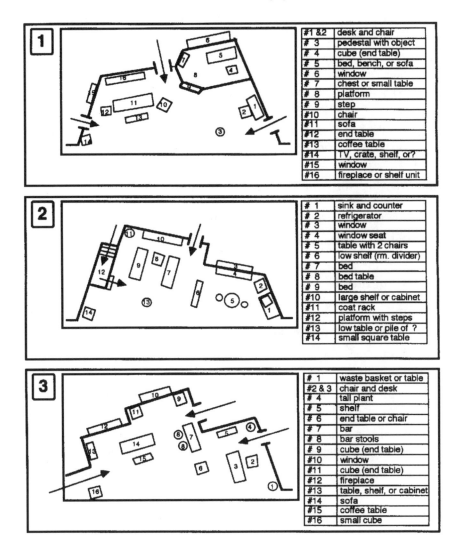

#1 &2	desk and chair
# 3	pedestal with object
# 4	cube (end table)
# 5	bed, bench, or sofa
# 6	window
# 7	chest or small table
# 8	platform
# 9	step
#10	chair
#11	sofa
#12	end table
#13	coffee table
#14	TV, crate, shelf, or?
#15	window
#16	fireplace or shelf unit

# 1	sink and counter
# 2	refrigerator
# 3	window
# 4	window seat
# 5	table with 2 chairs
# 6	low shelf (rm. divider)
# 7	bed
# 8	bed table
# 9	bed
#10	large shelf or cabinet
#11	coat rack
#12	platform with steps
#13	low table or pile of ?
#14	small square table

# 1	waste basket or table
#2 & 3	chair and desk
# 4	tall plant
# 5	shelf
# 6	end table or chair
# 7	bar
# 8	bar stools
# 9	cube (end table)
#10	window
#11	cube (end table)
#12	fireplace
#13	table, shelf, or cabinet
#14	sofa
#15	coffee table
#16	small cube

CRITIQUE

To the director

1. Did the inspiration for the scene come from the scenario, or from the ground plan?

2. If inspiration was from the ground plan, did this inspiration come by thinking about possible movement patterns in the abstract (i.e. before trying to attach any meaning to the movements), or was it the specific set pieces that sparked the idea?

3. Was the ground plan easy or difficult to work with? What did you like and dislike about the plan?

To another director who worked with the same plan

1. How did the movement patterns of this scene compare with your own?

2. Did any of the movements seem to go against the design of the ground plan?

To the rest of the class

1. Were all of the set pieces used? Was contact with each of the set pieces convincing, or did it seem too random and/or forced?

2. Was the location of the on-stage setting clear and detailed?

3. Both scenarios involve something that happened or will happen off-stage. Was the off-stage activity and/or location made clear? Was it kept as the main focus of the scene?

4. Was the unspoken communication convincing? Did the director convey this more through showing or telling (i.e. through action or words)?

5. Did the movement work with or against the ground plan? Was it effective?

6. Did the director work with or against the ground plan?

7. Favorite moment? Least favorite moment?

POWER PLANNING
(Creating Power Areas in a Ground Plan)

The Perception of Power
is power.

— David Garth

OVERVIEW

Practice the provided scale exercises, and then using only six chairs, a table, and a bottle, create a ground plan in which *one chair becomes the most powerful object* in relation to the other chairs, the table and bottle.[4] Any of the objects can be moved or placed on top of each other, or on their sides, or whatever, but *none of the objects can be removed altogether from the space*. Use this ground plan to create a situation and dialogue for a three-character scene based on one of the following themes:

• *Power is poison.*
— Henry Adams

• *Power is the ultimate aphrodisiac.*
— Henry Kissinger

• *Power is not a means, it is an end.*
— George Orwell

• *Political power is...the organized power of one class to oppress another.*
— Friedrich Engels and Karl Marx

• *Power is a drug, the desire for which increases with habit.*
— Bertrand Russell

DISCUSSION

Above all else, this exercise is an excellent reminder that a ground plan creates focus even if there are no actors on stage. By the way the set pieces are positioned, some of them will be given more emphasis than others. Set pieces need to be grouped into effective compositions; in many ways, they are like actors, and all the dynamics of staging such as stage area, right and left movement, contrast, etc. apply just as readily to set pieces as they do to actors. In the design process the director will often

---

[4]This ground plan exercise, minus the theme-scene idea comes from Augusto Boal, *Games for Actors and Non-Actors*, translated by Adrian Jackson, (London and New York: Routledge, 1992), p. 150.

work with the designer to determine not only what set pieces to include, but which of them are to be the more important elements. This exercise, by asking for a single chair to be the prominent item, parallels the typical director/designer concern over which set pieces to emphasize.

Unlike the last exercise, this time an actual ground plan has to be created, but the design task is manageable because there is a limited number of set pieces, and the only necessary requirement is to end up with a "power chair." The design demands are deliberately simplified since this is the first formal ground plan work required. The very fact that there isn't any text provided makes this exercise not that far removed from the previous justified movement work. It's very similar to the last exercise, except that in this case the pieces of the plan have to be arranged. There are many solutions to the problem of making one chair the most powerful position on stage — enjoy finding as many as possible.

As usual, there is more than one way to approach this exercise. The impetus for creating a situation can come from the theme, and/or it can come from the ground plan. Since the only specific requirement is to spotlight a single chair, an excellent way to generate ideas is to make several ground plans that meet this criteria. With multiple plans to pick from, the exercise becomes very similar to the previous one — as it were, a gentle, very friendly "mutation." As with the last exercise, an excellent way to generate ideas for possible situations is to trace the movement patterns of a particular plan without worrying about what the moves might mean. Working this abstractly is somewhat like the art exercise that asks you to create a drawing from random scribbling. Another practical way to analyze a given ground plan is to figure out not just the number one power position, but the pecking order possibilities for the various other set pieces as well.

WORKING IN SCALE

It is imperative that a director know how to work in scale. Thumbnail sketches are great for quick conceptual thinking, but until a thumbnail design is translated into scale, there is no guarantee the setting will work. A procedure for creating ground plans by cutting and tracing in scale is recommended and described a bit later. In order to do this procedure you will need to be able to use an "architect's scale," which is a special triangular ruler made to measure in various scales. Developing a proficiency for using this ruler is an important objective of this exercise, and the student director needs to discover that working in scale is an indispensable part of the job. Another reason for limiting the set pieces in this exercise is to keep the scale work as manageable as possible. Successful director/designer collaboration requires knowing scale in order to talk intelligently to each other, and even when the plan is finished, the director will need to use an architect's scale to be able to "read" it.

The scales on the ruler have a grid for not only the feet, but the inches as well. Notice that the number of lines in the inches grid vary depending on the scale. To measure a given distance, find the scale on the ruler that you intend to work with, and then place the "0" on one point and count the number of feet. Then adjust the ruler so that you can calculate the number of inches. Some people catch on very quickly to this work, whereas others need to be shown exactly how to do it. Before attempting to design a ground plan, take the time to work through the scale exercises.

SCALE EXERCISES

Blown Out Of Scale Problems

The following diagrams are ***magnified*** views of the inches segment of your architect's scale. Each grid equals one foot, but the number of lines dividing up the foot differ depending upon the particular scale. These exercises are designed to make it easier to understand the differences between the various scales on the ruler. The four diagrams are ***not in scale***; they have been magnified so that it is easier to see the individual lines.

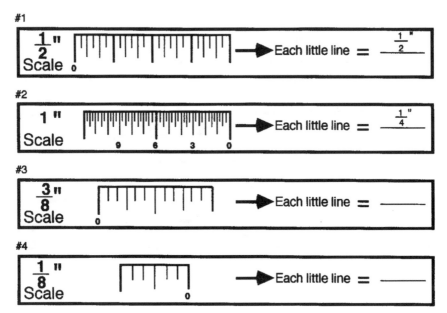

SCALE EXERCISES *(Continued)*

For this next series of exercises, use your architect's ruler to figure out the following measurements:

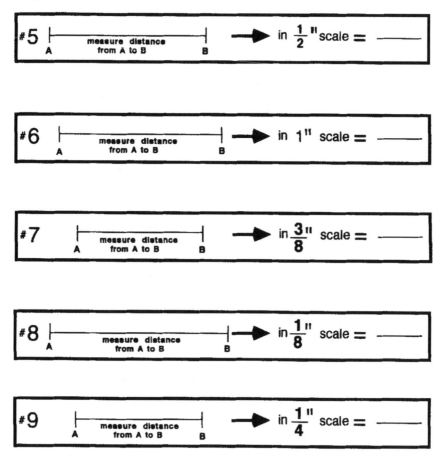

PROCEDURE

1. Special supplies needed for this exercise are: 1) colored paper and 2) an architect's scale.

2. Using a sheet of white, unlined paper, draw a frame to represent a playing space of *18' x 20' in ½ inch scale* as shown:

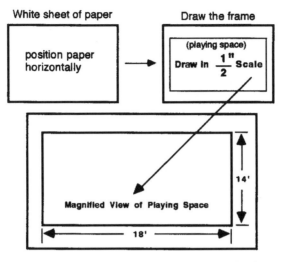

White sheet of paper

position paper
horizontally

Draw the frame

(playing space)

Draw in $\frac{1}{2}^{\prime\prime}$ Scale

Magnified View of Playing Space

14'

18'

3. Draw a center line as shown:

4. Draw to ½" scale, on a colored sheet of paper, *each* of the required set pieces. Then, cut *each* of them out.

Label center line like this:

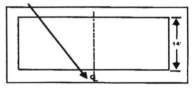

14'

5. Experiment with different designs by moving the pieces of colored paper into various patterns.

6. When you have discovered an arrangement you like, *trace around each of the set pieces*, and the ground plan is finished.

Experiment with different configurations:

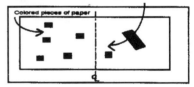

Colored pieces of paper

7. Make several designs, using this cut and trace method, and then let one of them inspire an idea for a three-person scene that dramatizes one of the five quotations about power listed on page 123.

CRITIQUE

To the director

1. Did the inspiration for the scene come from the theme or from the ground plan, or both?

2. If inspiration was from the ground plan, did this inspiration come by thinking about possible movement patterns in the abstract (i.e. before trying to attach any meaning to the movements), or was it the specific set pieces that sparked the idea?

3. Was the ground plan easy or difficult to work with? What did you like and dislike about the plan?

To the rest of the class

1. Was the situation (the *who*, the *what*, and the *where*) well communicated? Was the scene theatrically effective, or did it come across as a class exercise?

2. Did one chair truly become the most powerful chair? Was the chair also in a powerful stage area, or was it made powerful in another way? What compositional factors were brought into play in arranging the set pieces?

3. Was the scene more visually or verbally oriented? Or was there a balance?

4. Did any of the movements seem to go with or against the design of the ground plan? What movements were especially interesting?

5. Was the ground plan visually effective?

6. Did the director work with or against the ground plan?

7. Favorite moment? Least favorite moment?

GESTALT GROUND PLANS
(Experimenting With Gestalt Psychology Concepts)

(Creativity is)
the power to connect
the seemingly unconnected.

— William Plomer

OVERVIEW

Create a scene with a very specific location in which the *three* characters on-stage pursue an activity while something that involves all three of them is taking place somewhere else.[5] Create a ground plan for this scenario by basing it on *one* of the following Gestalt psychology concepts:

- Proximity
- Similarity
- Line of direction
- Contrast

GESTALT THEORY:

Gestalt is a German word that is very difficult to translate into English; the word encompasses such things as form, shape, configuration and pattern. The term is derived from the work of late nineteenth-century Austrian and German psychologists who experimented with the role of pattern-seeking in human behavior. The result of these studies is Gestalt psychology whose practitioners argue that "every perceptual image consists of more than the sum of its parts; it also possesses a *gestalt*, a patterning force that holds the parts together."[6] In other words, Gestalt psychologists believe that perception is like a magnetic field that is able to bring sensory imagery together into holistic patterns, or *gestalten*.

According to Gestalt theory, perception *obeys an innate urge toward simplification* by assembling complex stimuli into *simpler groups*. This perception process is totally automatic — we don't think about it, it just happens. While all things are similar in some respects and different in others, comparison only becomes meaningful when there is some type of common base. In other words, there has a relevant

---

[5]The scenario idea, minus the Gestalt ground plan concept, is based on an exercise by Viola Spolin called, "What's Beyond?" See Viola Spolin, *Improvisation for the Theatre*, (Evanston: Northwestern University Press, 1973), p. 131-132.

[6]Robert H. McKim, *Thinking Visually*, (Belmont: Wadsworth Publications, 1980), pp. 61-62.

degree of connectiveness for the similarities and differences to rate as meaningful. Rudolf Arnheim in his excellent study, *Art and Visual Perception,* demonstrates this idea with the following anecdote:

> In an experiment with preschool children, Giuseppe Mosconi showed six pictures, of which five represented large animals, one a warship. The subjects were asked to tell which of the pictures was "most different" from a seventh, representing sheep. Although adults and older children pointed to the warship without hesitation, only four out of fifty-one preschoolers did the same. When asked why the did not pick the ship, they responded: "Because it's not an animal."[7]

The overall point is that ***meaningful comparisons will not be made between unrelated things.***

In the previous exercise, the point was made that designing a ground plan is very similar to blocking actors. With this exercise, this point becomes even more obvious because there are many examples to back it up. Both set design and staging practices are influenced by many of the same factors. For instance, just as focus needs to be given to specific actors in a grouping of characters, focus often needs to be given to specific parts of a ground plan. A fringe benefit of this exercise is that the gestalt principles discussed can be just as valuable in blocking actors as they can be in creating ground plans.

The following discussion shows the various types of comparison that come into play, including:

- Proximity (or similarity of location)

- Similarity (of size, shape, spatial orientation, color, or direction)

- Line of direction

- Contrast

In discussing and providing examples of these various groupings, it will soon become obvious that many of the categories overlap. When overlapping does occur, it is interesting to try to determine what the dominant comparison happens to be.

---

[7]Rudolf Arnheim, *Art and Visual Perception: A Psychology of the Creative Eye,* (Los Angeles: University of California Press, 1974), p. 79.

PROXIMITY (OR SIMILARITY OF LOCATION)

These ten different shapes are grouped together by ***proximity***. We see two separate groupings. Why not merely ten separate shapes? Or two other groups? Or five groups of two?

Proximity

SIMILARITY

The white and black circles are grouped into a *line* and *triangle* by ***similarity***. The attraction of like things can be with similar sizes, shapes, directions, colors, or even textures. As with similarity, these kind of groupings occur involuntarily — our nervous system automatically groups these visual complexities for us.

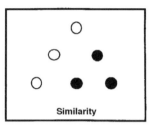

Similarity

LINE OF DIRECTION

The random shapes are perceived as serpentine because of the grouping effect known as the ***line of direction***. Just as movement is important in blocking actors, creating a sense of movement can also be a very effective "tool" to consider in designing a ground plan.

Line of Direction

CONTRAST

Anything that is distinctly different from a group of similar things will automatically receive emphasis. The diagonal bar clearly catches our attention, due to the factor of ***contrast***. As with blocking actors, contrast in ground plans is possible via area, plane, level, or angle.

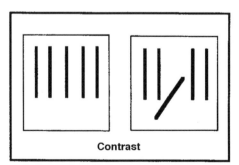

Contrast

SIMILARITY GROUPINGS — ADDITIONAL EXAMPLES

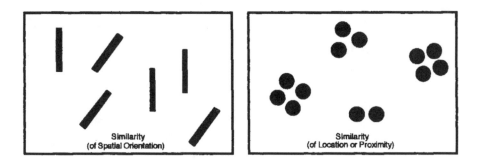

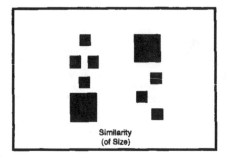

Similarity
(of Size)

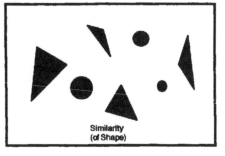

Similarity
(of Shape)

Similarity
(of Spatial Orientation)

Similarity
(of Location or Proximity)

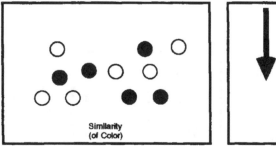

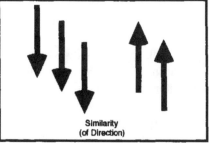

Similarity
(of Color)

Similarity
(of Direction)

FURTHER NOTES

As the previous examples have shown, grouping by similarity (the attraction of like things) can be made several ways. Groupings of similarity can be made via such perceptual factors of shape, color, spatial location, spatial similarity, and size. Once again, it's well worth mentioning that these principles are every bit as applicable to blocking actors as they are to creating ground plans. Think of how valuable gestalt concepts could be, for instance, in staging crowd scenes.

A closer look at the given diagrams will also reveal that it is very difficult to completely separate the types of groupings. For instance, in the diagram demonstrating similarity of size, this may be the dominant sorting factor, but similarity of location (or proximity) is also fairly evident. More often than not, ***combinations of perceptual grouping*** will be brought into play, rather than just a single sorting factor. Just as staging involves combining factors of level, plane, area and body position, the art of creating an effective ground plan necessitates an eye for combining several factors.

This ground plan exercise is more advanced than the previous one because there are no restrictions placed on the number of set pieces that can be used. Generally the biggest trap when there are no restrictions is using too much rather than too little. Keep in mind that the aim of set design, as with any art, is to spark the imagination, not flood it with a surplus of unnecessary detail. Sometimes directors and designers over design by trying to show too much, which has the net effect of deadening rather than stirring the imagination. Economy of expression is every bit as pertinent to set design as it is to acting. Crystallizing a location through economy exemplifies the all-important point that a stage setting is not a real place, but a symbol of a real place.

As with the previous ground plan exercises, there still isn't a text. A typical situation for this exercise might be a group of office workers doing their various jobs while they know in the next room that a board of directors' meeting has been called to reduce staff. The off-stage activity creates the tension that drives the scene, so it is very important to make sure this activity is very clear. The danger with this scenario is that the director, in an attempt to clarify the off-stage activity, will rely too much on the verbal rather than the visual. There is a danger that the characters will feel the need to "spell it out" by doing too much telling, and not enough showing in the scene. Relying on too much telling is the equivalent of indicating where the actor or director does more than is necessary to communicate the reality of the situation. Here, as well, the best dictum is: less means more effectiveness.

Given that the scenario is more detailed than the previous scene, chances are most directors will find inspiration for a situation from the provided scenario rather than from a randomly drawn ground plan. If the situation comes before the ground plan, then this exercise begins to fit into the conventional text first design process. It

133

doesn't absolutely have to follow this process, however; the inspiration can still come first from the ground plan. As a suggestion, if you're having trouble conjuring up a situation, try creating various ground plans based on gestalt principles. Doing this will not only reinforce your understanding of the gestalt principles, but a particular plan may very well scream for a specific situation to come forth.

CRITIQUE

To the director

1. Did the inspiration for the scene come from the scenario or from the ground plan, or both?

2. If inspiration was from the ground plan, did this inspiration come by thinking about possible movement patterns in the abstract (i.e. before trying to attach any meaning to the movements), or was it the specific set pieces that sparked the idea?

3. Was the ground plan easy or difficult to work with? What did you like and dislike about the plan?

To the rest of the class

1. Was the off-stage activity that involved all of the characters clear? Was it believably communicated, or was there too much telling and not enough showing? In general, was the situation (the **who**, the **what**, and the **where**) well communicated?

2. What gestalt principles were in effect? What was the dominant principle, and were there any secondary, overlapping ones?

3. Was the scene more visually or verbally oriented? Or was there a balance?

4. Was the ground plan visually effective? Did any of the movements seem to go with or against the design of the ground plan? What movements were especially interesting?

5. Was the staging generally effective? Did any movements appear unmotivated?

6. Was there a definite beginning, middle, and end to the scene? Was the scene effective theatre, or did the scene come across only as a completed class exercise?

7. Favorite moment? Least favorite moment?

PATTERN PLAY
(Pattern-Generated Ground Plan and Scene Work)

*Vision is the art
of seeing things invisible.*

— Jonathan Swift

OVERVIEW

Begin by picking either situation #1 or #2 described below. Both situations involve two on-stage characters pursuing an activity while something that involves both of them is taking place off-stage, or as Viola Spolin describes it, "in the beyond."[8] The "beyond" is constantly on their minds, but it is never openly discussed. Use the given pattern as a creative catalyst in designing an effective ground plan for this scene. The improvised dialogue is rehearsed sufficiently so that it is "set," and the scene is over as soon as the "what's beyond" is explicitly mentioned.

THE PATTERN

Use the following pattern as a guide in creating an effective ground plan for this scene. Think of the pattern as "movement tracks" for the characters to use. The challenge is to create a ground plan that fully encourages and fully justifies these "movement tracks." The finished ground plan does not have to look like the given pattern, but the ground plan does need to provide a stimulus that ultimately creates movement patterns that conform to the pattern. Some groups might decide to tape the pattern on the floor so as to be constantly reminded of the available pathways.

There are a number of ways to conceptualize a pattern-generated ground plan. One is to determine the essential set pieces, and then use the "movement tracks" of the pattern to figure out where the set pieces might best be placed. The other possibility is to look first at the "movement tracks," and only then try to decide what set

---

[8]Credit for the "what's beyond" part of this exercise must be given to Viola Spolin. See her *Improvisation for the Theatre*, (Evanston: Northwestern University Press, 1963), pp. 131-132.

pieces might cause such movement. The difference between these two approaches is subtle, and in some cases a director might discover that a combination of these approaches works best. Maybe, for instance, the director decides from the beginning that there has to be a large office desk in the scene, and from the pattern the ideal placement becomes immediately obvious; but from here on, the movement tracks, rather than the preconceived set pieces, become the primary catalyst for designing the rest of the ground plan.

THE SITUATIONS

Both of these situations require two actors. Other characters are implied in the basic situations, but they never actually appear on stage — they are part of the "what's beyond." Again, remember that the scene is over as soon as the "what's beyond" is *explicitly* mentioned.

SITUATION 1
Where . . . . Office
Who . . . . Coworkers
What . . . . Working at their respective jobs
What's beyond . . . . . Meeting of the board of directors, re: reducing staff
SITUATION 2
Where . . . . Bedroom
Who . . . . Husband and wife
What . . . . In bed trying to sleep
What's beyond . . . . . Young daughter is entertaining her date in the living room

DISCUSSION

This exercise is an excellent stepping stone to Scene 19. Unlike the next scene, where there are a multitude of patterns and situations to select from, here there are only two situations and one pattern to take into consideration. When learning something new, fewer choices can ultimately be liberating; moreover, it is interesting for student directors to see how other directors in the workshop work with the same situation and pattern. Also, beginning with a relatively simple, two-person scene is easier than the three-person scene required of Scene 19.

The finished ground plan may or may not immediately suggest the given pattern; all that is vital is that it inspires the characters to use the pathways inherent in the pattern. Any ground plan, pattern-generated or not, will fail if it doesn't create theatrically dynamic pathways of meaningful movement. Yes, the provided pattern limits movement choices, but the built-in "movement tracks" still provide a vast array of possibilities. Think of the pattern as nothing more than a visual aid for a justified movement exercise. Any movement along the provided pathways is fair game,

136

so long as it is justified. Above all else, pattern-bound though your plan and scene has to be, make sure that in every respect, it is quality theatre.

VARIATIONS

Much can be learned by repeating this exercise. In subsequent attempts, the workshop directors will very likely want to create their own situations. This exercise can be an excellent vehicle for learning various staging concepts; for instance, I have used Pattern Play as a practice exercise for learning direct, indirect or counter focus.[9]

Each time the exercise is repeated there is also the option for the workshop to use a different pattern, such as the ones included below.[10] Or perhaps two designs can be worked on, one after the other, in order to demonstrate a particular ground plan point. For example, diagram #1 and #2 (and also #3 and #4) differ from each other only with respect to the angle of the lines. Most likely diagram #1 would generate a "raked" ground plan, whereas diagram #2 would probably foster a full-front set.[11] Used together, either with the same or different designs, they could be very useful in demonstrating the difference between raked and full-front ground plans.

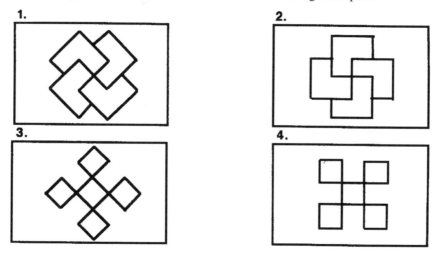

The primary value of all pattern-generated exercises is that they make visible what to the uninitiated is often invisible. The inexperienced eye is often unable to see the vital pathways of a given ground plan. The very process of pattern-generated exercises makes it virtually impossible not to tap into this circulatory, life-giving force of the playing space. By their very nature, all ground plans are pathways for movement, but the value of pattern-generated exercises is that they put a very strong spotlight on paths.

---

[9]For a discussion of direct and indirect focus, see p. 171. For a discussion of counter focus, see pp. 174-176.

[10]See p. 81 and pp. 144-146 for other possible patterns.

[11]For a discussion of raked versus full-front ground plans, see p. 116.

Pattern-generated exercises are also excellent ways of breaking away from the habitual handling of space. Habit is by its very nature often an unconscious activity, and even the most creative of directors runs the risk of unconsciously gravitating to favorite movement patterns. Working with a given pattern can force us into spatial solutions that otherwise we would never seriously consider, and so this kind of work has the potential of pulling us out of our customary ruts, and giving us new pathways to explore.

CRITIQUE

To the director

1. What was the catalyst for creating the scene — the needed set pieces, the pattern, or a combination of both?

2. Were there any parts of the pattern that were especially difficult to motivate?

3. Was the ground plan easy or difficult to work with? What did you like or dislike about the plan?

To the rest of the workshop

1. Was the situation (the *who*, *what*, and *where*) clearly established? Was the "what's beyond" well played?

2. Were there any interesting psychological areas created? How were the characters related to the pattern?

3. Was the overall situation interesting? Would the scene stand on its own, meaning if someone didn't know the exercise, would this still be considered effective theatre? Was there a definite beginning, middle, and end?

4. What power positions were created? Were any gestalt principles in effect?

5. Favorite moment? Least favorite moment?

PATTERN PLAN SWAP
(Swapping Pattern-Generated Ground Plans)

(Creativity is)
A type of learning process where teacher and pupil
are located in the same individual.

— Arthur Koestler

OVERVIEW

The overall objective of this exercise is to experiment with using patterns as a means of generating ground plans. A specific ground plan based on a specific pattern is created and then exchanged with another director. Each director will direct *two scenes* — one based on his pattern-generated ground plan, and the other based on a ground plan provided by another director. These two ground plans are then used to create two contrasting, three-character, scripted scenes.

Begin by selecting a situation from the numerous choices on pages 141-144. With this situation in mind, select a single pattern from the many possibilities on pages 144-146. Use this pattern to serve as a conceptual guideline for creating a ground plan that works well for your situation. Keep a copy, but swap your ground plan with another workshop director. The swapped plan *should not reveal the pattern the ground plan was derived from* since the fun of the swap is to see whether another director is able to discern the pattern you had in mind. Also in the interest of keeping the swapped plan as open to interpretation as possible, *do not spell out exactly what the stock rehearsal set pieces are meant to represent*. Create a fully developed scene for each ground plan. In the workshop we will first watch the "original" staging — done by the director who created the ground plan, then we will watch the "second generation" — done by the director who was given this ground plan to work with.

DISCUSSION

This exercise is clearly a natural progression from the previous one, since both are intently centered around pattern perception. This exercise is also very similar to *Scene #10 Justified Patterns*.[12] The previous justified exercise was more focused on blocking rather than ground plans, but the basic task of using a pattern as a guide in creating a ground plan was still the same. It's important to emphasize that the finished ground plan does not have to look like the chosen pattern, *but the ground plan does*

---

[12]See pp. 79-82.

need to provide the stimulus that ultimately creates movement patterns that conform to the pattern. A good ground plan will always encourage specific patterns of movement, but the challenge of this exercise is to begin with a specific pattern in mind, and figure out how to keep it intact throughout the design and staging process. It's not absolutely necessary for the audience to be able to discern the total pattern. Maybe the director wants the audience to see the overall shape of the pattern. Or maybe the director is only interested in having the pattern provide individually interesting movements, independent of the basic outline of the pattern. Since each director presents two scenes, there will be more than the usual number of scenes brought to the workshop, and there should be examples of both of these approaches — pattern noticed and unnoticed — in the workshop performances.

The lines of the pattern can be thought of as movement "tracks" for the characters, but obviously these tracks have to be motivated, and this is where the ground plan design becomes important. In this exercise, the intent of the ground plan is to motivate the actors to move in the "tracks" as dictated by the pattern. The placement of entrances and exits along with the arrangement of the set pieces provide the pivotal means of creating effective movement tracks. Together they form the "axes" of the ground plan, and these axes may very well conform to specific lines of the pattern. This is an excellent exercise to demonstrate the importance of axes, and the importance of these imaginary lines or tracks should not be underestimated.[13] Keep in mind that there are countless ways to move within a given pattern, and that each character will very likely use the pattern differently from the others. Maybe, for instance, a character uses only a particular part of the pattern, or maybe the use of pattern changes as the scene continues.[14]

Why is it necessary to have a pattern in mind? True, directors and designers do not always have a specific pattern in mind when working out a setting, but as an exercise this can be very valuable because it stresses the importance of pattern in ground plan and staging work. A director may not begin with a specific pattern in mind, but a director always needs to keep an eye open for pattern possibilities when working with a ground plan. Working with specific patterns in this exercise also has the advantage of helping us break away from our customary ruts; as creatures of habit we automatically gravitate, oftentimes unconsciously, into using the same blocking patterns over and over again, and this exercise is one of the best possible ways of pushing us onto entirely new pathways. The swapping process is fun because the director gets to see how another director interprets his ground plan. But apart from this curiosity, the swapping is also valuable because it encourages two different ways of working. Since the situations are relatively specific, most directors will begin with the situation and progress to the ground plan. With the swapped material, however, more likely than not, the ground plan becomes the catalyst for creating a situation.

[13]See p. 116 for a diagram and discussion pertaining to axes of a ground plan.

[14]See p. 80 for a further discussion of pattern dynamics.

Using someone else's ground plan is like wearing someone else's clothes, but as uncomfortable as it may feel at first, it also has the benefit of getting the director to break away from his habitual, overused blocking patterns.

AVAILABLE SITUATIONS

All of these situations are for three-character scenes. If by chance you happen to think that the same situation would work for both ground plans, feel free to do so. This would have the advantage of stressing the differences brought about by the ground plan. On the other hand, you may use a different situation for each ground plan if you feel that this would be best.

1. Two teenagers have been summoned to the principal's office. They are believed by the school's administrators to be the "ring leaders" in a group of pranksters whose most recent accomplishment was coating the locker rooms with shaving cream. The principal wants to get to the bottom of the situation and the students, while not entirely innocent, are certainly not the "ring leaders."

2. The traditional "good cop/bad cop" dichotomy is set up in the interrogation room of the local police station. While the accused, who is believed to be responsible for selling drugs at the local grade school, gradually becomes more concerned about his/her safety as the "bad cop" takes over, the scene concludes with no one gaining any ground.

3. Two gay lovers are enjoying a day in the park when their time together is interrupted by a person offended by their lifestyle. In the course of the confrontation, the pair tries to leave peacefully, but to no avail. A physical struggle erupts.

4. A shoplifting duo is striking a local business. The owner, well aware of the pair's reputation, keeps a close watch on them as they peruse the store. The owner confronts the two when he/she believes he/she has caught them taking items. Much to the owner's embarrassment, the pair is not stealing and they berate him/her for the confrontation.

5. A spouse comes home early from work to surprise his/her significant other. The surprise is turned around when he/she finds his/her spouse intimate with an unknown guest. The scene is resolved with the exit of the guest.

6. Two lovers are walking in a seaside park, basking in the scenery and one another. A homeless person, destitute and hungry, begins begging for aid. The discomfort of the lovers increases the tension and anger of the homeless person until a verbal explosion results.

7. A major fashion magazine has contracted two top models and a world-famous photographer for a shoot in Milan. As the shoot progresses, it becomes more obvious that positive personality was not a determining factor in hiring any of the three. As the models vie for camera time, the photographer becomes more agitated until he/she walks off the shoot in disgust.

8. Two children are engrossed in a game of their own creation. They are obviously having a wonderful time and are perfectly happy...until a younger sibling comes on the scene. As the littlest one enters, he/she wants to add his/her own touches to the game, much to the frustration of the others. The scene ends with no one playing.

9. It is move-in day for a new couple. They are thrilled with their new apartment and have recruited the help of a good friend in the moving process. The helper's patience becomes more thin with each time the "decorator" of the two decides that a piece of furniture should be moved. The helper's frustration hits a high pitch as the "decorator" requests a fourth change for a major piece of furniture.

10. The Last Will and Testament of a family matriarch is being read. The two survivors and the attorney are meeting in a dank office to go over the will. As the family members hear of the matriarch's plan to leave her entire estate to her twenty-four cats, they immediately make plans to have the Will voided. The attorney, a long-time friend of the matriarch, sees the selfishness of the duo and defends the dead woman's wishes with a vengeance. The scene ends with the cats on the winning side...for this round.

11. It is a child's bedroom. The child lies uncomfortable with a fever in his/her bed with a doctor carefully poking and prodding to determine the ailment. A single mother/father waits nervously by for the doctor's prognosis. The scene ends with the mother/father having to hear that his/her only child is dying.

12. It is the first day of school. A new kid arrives on the scene, nervous and excited at the same time. A duo checks him/her out from afar, and deciding that he/she might be okay, approaches him/her for a welcoming. The scene ends with the threesome having fun together on the playing field.

13. A couple is preparing to purchase their first home. They have arrived at the bank, where a loan officer awaits them for a discussion of the mortgage details. As the couple's file is opened, the banker begins asking about a department store credit problem one of the couple had in 1980; he/she is none too kind in the questioning. The couple can't

afford to be rude because this loan is too important to them. The scene ends with the banker softening on the pair and the loan being granted.

14. Two friends have gone out for a casual evening together. As they enjoy a drink in a local bar, one of the duo catches sight of another old friend — but this one was a romantic interest. It is not long before the former lover becomes the focus of attention and the twosome leave together, forgetting all about the casual drink partner.

15. It is a couple's first date and they are together at an exclusive restaurant. It also happens to be the first day at work for their waiter, Pat. Everyone is nervous and for Pat the result is a series of clumsy mishaps which lead to the date going awry. The interchange with the waiter makes it clear that this couple will not be together for long.

16. A brother and sister are at an outing together. As they enjoy the day at the beach one of them eyes an old flame coming their way. The sibling, well aware of how hurt his/her brother/sister was as the relationship ended, begins feeling defensive. As the former lovers begin chatting comfortably, even flirtatiously, the brother/sister begins interjecting. The scene ends with the former lover exiting, not really sure about what has just happened; the brother/sister embarrassed; and the confrontational sibling proud of his/her accomplishment.

17. A Parisian chef is engrossed in training two new students about the fine culinary arts. With all of the bravado possible, he/she is teaching about pastry baking. As the lesson progresses, each of the students begins to show his/her own skills by making suggestions and taking over the baking process. The chef becomes exasperated as the students become more and more enthusiastic. The scene ends with the chef's angry exit while the students continue to work happily at the pastry board.

18. Parents are in the middle of a financial debate at the dinner table. Their child plays quietly nearby. However, as the parent's disagreement escalates, the child becomes more agitated and louder. The scene ends with the parents confronting the child and deflecting their anger about their situation to their son/daughter.

19. An employee meets with his/her immediate boss and the company's manager. The employee believes he/she is to be promoted, but quickly learns that his/her position is to be eliminated. The remainder of the meeting consists of the supervisor's pledges that the company will do all it can to ease the former employee's transition, while the manager tries to terminate their meeting so he/she may continue laying off other employees.

20. The Winter Olympics are just around the corner and preparations are making athletes and trainers alike tense. An ice-skating coach is working with a pair of medal hopefuls, desperately trying to lead them into understanding an intricate turn. Their lack of skill is matched only by their desire for success. The scene concludes with the frustrated coach giving up.

AVAILABLE PATTERNS

In swapping ground plans, remember ***not*** to indicate what pattern was used to generate the plan. Also, in the interest of keeping the swapped ground plans as open to interpretation as possible, and since only the stock rehearsal pieces are to be used, do not provide any information that would necessarily give away the situation. In addition to these patterns, you can choose from any of those on page 81.

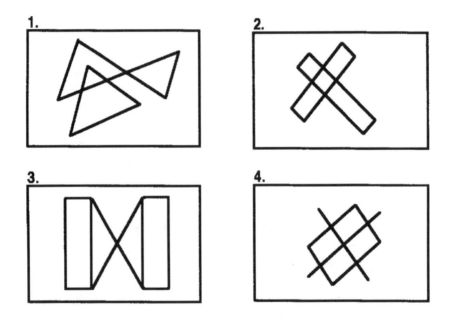

POSSIBLE PATTERNS *(Continued)*

5.

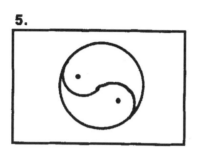

6.

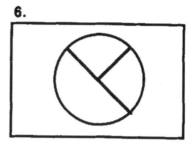

7.

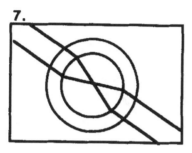

8.

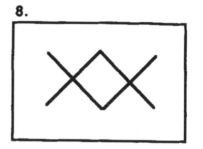

9.

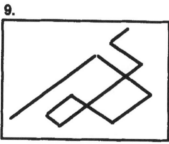

10.

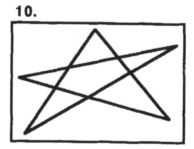

11.

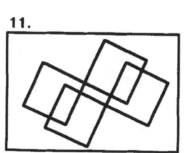

12.

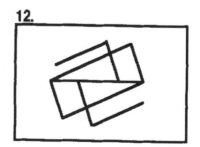

POSSIBLE PATTERNS *(Continued)*

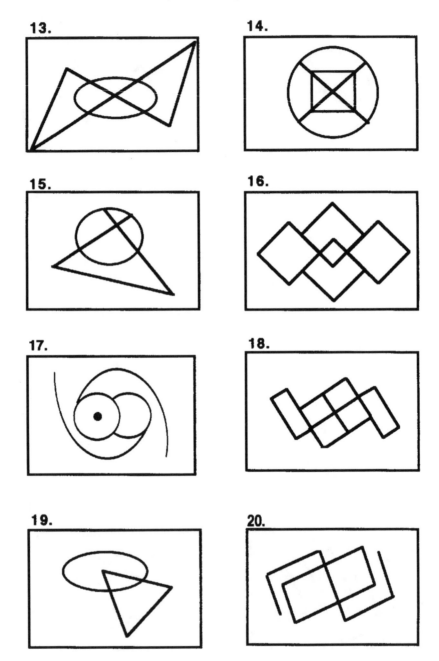

CRITIQUE

To the originator of the ground plan

1. How did your staging on your own ground plan compare to the scene done by the director using your ground plan? Was there a similarity or difference in the movement patterns between the two scenes? Did the ground plan inspire similar or very different situations?

2. Did the director using your plan seem to hook into your original pattern, or fight against it?

3. Was the ground plan easy or difficult to work with? What did you like and dislike about the plan?

To the "second generation" director

1. What pattern did you feel was the director's inspiration? Did you use this pattern, or come up with another one?

2. What was it about the ground plan that gave you the idea for the situation?

3. Was the ground plan easy or difficult to work with? What did you like and dislike about the plan?

To the rest of the class

1. What pattern did you feel was the director's inspiration?

2. Was the ground plan visually effective? Was the staging generally effective? Did the director work with or against the ground plan?

3. What movements were spotlighted with the ground plan? Were there distinct psychological areas? What movements were especially interesting?

4. Was the situation (the *who*, the *what*, and the *where*) clearly communicated? Was the scene theatrically effective, or did it come across as a class exercise? Was the scene more visually or verbally oriented? Or was there a balance?

5. Were any gestalt principles in effect?

6. Were power positions created?

7. Favorite moment? Least favorite moment?

TIME TO LET GO
(Creating a Ground Plan From Subtext)

Too many people live too much in the past.
The past must be a springboard, not a sofa.

— Harold Macmillan

OVERVIEW

You are provided with almost everything! — a specific situation, characters, dialogue, and moment-for-moment motivation. What more could you possibly want — a ground plan? Well, since almost everything else has been provided, how about you creating an incredibly dynamic ground plan? Then, stage a sensational scene to show it off.

DISCUSSION

Since everyone will be working with exactly the same material, ***the challenge for each director is to create a "signature scene"*** — a scene nobody else but the specific individual could create. Given that all of the scenes are identical in terms of situation and subtext, this exercise demonstrates, above all else, the tremendous effect a ground plan has upon the overall staging of a scene. A well-designed, carefully thought out ground plan makes the blocking process flow easily. The ground plan is the all-important foundation for effective blocking; without such a foundation, no matter how brilliant everything else might be, the net result will be very disappointing. Keep in mind that an effective ground plan should dynamically demonstrate the scene's psychological areas and conflicts.

Usually in directing a script (a text), it is important for actors and directors to create appropriate ***subtext*** for each moment in play. Subtext literally means that which is beneath the text, and the challenge is usually to explore the meaning behind the spoken lines. In this exercise, all the subtext is completely provided, but the challenge in this case is to find dynamic ways to stage it. The exercise is designed for you to discover that ***subtext exists for movements, as well as lines***. Since there is an actual script to work with, this exercise comes very close to approximating the typical directing situation. The task is made slightly easier than usual because all of the subtext has been provided, but this is still the most advanced exercise so far because there is considerably more detail demanded by the situation that has to be integrated into the ground plan.

This, along with the following exercise, is the perfect transition into the next chapter because it uses what's called an ***open scene*** for a script. With an open scene, all that's usually provided is the virtually meaningless dialogue which is deliberately designed to be as "open" as possible to multiple interpretations. Here the open scene is in effect "closed" because it has been completely interpreted, but it has an advantage of serving as a model for the upcoming open scene exercises. This tactic of providing a model for "osmotic" learning[15] has been a consistent part of the training process, and both this exercise and the next one allow intimate study of open scenes without actually having to, as yet, do this kind of work. The value of having a detailed model of an open scene to work from will soon be appreciated in the work ahead.

SUGGESTIONS

1. Carefully study the provided "activity-subtext" analysis of the scene (see pages 151-153), and try to determine the needed set pieces. There are several ways to do this. The most obvious way is find yourself a set designer, but let's assume that either you don't have enough money to hire one, and/or you fully buy into the educational value of having to create a ground plan by yourself at this point. You might begin by trying to recall the details in a real bedroom that somehow seems right for the scene, and then modify it in order to make it stage worthy. Or you may peruse a magazine such as *Better Homes and Gardens* as a way of getting ideas; whether from real life or magazines, the room you design may very well be a combination of more than one room. Or you may simply start by creating various thumbnail ground plans.

2. In your mind at this point there is probably an "ideal" of what this room should look like. Figure out a way to best convey this "ideal" using the available black rehearsal set pieces. At some point in your conceptualizing you will very likely want to use the cutting and tracing procedure that was previously recommended, where colored paper is used to experiment with various configurations.[16]

3. Draw your final draft to scale, making sure to include:

   • The scale you're working with

   • A center line

   • All elevations

4. In staging the scene, follow the steps provided in the activity-subtext analysis very closely, and ***do not add or subtract any stage business or lines***.

---

[15]For a discussion of "osmotic learning," see p. 112.

[16]See *Scene 16: Power Planning*, p. 123.

Activity-Subtext Analysis

SCENE TITLE: **Time to Let Go**

CHARACTERS: **One is** *Wife*

                        Two is *Husband*

LINES: One: **Oh.**

                      Two: **Yes.**

                      One: **Why are you doing this?**

                      Two: **It's the best thing.**

                      One: **You can't mean it.**

                      Two: **No, I'm serious.**

                      One: **Please.**

                      Two: **What?**

                      One: **What does this mean?**

                      Two: **Nothing.**

                      One: **Listen.**

                      Two: **No.**

                      One: **So different.**

                      Two: **Not really.**

                      One: **Oh.**

                      Two: **You're good.**

                      One: **Forget it.**

                      Two: **What.**

                      One: **Go on.**

                      Two: **I will.**

DESCRIPTION OF SCENE

The couple lost their only child before the baby reached the age of three. Since the couple had only one child late in their marriage, they were unable to have any more. The tragic death occurred about six months ago. The wife has often been found sobbing hysterically over the child's box of toys. The day has come when the husband is determined to get rid of the toys, because of the way they continue to haunt him and his wife.[17]

Activity-Subtext Analysis

Note: the dialogue has been bolded in order to make it easy to distinguish it from the action.

#	ACTIVITY	SUBTEXT
1	She enters bedroom	to find something to distract herself
2	She finds and opens book	to grab first available diversion
3	She sits on bed	to calm herself
4	She pages through book	to occupy her mind
5	She hears noise; starts; recovers	to suppress her fears
6	She crosses to door	to somehow stop what she expects
7	He enters with basket	to make her understand his plan
8	She says, "**Oh.**"	to get him to stop
9	He says, "**Yes.**"	to make her understand he will not back down
10	She touches the toys	to somehow touch her child as well
11	She asks, "**Why are you doing this?**"	to cause him to change his mind
12	He says, "**It's the best thing.**"	to persuade her that he is doing this because they need it
13	She takes the basket	to stay close to the toys
14	She says, "**You can't mean it.**"	to intimidate him
15	She kneels, puts toys on the floor	to keep them near her
16	He moves to put a hand on her shoulder	to comfort her
17	He says, "**No, I'm serious.**"	to get her to comprehend that he will not be dissuaded
18	She picks up a doll from the basket	to cling to it
19	She says, "**Please.**"	to get him to back off
20	He says, "**What?**"	to force her to at least speak of it
21	She holds the doll like a baby	to bring back the feeling of comforting

[17]This particular open scene was created by Wandalie Henshaw who has the distinction of being the inventor of the "open scene." She developed this exercise in the late sixties. See Wandalie Henshaw, "The 'Open Scene' as a Directing Exercise," *Educational Theatre Journal* 21, (October 1969): 275-284.

#	ACTIVITY	SUBTEXT
22	She says, "**What does this mean?**	to arouse his grief
23	He says, "**Nothing**."	to maintain control
24	He turns away	to find a less devastating sight
25	She picks out music box	to find a more powerful weapon
26	She plays it	to pull him into her perspective
27	She says, "**Listen**."	to remind him of better times
28	He says, "**No**."	to fight the music's effect
29	He crosses to other side of room	to regain firmness and purpose
30	She rises and faces him	to confront him combatively
31	She says, "**So different**."	to accuse him of insensitivity
32	He turns to face her	to stop the charge
33	He says, "**Not really**."	to accept his own vulnerability
34	She says, "**Oh**."	to acknowledge his feelings
35	She goes to him	to make peace
36	She embraces him	to apologize and comfort
37	They hold each other	to gain strength
38	He looks at her	to check if she is ready
39	He holds onto her, says, "**You're good**."	to assure her that she has the strength to give the toys up
40	She slowly returns the toys	to say good-bye to the child
41	She stand up, looks away	to end her attachment
42	She says to herself, "**Forget it**."	to discipline herself
43	She picks up basket	to test herself
44	She hands basket to him	to free herself from any temptation to change her mind
45	He says, "**What?**"	to get a verbal commitment from her
46	She quietly says, "**Go on**."	to encourage him to do it quickly before he weakens
47	He says, "**I will**."	to accept the offer firmly and close the discussion
48	He exits with toys	to accomplish his task
49	She listens to music box fading as it gets farther away	to linger an instant longer in the past
50	She sits on the bed	to support herself
51	She lies down and curls up on the bed	to comfort herself and help her resolve

CRITIQUE

1. Did the ground plan help spotlight the important moments of the scene? What moments were spotlighted? What specific set pieces were given more emphasis than others? What was effective or ineffective about the ground plan?

2. Assuming you were unfamiliar with the scene, was it clear *who* the characters were, and *where* the scene took place? Could the scene stand on its own?

3. Were any gestalt principles in effect? Were power positions created?

4. Was the staging effective? Were there distinct psychological areas? If so, what were they? Was there a visual progression? Were there any effective visual pauses?

5. Were any activities changed from the given "activity-subtext" analysis? Did the characters seem to use an inner dialogue?

6. Surprises? A moment or specific approach you hadn't considered? How did this scene compare with the one you directed?

7. Favorite moment? Least favorite moment?

SUBTEXT SWAP
(Experimenting With Another Director's Subtext)

Man's desires are limited by his perceptions:
None can desire what he has not perceived.

— **William Blake**

OVERVIEW

This is a exchange exercise where two directors create their own separate scenes, and then swap their subtext and dialogue, but *not their ground plans* with each other. Each director will direct *two scenes* — one based on his own situation and subtext, and the other based on a situation and subtext given to him by another director. In the workshop we will first watch the "original" staging — done by the director who created the situation, and then we will watch the "second-generation" — done by the director who was given this situation and subtext to work with.

Begin by using a painting, graphic or photograph as a starting point for conjuring forth a situation. It is critical that the selected visual *transcend the obvious surface level* of the intended scene — let the image be connected in some way to the "essence" of the piece. The picture may also offer insights into texture, color schemes, overall mood, kinesthetic qualities, or specific images inherent in the piece. With the picture-generated situation firmly in mind, develop a fully detailed "activity-subtext" analysis for the scene modeled after the one used in previous exercise (see pages 151-153).

DISCUSSION

In terms of working with the subtext given to you by another director, this exercise is virtually identical to the previous one. The major distinction between this exercise and the last one is the *picture-generated* part of the work. Directors and designers in their conferences frequently play the game of asking: If this play were a picture, what specific picture would it be? Using a picture is an excellent way to generate not just ground plan ideas, but related production concept ideas as well. Both this exercise and the previous one are perfect transitions into the open scene work ahead because a featured part of this work is creating and working with subtext, which is a vital component of open scene work. Subtext, as director Constantin Stanislavski loved to remind us, is that which is literally beneath the text that motivates the actor to say what he says. These last exercises make it very clear that subtext affects movements as well as lines. Developing subtext is one of the major ways in which a theatre artist is able to put his own "thumbprint" on the work.

155

CRITIQUE

To the originator of the ground plan

1. How did the staging of your own scene compare to the scene done by the director using your subtext? Was there a similarity or difference in the ground plan? Was the ground plan effective? Why?

2. Surprises? Aspects you hadn't thought of in watching your scene directed by someone else?

3. Were any changes made in your "activity-subtext" analysis?

4. What was the link between the artwork and your scene?

To the "second generation" director

1. Surprises? Aspects you hadn't thought of in watching the original scene?

2. Was it difficult translating someone else's subtext?

To the rest of the class

1. Which ground plan worked best? Or were they both effective in different ways? Did the directors tend to work with or against their ground plans?

2. Which scene did you like the best? Or were they each in their own ways effective?

3. What movements were spotlighted in the ground plans? Were there distinct psychological areas? What movements were especially interesting?

4. Was the situation (the *who*, the *what*, and the *where*) clearly communicated? Were the scenes theatrically effective, or did they come across as a class exercise? Were the scenes more visually or verbally oriented? Or was there a balance?

5. Were any gestalt principles in effect? Were power positions created?

6. Was the link between the artwork and the scene evident?

7. Favorite moment? Least favorite moment?

CHAPTER 5
OPEN SCENE EXERCISES

Training exercises ultimately need to prepare the director for working with text, since in most cases, directing is still a text bound task. Up to this point in the training there have been several advantages to keeping free from written text, but now there is an increasing need to let specific scripts become the springboard for creative work. At the same time, there are still many more concepts to explore, and spending too much time with script analysis is just that much less time that can be spent on specific staging work. The solution to this dilemma is to use very short scripts. Consider the following extremely short script:

> One: Ah.
>
> Two: So?
>
> One: All set?
>
> Two: No.
>
> One: Well.
>
> Two: Yes.

Not much of a text! Such a skeletal script devoid of plot, theme, characterization or mood is known as an "open scene."[1] The dialogue is the dramatic equivalent of an ink blot test because by itself it means nothing, but it is "open" to a great number of interpretations. The above dialogue could just as easy be a drug bust between a dealer and a narc as it could be two friends at a clothing store picking out a new outfit. Open scripts vary from around six to thirty lines, and most of the scripts we will use in the following exercises average around twenty lines.

It's hard to believe that the "open" scene, now a mainstay of acting and directing classes, has not really been around that long. Acting teachers were the first to use open scenes, recognizing that in early training there were definite benefits to keeping away from formal texts. It wasn't, however, until the late sixties that the open scene became a recognized tool for directing classes. The first person on record to use an open scene as a directing exercise was Wandalie Henshaw, who taught directing at University of Victoria, British Columbia, Canada.[2] According to her

---

[1]Sometimes they are referred to as "contentless scenes." Both terms highlight the fact that the script is an empty vessel waiting to be filled.

[2]For all anybody knows, other directing teachers may have used open scenes as well, but Wandalie Henshaw was the first to publish her experiences in an article titled, "The 'Open Scene' as a Directing Exercise," *Educational Theatre Journal* 21 (October 1969): 275-284.

article, she only did one basic exercise with open scenes. Her exercise had students do the same open scene four contrasting ways, picking from wide range of genres and styles. In her own words she describes the exercise:

> Each student is given a list of broad or specific types and styles on which to model his four approaches: comedy, farce, tragedy, melodrama, situation comedy, comedy of manners, low comedy, absurdist comedy, realism, naturalism, expressionism, formalism.[3]

It is a great exercise, but as far as tapping into the potential of open scenes for director training, it is but the tip of the proverbial iceberg. There are many more areas to explore besides genres.

Apart from cutting the demands of script analysis down to practically nothing, the chief advantage of the open scene for directing exercises is that the sparseness of the text forces the director to invent and explore the power of subtext. The substance of the scene has to occur beneath the lines because the lines by themselves are far too sketchy to dictate plot, character, or behavior. Having completed the final two ground plan exercises, workshop directors have already discovered the importance of subtext. Open scene exercises cry out for the director to create meaningful stage business and motivated blocking. Since the driving force of open scene work is subtext, the text should be strictly adhered to, changing not so much as a single word. Used this way, the open scene has the advantage of keeping the beginning director from relying on too much telling and not enough showing. Even with a solid, silent scene foundation where the emphasis is totally on the visual, student directors will sometimes backslide into depending too much upon the verbal.

There is still some script analysis work because with so little to hook onto, utmost critical attention must be used to, as Henshaw herself puts it, "extract the last scrap of meaning, the barest hint of motivation, the vaguest suggestion of possible movement or business."[4] Although it may not seem so at first, most open scenes are not completely open. Implicit in the given dialogue might be a master-slave kind of relationship where one character is the aggressor, or maybe one of the characters is more inquiring than another. Even if lines for an open scene are selected at random by a computer program, there is usually some kind of implied relationship suggested by the text. A good open scene, as with any good script, will also tend to have interesting twists and turns, and the director needs to keep a lookout for these built-in hints.

The exercises of this chapter all use open scenes, but apart from this, they have widely different objectives, and as a group they are much more heterogeneous than the previous exercises. The seven exercises of this chapter are:

---

[3]Wandalie Henshaw, "The 'Open Scene' as a Directing Exercise," *Educational Theatre Journal* 21 (October 1969): 276.

[4]Ibid.

SCENE	TITLE	DESCRIPTION
Scene 22	To Direct or Indirect	Experimenting with direct and indirect focus in triangular compositions.
Scene 23	The Brecht Test	Experimenting with counter focus and testing Bertold Brecht's notion that blocking just by itself, divorced from all dialogue, should be fully able to communicate the storyline. The scene is presented both regularly and silently to test this idea.
Scene 24	Obstacle Course	Experimenting with using duoemphasis and creating obstacles. Physical and psychological obstacles are studied as a means of revealing character and heightening excitement. Similar to Scene 21 in that strong visual communication is checked by performing the scene twice — once with and without dialogue.
Scene 25	Single and Silent	To experiment with creating a scene centered around a silent character, and to explore the uses of secondary emphasis.
Scene 26	Before and After	Experimenting with the differences in having movement come before or after a line.
Scene 27	Rant 'N Rhythm	To explore the various ways that rhythm is capable of affecting the dynamics of a scene.
Scene 28	Riffs of Rashomon	Staging three scenes, seeing the same event through the eyes of three different characters.

Diversity more than anything else is the overall point of these exercises. The silent scenes of Chapter 1 had the common objective of avoiding the "taking heads" syndrome, and the justified and ground plan exercises each had single-minded goals, but the exercises of this chapter are considerably more diverse and multifocused. Open scenes become not the end, but the means of exploring a wide variety of topics. Among other things, the first four scenes explore compositional techniques whereas the next four are centered around the timing, rhythm, and point of view. As usual, the seven exercises of this chapter are ranked in order of difficulty, but in some cases this becomes pretty arbitrary.

For future reference it also worth mentioning that many of these open scene exercises could be easily adapted to longer "closed" scripts. Just as no open scene is completely open, no closed script is completely closed. Definitely *The Brecht Test* and *Rant 'N Rhythm* are excellent exercises for formal scene work, but even an exercise such as *Riffs of Rashomon* could, in some cases, work pretty well simply by creating an improvisation that is outside of the actual text, but well within the world of the play.

SAMPLE OPEN SCENES

The following open scenes utilize two to six characters. Keep in mind that open scenes can be excellent exercises for directors and actors working on formal scripts, as well. Using open scenes to substitute for a particular sequence in a play can encourage actors to rely more on their objectives (their subtext), and less on the lines themselves. It is possible that after working with some of these sample scenes, the group will want to write their own. Maybe each team is asked as a group to develop an open scene, or maybe there are individual volunteers. In any case, these are some possibilities:

Two-Person Scenes

#1	
One:	Oh.
Two:	Yes.
One:	Why are you doing this?
Two:	It's the best thing.
One:	You can't mean it.
Two:	No, I'm serious.
One:	Please.
Two:	What?
One:	What does this mean?
Two:	Nothing.
One:	Listen.
Two:	No.
One:	So different.
Two:	Not really.
One:	Oh.
Two:	You're good.
One:	Forget it.
Two:	What?
One:	Go on.
Two:	I will.

#2	
One:	Well?
Two:	Well?
One:	Who?
Two:	Guess.
One:	Impossible!
Two:	Try.
One:	Never.
Two:	Sure.
One:	I don't think…
Two:	You do too!
One:	Do not!
Two:	Stop it.
One:	I will not. Not until…
Two:	I have had it with this…
One:	Well, you're just going to have to…
Two:	Listen to me for a minute. We could…
One:	Now I've heard enough.
Two:	No. Really.
One:	No. Really.

Two-Person Scenes (*Continued*)

#3

One:	I used to think it was.
Two:	We all did.
One:	What do you think?
Two:	About what?
One:	Ask me.
Two:	I don't think so.
One:	Why not?
Two:	I. Well, I…
One:	Huh.
Two:	Same to you.
One:	What did you say?
Two:	Nothing.
One:	Every time…
Two:	Not that?
One:	Yes, that.
Two:	Enough.
One:	Yes.

#4

One:	That better be it!
Two:	What do you mean?
One:	If you knew what I did.
Two:	You'll be sorry.
One:	No, I don't think so.
Two:	That's ridiculous.
One:	Is it?
Two:	There's not enough time to consider doing anything else.
One:	What do you mean?
Two:	No, it's not what you think.
One:	But what else is left?
Two:	You've known all along, haven't you?
One:	Not really.
Two:	Then help me with this.
One:	So that's it, isn't it?
Two:	Yes.
One:	Then try this before it's too late.
Two:	Okay. That better be it, though.

Three-Person Scenes

#5

One:	In here?
Two:	Yes.
Three:	Over here.
Two:	You're wrong.
Three:	I'm sure.
Two:	You're really…
One:	Quiet.
Two:	Fine.
Three:	Here we go.
One:	This is it?
Three:	Yes.
Two:	See.
One:	Quiet.
Three:	Yeah.
Two:	Fine.
One:	This is a little bit…
Three:	It'll be fine.
One:	Do you really think so?
Two:	I'm not saying anything.
One:	Quiet.
Two:	Fine.

#6

One:	Where did they go?
Two:	When?
One:	Not long ago.
Three:	At all.
One:	Who?
Two:	I don't understand.
Three:	Fun and games.
Two:	Let's go.
Three:	Not before…
Two:	Leave.
Three:	No.
Two:	Why did you…
One:	Who?
Two:	Let's get out of here.
Three:	What did you think would happen?
One:	No.
Two:	Not this.
Three:	You're wrong.
Two:	We'll leave.
Three:	I'll see you later.

Three-Person Scenes (Continued)

#7

One:	It's coming.
Two:	I can't.
Three:	You can.
Two:	I can't.
One:	You can.
Three:	Others have.
Two:	Not me.
One:	It's okay.
Two:	No, it isn't.
Three:	Just this once.
Two:	No, I can't.
One:	Do you want to quit now?
Two:	Why shouldn't I?
Three:	You know better…
Two:	I can't.
One:	You can.
Three:	You can.
Two:	No.
Three:	See, you did it.

#8

One:	You're not stopping!
Two:	You're not either.
Three:	Sorry. I got carried away.
Two:	There, I got it.
One:	You're going to get it!
Three:	So, let's take things a step at a time, okay?
Two:	So come on, stop!
One:	I will if you will.
Three:	Wait a minute, that's…
Two:	So now who's upset?
Three:	You're not.
One:	Stop it! Stop it right now.
Two:	Look what I found.
Three:	What?
One:	So who cares?
Two:	I do.
Three:	It's safe to stop now.

Four-Person Scenes

#9

One:	Will you please come here.
Two:	I can't.
One:	Why not?
Three:	Can't you see why?
One:	I can't see anything.
Two:	That's not what I mean.
One:	It's important, really…
Four:	What do you want from me?
Two:	Nothing, except…
Four:	You can't do that.
Three:	This is crazy, really crazy.
Four:	I've heard enough!
Two:	You just don't get it.
Three:	That's not the point.
Four:	Then you tell me.
One:	Stop it. Okay?
Two:	Where is it?
Three:	I knew it wouldn't work.
Four:	Forget it, it's done.
One:	Yeah. Forget it.

#10

One:	What is it about?
Two:	I don't know.
Three:	Well, who does?
Two:	He/she does.
Three:	I just got here.
Two:	So, you don't know.
Three:	Not really.
One:	Do you, or don't you, know?
Three:	I…well…I'm not absolutely…
One:	Well…do you know?
Four:	What?
One:	What it's all about. I asked them.
Four:	And they didn't know.
Two:	That's all that anybody knows.
Four:	And you expect me to know.
One:	Well, I thought…
Four:	Oh, boy.
Three:	Hard to believe, isn't it?
Two:	I haven't seen anything like it.
One:	Someone. Anyone.

Four-Person Scenes (Continued)

#11

One:	**That's disgusting.**
Two:	**That's all you can think of.**
One:	**Many times. Try it again.**
Three:	**There has to be a way.**
Four:	**So, let's get out of here.**
Three:	**I can't believe it.**
Four:	**Hurry up. Come on.**
One:	**Don't trouble yourself.**
Two:	**Only when I want to.**
Three:	**Find another way.**
Two:	**That will never happen.**
One:	**Exactly what we expected.**
Four:	**Back off, I mean it.**
Two:	**At least try it.**
Three:	**That really is disgusting.**
Two:	**Thanks a lot.**
One:	**It's not that easy.**
Three:	**Save it for later.**
Four:	**Easier said than done.**
One:	**Not now. It's too late.**

#12

One:	**Not until I'm ready.**
Two:	**Go ahead, put it in.**
Three:	**There's no way.**
Two:	**Take this, you'll see.**
Four:	**Make my day.**
One:	**Cut it out!**
Three:	**So that's it.**
Two:	**Save a little for later.**
One:	**You're really mixed up.**
Four:	**Take your time.**
One:	**It's beyond me.**
Two:	**What a let down.**
Four:	**I don't get it.**
Two:	**Come on.**
Three:	**Try that one more time.**
One:	**Next time will be better.**
Four:	**Double your pleasure.**
Two:	**Do I have to?**
One:	**That's a great deal.**
Three:	**Headline news.**

Five-Person Scenes

#13

One: I've been looking everywhere.
Two: Not hard enough.
One: I did.
Three: You should have tried harder.
Four: See, I found it.
Five: Me, too.
One: Where was it?
Two: You really didn't know.
One: No.
Three: That certainly says a lot.
One: I don't get it.
Four: Certainly does.
One: Is that for me?
Five: Who else?
Three: That's incredible.
One: But, I...
Five: It's okay. You'll get it.
One: With them...
Two: Oh.
Four: Yeah. Sure.

#14

One: It's the only thing I want.
Two: The only thing.
Three: But there's many choices.
Four: Incredible!
One: You said it.
Two: Believe it or not.
One: Look at me.
Two: I'm looking.
Five: Are you both ready?
One: Yes. Why does everyone...
Two: Wait...
One: Nobody really cares.
Three: Now, that's not fair.
Two: There is a point to this.
Five: You bet there is!
Three: You'd better listen.
Four: Yeah.
One: Fine.
Five: I feel better.
Two: Me, too.

Five-Person Scenes (Continued)

#15

One:	Is that all you can say?
Two:	What do you want?
One:	That's really nice.
Three:	Pride cometh before the fall.
Four:	I don't think that's it.
Five:	I just wish I had one.
Two:	It's hopeless.
Four:	Just calm down.
Two:	It's like a bad dream.
Three:	Who's keeping score?
Four:	Sinus problems and bursitis.
One:	I'm really sorry.
Two:	That sure was a mistake.
Three:	Do you do it often?
Five:	Maybe once a week.
One:	You sure it's okay?
Five:	Close your eyes.
Four:	I'm so dehydrated.
Five:	Why is that so hard?

#16

One:	This is the first time for me.
Two:	Am I close?
One:	I can tell by the way you sit.
Two:	What do you mean?
Three:	I can't keep up with it.
Four:	It's a time bomb, isn't it?
Five:	I just can't go on this way.
Four:	Is that all you want?
One:	The hell with it.
Two:	Maybe it's me, or...
Three:	I'm tempted to find out.
Five:	Out with it.
Four:	Yes, yes I will.
Two:	Isn't that strange?
Three:	What a shame.
One:	Stop staring at me.
Four:	Just another bad choice.
Five:	Why?
Two:	That's what I thought too.
Three:	It's not my first time.

Six-Person Scenes

#17

One:	It's a characteristic.
Two:	I don't think so.
One:	Sure it is.
Two:	Look more closely.
Three:	I've never seen anything like it.
Four:	You're kidding.
Three:	Would I kid about this?
Four:	I guess not.
Six:	See what I mean?
Five:	What are you saying?
Three:	I overheard, and I don't....
Two:	How rude. That's terrible.
Six:	Not really. Think about it.
Four:	It's expected.
One:	Here, this will be better.
Five:	Of course.
Two:	Calm down.
One:	I will not.
Five:	I've got to get some air.
Four:	Quiet.

#18

One:	I doubt that.
Two:	What would you do if...
Three:	Such as what?
Two:	Such as — how to help you.
Four:	I couldn't help it.
Five:	We can't stop them.
Six:	Now wait just a minute.
Five:	I don't like it.
One:	She/he's out there.
Two:	Tell what I said.
Five:	Well, what's that prove?
Six:	Not much around here.
Three:	How about it?
Four:	What will you do, stop?
One:	Stop or go on...who cares?
Two:	I'm not that thin-skinned.
Three:	I'll look the other way.
Six:	You call that worth it?
Five:	As long as it's not for me.
Four:	What a great way to go.

TO DIRECT OR INDIRECT
(Experimenting With Direct and Indirect Focus)

*Attempt the impossible
in order to improve your work.*

— Bette Davis

OVERVIEW

Working with a three-character "open scene" (see pages 162-163), create interesting characters, a meaningful situation, and a dynamic ground plan that fully motivate the given dialogue. If suggestions for a situation are needed, those on pages 141-144 may be of some help. Since the intent of this exercise is to develop proficiency in using *direct and indirect focus*, choose from one of the two following structures:

- Alternate between direct and indirect focus at strategic turning points.

- Consistently use indirect focus, but change to direct focus for the climax.

A FIRST OPEN SCENE EXERCISE

In our earlier work, the challenge was to justify the given movement, but now it's the dialogue's turn to be justified. Before attempting this exercise, it would be a good idea to practice working with two-person open scenes. Two-person scenes are not only easier to stage, but creating subtext for two actors is definitely easier than it is for three. A little practice with open scenes leads to the discovery that *it's not so much the words, but feelings behind the words that are important*. In many respects, an open scene is little more than a glorified gibberish exercise.[5] The dialogue is so fragmented and so skeletal as to be but a small step away from pure gibberish. Words alone do not by any means express all there is to a dramatic moment, and open scene work is one of the best ways to discover that an expressive *physical* language is vital to good theatre. The most resistance to open scenes comes from directors who are still overly dependent upon the words — relying too much on the telling and not enough on the showing. Directors bound too much to the power

---

[5]Gibberish exercises, as developed by Viola Spolin, require the actors to use abstract sounds in place of actual words. Without the aid of recognizable words, the meaning has to be conveyed through physicalizing and tone of voice. For more discussion about gibberish, see Viola Spolin, *Improvisation for the Theatre*, (Evanston: Northwestern University Press, 1973), pp. 120-126.

of the spoken word often encourage their actors in open scenes to rely on indicating, because indicating stems from a fear that what's being done is not enough. They will also be the first to want to change or add lines in order to make the situation fit. Any kind of stage business or line reading is fair game, but with open scene exercises, changing so much as a single word is cheating because it destroys the intent of the exercise. Adding stage business, pauses, and switching tactics in midsentence are fine and highly recommended, but play by the rules and *stick exactly to the given dialogue*. When open scenes work, they demonstrate the communicative power of subtext, and the importance of showing instead of telling. With enough open scene practice, comes the revelation that subtext and stage business can combine to become a very powerful visual vocabulary.

TRIANGLES

Along with effectively justifying an open scene, the intent of this exercise is to experiment with triangular groupings by using direct and indirect focus. Compositions of three or more actors frequently rely on triangular groupings. Triangular compositions are readily accepted not just because they are aesthetically pleasing and practical, but because in everyday life people inadvertently arrange themselves in triangular groupings as way of keeping eye contact with each other. Three people attempting to talk to each other in a straight line would have difficulty, but three people in a triangle can interact easily. In general, flat triangles, where the apex is not far enough away from the base line, are best avoided because they don't read very well from the audience, plus they fail to articulate the relationships between the characters. The typical arrangement is to let three actors form the corners of the triangle, but when there are more than three actors, the legs of the triangle can be broken by inserting actors at various positions along the legs. It is also possible, as in a cocktail party scene, to have clusters of actors at each of the three main points of the triangle. Triangular compositions are inherently dynamic because of the diagonal lines, and because there is a very definite focal point. In any given triangle, the actor at the apex of the triangle will take focus, but triangular compositions have the distinct advantage of allowing focus to shift easily from one corner of the triangle to another. As will be demonstrated, the focal point can be created either through *direct* or *indirect* focus. In this scene, practice varying the triangular compositions by using one or more of the following methods:

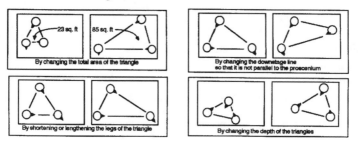

170

The size and shape of triangles can be varied almost infinitely. Triangular compositions make it very easy for the director to shift focus from actor to actor; by a simple shift in head and/or body position the focus can quickly shift to any corner of the triangle. Triangles are a wonderful staging technique, but if they are overused or not varied they can easily become monotonous. Remember there are several other ways to achieve emphasis.

DIRECT AND INDIRECT FOCUS

Direct focus is when two actors look at or face the third. *Indirect* focus is when the eye of one actor looks at or faces another actor who is the one looking or facing the focal point. Both direct and indirect focus can also be used effectively in compositions with more than three actors — no matter what the number, the important issue is simply whether the lines of focus are directly or indirectly connected. A mistake beginning directors frequently make is shifting focus too rapidly. The audience has to have time to assimilate the impact of the composition, and the characters need time to act and react in a particular position.

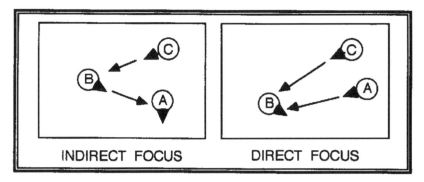

INDIRECT FOCUS   DIRECT FOCUS

PSYCHOLOGICALLY SPEAKING

Side by side with the technical grasp of triangular compositions, there needs to be a grasp of the psychological ramifications. There is a world of difference between the feeling conveyed between indirect and direct focus compositions, just as there is considerable difference in the emotional effect between a triangle whose base line is parallel to the proscenium versus one whose base line is angled. There are ample ways of creating effective visual progressions. Certainly progressing from indirect focus to a climactic direct focus is one such possibility. Whether the triangle emphasizes apartness or togetherness speaks volumes, as do changes in the size of the triangle; maybe, for instance, as the tension mounts, one or more of the legs of a triangle change in length. The lines of the shifting triangles can create shifting lines of communication and/or shifting degrees of tension.

CRITIQUE

1. Was the situation (the ***who***, the ***what***, and the ***where***) well communicated?

2. Were the triangular compositions justified and visually effective? Did the triangular compositions and focus shifts create effective story-telling? Which ways were used to vary the triangular compositions:

   • Shortening or lengthening of the legs?

   • Changing the total area of the triangle?

   • By changing the downstage line so that it is not parallel to the proscenium?

   • By changing the depth of the triangles?

3. When and with what strategy did the director use direct and indirect focus:

   • Alternated between direct and indirect at strategic turning points?

   • Consistent use of indirect focus up until the climax?

4. Was there an overuse of focal shifts? Was there any kind of progression (lesser to greater, or vice versa)?

5. Was the ground plan effective? Were there any effective power positions? Were psychological areas put to use, and were there any gestalt principles in effect?

6. Was indicating at any point a problem?

7. Favorite moment? Least favorite moment?

THE BRECHT TEST
(Visual Pantomime and Counter Focus Work)

What is now proved
was once only imagined.

— Proverb

The challenge of this exercise is twofold. One is to experiment with Bertolt Brecht's notion that blocking is the backbone of the production; ideally he felt that the blocking should be able to tell the main story of a play — and its contradictions — by itself, so that a person watching through a glass wall unable to hear what was being said would still be able to tell the main story of the play. To test Brecht's idea, the director will perform his open scene silently as a *visual pantomime* and then regularly with dialogue. The second challenge of this exercise is to experiment with *counter focus*.

Working with a three- to six-character open scene (see pages 161-168), create interesting characters, a meaningful situation, and a dynamic ground plan that fully motivate the given dialogue. As with the previous exercise, work with triangular compositions, but in addition to direct and indirect focus, experiment with the use of counterfocus. Be sure to allow enough rehearsal time for your actors to *fully memorize* all dialogue and business. You will be asked to perform the scene *two* ways:

- Once *without dialogue* to check whether there is strong visual communication without the help of text.
- A second time regularly *with dialogue*.

THE TEST — A VISUAL PANTOMIME

Effective blocking means carefully controlling the audience's attention so that they catch what is important at any given moment. Unlike film and television directors who have the advantage of close-ups and shifting camera angles and distances, the theatre director is given the equivalent of only a "long shot" to work with. Since the audience is generally privy to seeing the entire setting all of the time, only the consummate skill of the director can shift an audience's concentration from place to place as needed. Unlike the film director who can obliterate all unwanted detail by the use of a close-up, the stage director has to rely on comparatively more subtle and complex techniques to keep the spectators' eyes where he wishes them. Successful staging supports Bertold Brecht's notion that a visual pantomime can carry the meaning of a play without the benefit of any text. Take away the text, as happens when turning the volume of a television off, and it is surprising how some shows are largely incomprehensible, while others are engagingly communicative. Were we to watch a well-staged play in a language unknown to us, apart from the fact that the entire play would turn into a colossal gibberish exercise, the effective picturization would carry a surprising amount of the meaning. The intonation, tone, volume and intensity of the words would also provide hints about meaning, but all these hints would be lost with ineffective staging.

With *The Brecht Test*, the scene is first performed as a visual pantomime without the benefit of even abstract or gibberish sound, and the challenge, as always, is to have the **who**, **what**, and **where** be as comprehensible as possible. It is a "test" well worth taking because it tells the director in no uncertain terms whether or not he is having a problem creating strong visual communication. Performing the scene as a visual pantomime is virtually the same as the silent scene work with which we started. A respectful returning gaze to the silent start of our workshop is always worthwhile because it fortifies, in the most theatrical way possible, the need for effective movement and composition. *The Brecht Test* is a genuine "test" because the silent version is presented first *without any introduction whatsoever*, and either the storyline comes across or is lost to the audience. The overly anxious director who insists on a lengthy introduction has already failed the "test." Even if specific directors do fail the test, however, they will very likely discover through the work of others that a visual vocabulary is well worth cultivating into a practical language of the theatre. Just to successfully perform an open scene regularly with dialogue, there has to be a considerable amount happening between each of the actual lines, and so there is, in general, a high demand placed upon the visual just to get the scene itself to work. The sketchy dialogue of an open scene demands strong visual communication to make it work, and a silent rendition of an open scene is simply a further intensification of this need. Performing the "test" is easily done with any kind of scripted scene. The test is built into the next exercise as well, but it could also work with any of the exercises of this chapter. Taking this kind of test periodically during this phase of the training is well worth the time.

COUNTER FOCUS

Besides the concept of the "test," the objective of this exercise is to experiment with counter focus. Counter focus adds variety to compositions and can strengthen picturization. Counter focus means a focus that is opposed to the main focus. We have already seen from working with direct focus that when other actors focus on a particular actor the audience tends to do the same. With indirect focus there is a roundabout path that ultimately leads to the dominant actor. But with counter focus, the eye is directed completely away from the primary focus, and this sets up a competitive tension between the two. The emphatic figure keeps its primary focus by being placed in a stronger stage area or by being in a stronger body position; certainly costume color, level, and lighting are also potential tools to keep the focus on the emphatic character. In some instances counter focus can even increase, rather than weaken the emphasis given to an emphatic character. Part of the reason for this is that the tension created by the counter focus is inherently more interesting than that without, plus it helps relieve the potential monotony of too many overly emphatic compositions. Especially when realism is valued, counter focus helps create verisimilitude — i.e. a convincingly "real" looking picture. Imagine the absurdity of an Ibsen play where all heads turned together from one character to another, and then back again. As with all compositional choices, a character in a counter focus must be motivated; love, hate, curiosity, agreement or outrage could all be reasons for a character to face away from an emphatic actor.

Below are diagrams to demonstrate the difference between direct, indirect, and counter focus:

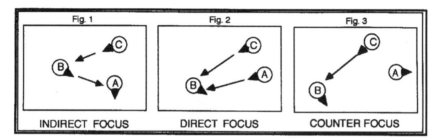

In Figure 3, character A creates a focus counter to the the primary focus given to the emphatic figure (character B). There is tension set up between characters B and A, but character B still has the primary focus. Although character A takes some of the focus, this focus is clearly subordinate to character B because of the weaker body position and weaker stage area. In Figure 3, there is actually a combination of direct focus (characters C and B) and counter focus (character A).

By adding more actors it is possible to have a combination of indirect and counter focus, as in Figure 4. Here character A has the primary focus, with character B having *indirect focus* on E and character F looking off-stage right in a *counter focus.* Even though character F is in

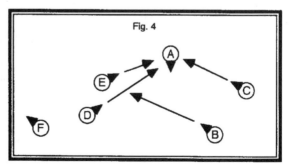

a strong stage area, the ¾ body position softens the effect, plus there is a great amount of strength given to character A just by the fact that three characters are directly focusing on this character. The greatest danger in working with focus is to consistently overemphasize the compositions, but when used judiciously, both indirect and counter focus are enormously effective techniques that help avoid this danger.

SUGGESTIONS

- If working in teams, it would save a lot of time in memorizing lines, if each team member *used the same open scene*.

- Create as much subtext as possible to motivate your actors, and to provide as much depth as possible for the work.

- Remember you will perform your scene twice — with and without dialogue. For the silent scene, *don't have your actors mouth the words* because it's distracting. Simply perform all blocking and business.

CRITIQUE

Silent Version

1. Did we know *where* the characters were? Did we know *who* the characters were, and *what* they were doing?

2. Was counter focus used? Was there any indirect focus? Were there any visual pauses?

3. Were you kept interested? Was it visually exciting? Would Brecht, given his high standards for visual clarity, have liked it?

Dialogue Version

1. Was there any additional information gleaned from listening to the dialogue? Could any of this missing information have been communicated visually? Was there a definite beginning, middle, and end to the scene?

2. Was the counter focus motivated? Was it generally effective?

3. Was there effective triangle variety? What kinds were used?

4. Was the overall staging effective? Was there a visual progression?

5. Did the ground plan help spotlight the important moments of the scene? What was effective or ineffective about the ground plan? Were there distinct psychological areas?

6. Did the characters seem to use an inner dialogue?

7. Favorite moment? Least favorite moment?

OBSTACLE COURSE
(Experimenting With Obstacles and Duoemphasis)

We combat obstacles
in order to get repose,
and, when got, the repose is insupportable.

— Henry Brooks Adams

OVERVIEW

Begin by selecting a four- to six-character open scene. In creating characters and a situation that fully justify the open scene, the challenge is twofold. One is to create heightened excitement through the use of *physical and psychological obstacles*. The second challenge comes in having to utilize both *direct emphasis* and *duoemphasis* effectively in staging the scene. Direct emphasis is what we have been doing all along, finding ways to give emphasis to a single character, but duoemphasis means giving equal emphasis to two characters simultaneously. Following the "testing" concept from the last exercise, the scene will be performed twice, once without dialogue to check whether there is strong visual communication, and once regularly with dialogue.

PHYSICAL AND PSYCHOLOGICAL OBSTACLES

In justifying the open scene, the overall challenge is to ***use* both *physical and psychological obstacles***. An obstacle, whether physical or psychological, keeps a character from getting what he wants. Objectives and obstacles are two sides of the same coin — which is why obstacles are sometimes referred to as counterobjectives; by blocking what a character wants (the character's objective), an obstacle has the potential of creating tension and suspense, which can help excite and involve an audience. Part of the reason obstacles can hold an audience's attention is because they create a sense of unpredictability. Just as there are major and minor objectives, there are ***major and minor obstacles***. The major obstacle is what a character has to struggle against to attain his "superobjective." For example, Laura's superobjective in *The Glass Menagerie* might be a desire to find love and approval in the real world by marrying someone like Jim, but her major obstacle is shyness. Minor obstacles are the smaller obstacles that parallel the smaller objectives (the beats) in a given scene. The minor objectives and obstacles all feed into and fortify the superobjective and major obstacle. Laura's smaller objectives in a particular scene might be "to hide her feelings" or "to comfort" and her minor obstacles might be her hurt feelings and being upset. Even in a comparatively brief open scene, there should be an effort to define both the major and minor obstacles for the principle characters.

Physical Obstacles: When you've locked the keys in your car, the locked car is definitely a physical obstacle. A ringing alarm clock waking the dead, waiting in too long a ski lift line with too little time, or facing a locked door when trying to escape from an attacker could all qualify as physical obstacles. Anything that externally blocks something from happening is a physical obstacle. Physical handicaps such as Helen Keller's deaf muteness, or Tieresias' blindness are physical obstacles which in both cases are ultimately overcome. Even clothing, when trying to run on the beach in high heels, or struggling with jeans that are a bit too tight, can be physical obstacles. Endless physical obstacles exist, and oftentimes searching for obstacles to throw in the path of your characters is a far more lucrative pursuit than simply searching for general activities to give them. Obstacles are sometimes provided by the playwright, but especially with minor obstacles, it is often up to the director to create them.

Characters tend to move more on stage than in real life, and a good ground plan needs above all else to be a good "obstacle course" for the characters to play against. Robert Cowen in his acting text reminds us that since the actor will always "take the straightest line to victory, it's necessary for the director (or the actor in his homework) to plant obstacles which will give his action some contour and bring out some 'characterizing' details."[6] In designing a playing space, whenever possible, consider not having everything within arm's reach of the characters. A cross to answer a ringing telephone is potentially more interesting and more character revealing than playing the moment with the character right next to the phone. Imagine a host and a guest engaged in conversation, attempting to decide what television program to watch. The host could simply get up and turn on the television, but it might be much more interesting to have him suddenly have to search for the remote (minor obstacle #1). And while he's looking around, maybe he reaches into his pocket and pulls out a cigarette, only to discover that he doesn't have a match (minor obstacle #2). The guest seeing his friend's frustration, takes out his pocket lighter, and the host crosses over to get his cigarette lit. As the host finally finds the remote, the guest has lit a cigarette of his own. Incorporating these two minor obstacles into the scene helps to engage the audience, and it creates character revealing detail. Physical obstacles are enormously helpful to actors because they are a real force to work against in a scene. Physical obstacles, unlike thoughts, are easier for an actor to react against because they are generally real objects and they don't have to be imagined, which makes them excellent triggers for the emotions.

Psychological Obstacles: When the barrier is internal rather than external, then the obstacle is psychological instead of physical. Usually the character's "major

---

[6]Robert Cohen, *Acting Power: An Introduction to Acting*, (Palo Alto: Mayfield Publishing Co., 1978), p. 94. Cohen's discussion of obstacle is excellent, providing many perceptive examples (see pp. 93-97).

obstacle" is psychologically, rather than physically centered. Phobias such as a fear of flying, falling, or dying, along with a fear of becoming violent could definitely become psychological obstacles. Sometimes the psychological barrier is a self-censoring voice from within the character, and the character is really struggling against his own disturbing thoughts and feelings. Sometimes these feelings of doubt, hatred, or anger are unconsciously projected onto others. Other times it actually is another character's viewpoint that becomes the obstacle. Sometimes a physical obstacle such as Laura's leg brace in *The Glass Menagerie* evolves into a psychological obstacle as well. In virtually all cases, psychological obstacles are inextricably bound to feelings, and this link was why Stanislavksi repeatedly stressed the value of psychological obstacles in his work.

Just as counter focus creates compositional variety, obstacles also stimulate dramatic variety. Obstacles offset predictability, and they also help to bring about transitions such as when one tactic is changed to another in the struggle to beat the obstacle. Creating obstacles brings about a heightened level of excitement and dramatic conflict. Audiences will empathize more when there are obstacles because it is easy to identify with the frustration. As a means of heightening the excitement level and dramatic interest of your scene, ***plan on using both physical and psychological obstacles***. Taken to the extreme, creating an overload of obstacles would probably result in out and out farce, which is a wonderful technique to remember when working with these forms, but for now, ***staying more realistically bound*** is more beneficial.

DUOEMPHASIS

Duoemphasis is to be used in staging the physical and psychological obstacles. Up to this point, we have mostly concentrated on ***direct emphasis***, which is where all the attention is directed on a single figure. This kind of direct emphasis can be very effective in some scenes, and especially for the peak moments of particular scenes, but in many cases there is a need to put emphasis on more than one person at a given time. Besides using *direct emphasis*, the challenge in this exercise is to bring *duoemphasis* into the picture.[7] ***Duoemphasis means that there is equal attention on both characters in a scene***. In other words, duoemphasis is a shared emphasis which permits the audience to shift its attention easily from one character to another. The artistic challenge with duoemphasis is finding contrasting ways to emphasize the two characters. Consider the composition shown in Figure 1. Characters A and D have duoemphasis. The major reason why characters A and

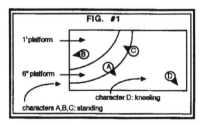

----

[7]This term was created by Alexander Dean and Lawrence Carra. Their text is still the definitive work on composition and picturization. See Alexander Dean & Lawrence Carra, *Fundamentals of Play Directing*, (New York: Holt, Rinehart and Winston, Inc., 1974), p. 131.

D have more emphasis than the others is because they are in comparatively more open body positions than the other characters. The fact that they are both in ¼ left positions creates a strong visual parallel between them. But apart from this similarity, they each achieve emphasis differently. Even though Figure D is on a higher level, Figure A achieves emphasis by being in a more open body position and farther downstage, whereas Figure D achieves emphasis by a contrast of level (everyone else is standing) and spatial separation. Keep in mind that shifting from duoemphasis to direct emphasis is an excellent way to create a visual progression and build to a climactic moment in the scene. For this exercise, ***plan on using both direct and duoemphasis***, and figure out an effective strategy for interrelating them. Remember also, that we will be performing this scene twice, once silently and once with dialogue.

CRITIQUE

Silent Version   .

1. Did we know ***where*** the characters were? Did we know ***who*** the characters were, and ***what*** they were doing?
2. Was duoemphasis used? How was it interrelated with direct emphasis? Were there any visual pauses?
3. Were the physical and psychological obstacles clear? Were they theatrically valid and interesting?
4. Was it visually exciting? Would Brecht, given his high standards for visual clarity, have liked it?

Dialogue Version

1. Was there any additional information gleaned from listening to the dialogue? Could any of this missing information have been communicated visually? Was there a definite beginning, middle, and end to the scene?
2. Was the duoemphasis motivated? Was it effective? Was it integrated well with direct emphasis? Was there a visual progression?
3. Did the major characters have a clear "major obstacle," as well as several minor ones?
4. Were there both physical and psychological obstacles? Which of these tended to dominate the scene? Did the obstacles seem at all times motivated?
5. Was the ground plan an effective obstacle course? Did it help spotlight important moments? Were there distinct psychological areas?
6. Did the characters seem to use an inner dialogue?
7. Favorite moment? Least favorite moment?

SINGLE AND SILENT
(Motivating a Silent Character and Secondary Emphasis)

*The silent man
is the best to listen to.*

— Japanese Proverb

OVERVIEW

Working with a four- or five-person open dialogue, *create a scene in which one of the characters is, for some reason, speechless*. The silent character *must be pivotal* to the basic action of the scene. Since one of the characters is to be totally silent, a cast of five will select a four-person open dialogue, and a cast of six will work with a five-person dialogue. The silent character needs to be pivotal to the situation, but in terms of composition, this doesn't necessarily mean that this character has to always have direct emphasis. *Along with creating a silent character in a speaking world, the intent of the exercise is to experiment with secondary emphasis.*

A NEW SLANT ON SILENCE

The line between silent and spoken scenes has been getting finer and finer. Starting in absolute silence, the overall progression of the training exercises has been from silence to speech, but the central theme all along has been need for strong visual communication. The justified movement exercises introduced dialogue, but the visual element was never forgotten because the exercises were all centered around a silent start (i.e. the movements). The ground plan exercises stressed the need for a strong visual foundation, and whereas the open scenes start with dialogue, it is pretty obvious that a great deal of visual drama needs to be added to the dialogue in order to make them work. If all this weren't enough, the *Brecht Testing* of the previous two exercises has proved that dialogue does not in any way diminish the need for effective visual pantomime. This exercise, by combining absolute silence and open scene dialogue, blurs the distinction between the sight and sound facets of performance even further.

The exercise creates a different slant on the use of silence, but the familiar theme concerning the need for visual clarity is still very much the same. Remember that it is essential that *the nonspeaking character be pivotal to the basic situation of the scene*. Silence always has the potential of commanding attention, but this is especially true when it is juxtaposed with speech. As has been aptly demonstrated in previous exercises, silence can take on either a positive or negative slant, but regardless of how it is perceived, make sure that it is at all times totally motivated.

SECONDARY EMPHASIS

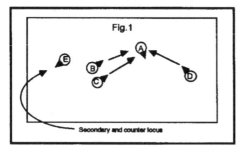

The silent character has to be pivotal, but this doesn't mean that this character has to have direct emphasis all the time. Along with integrating a silent character into a scripted scene, the challenge of this exercise is to experiment with *secondary emphasis*. Up to this point we have experimented with direct emphasis and duoemphasis.

Secondary emphasis occurs when a composition has a secondary or subsidiary center of attention. At first it may seem that secondary emphasis is virtually the same as counter focus. The difference between the two is that counter focus refers to a focus that goes against the primary center of attention, whereas secondary emphasis is simply an emphasis that is subsidiary rather than against the primary emphasis. In Figure 1, the counter focus happens to be the same as the secondary focus, but this is not always the case. In Figure 2, for example, characters B and C have the primary emphasis. Character C is slightly more upstage of character B, but they remain fairly equal because B's downstage advantage is balanced by C's closer to center advantage. The secondary emphasis is on character D, and character A has a counter focus. Unlike character A, character D is clearly tuned into the primary emphasis, but it is definitely not as strong as

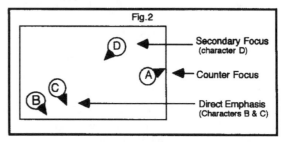

either of the downstage characters. A secondary emphatic figure may be in a composition that has only one emphatic figure (direct emphasis) or it may occur where there are several emphatic figures. To illustrate secondary emphasis, Alexander Dean uses the well-known biblical story of Solomon to make his point; as he explains:

> Two women appear before him claiming motherhood of a babe. He listens to both and then commands that the infant be cut in half and that one-half be given to each woman. The impostor agrees, but the real mother cries out to give the whole infant alive to the other woman.
>
> In staging this scene we have three emphatic figures: the king-judge, the mother and the other woman. The infant is of course

important, even though it has no lines; it is a clear illustration of secondary emphasis. The king and the women must have distinct and evenly delineated emphasis, the king perhaps slightly more than the women. The infant, however, must be placed in a position where the actual lines from the placement of the three emphatic figures will convene, where all three may focus by look as well as by line from the hand when referring to it. The infant never takes emphasis of itself.[8]

Another typical use of secondary emphasis is when a character gives a speech about another character who is silent, and the audience frequently glances at the silent character to see how he is reacting, and then back to the speaker. Sometimes it is very effective to have characters begin with a secondary emphasis, but to have them change at a critical moment in the scene to duoemphasis or even direct emphasis. Keeping a character who is at first relatively unimportant in an emphatic position throughout the scene is a big mistake, because when the time comes for the character to command our attention, the potential impact will have been lost. Sometimes a piece of furniture or a prop can take on a secondary emphasis. For instance, in *Scene 18: Time to Let Go,*[9] which involved a husband and wife having to take away their dead baby's toys, there is strong likelihood that the toys will acquire secondary emphasis.

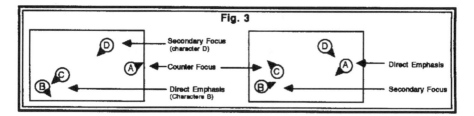

Fig. 3

Shifting emphasis can be accomplished by changing to a new composition, or it can be done by subtle shifts of body position. For instance, notice in Figure 3 the incredible difference in emphasis created by relatively minor adjustments. By simple shifts of body positions, the direct emphasis was switched from character B to character A. Character C shifted over to a counter focus, and character B took on a secondary focus. The point of this demonstration is to show how easy it is to create fluid transitions of emphasis.

Even though this exercise features only ***secondary emphasis***, this doesn't mean that other types of emphasis can't be used. Obviously, to have a secondary emphasis, there has to be some sort of "primary emphasis" in order to justify the difference in attention value. Duoemphasis or direct emphasis are both possibilities to keep in

---

[8]Alexander Dean & Lawrence Carra, *Fundamentals of Play Directing*, (New York: Holt, Rinehart and Winston, Inc., 1974), p. 135.

[9]See pp. 135.

mind when working with secondary emphasis. Secondary emphasis can be used in compositions that have but a single emphatic figure, or those that have several. Compositions can use any number of combinations of emphasis, such as:

- Direct and secondary emphasis

- Secondary and duoemphasis

- Duoemphasis and secondary

- Direct, duoemphasis, and secondary

And in as much as direct emphasis involves direct, indirect and counter focus, there is a wealth of compositional possibilities.

CRITIQUE

1. Was the silence at all times justified? Were there any moments which seemed forced?

2. Did we know **where** the characters were? Did we know **who** the characters were, and **what** they were doing?

3. Was secondary emphasis effectively put to use? Was any particular character/s associated with this secondary emphasis?

4. Were duoemphasis and direct emphasis also put to use? Did shifts of emphasis help to highlight specific turning points?

5. Was there a visual progression? Was the ground plan an effective obstacle course? Did it help spotlight important moments? Were there distinct psychological areas?

6. Were there physical or psychological obstacles?

7. Favorite moment? Least favorite moment?

BEFORE AND AFTER

(Experimenting With Movement Coming Before or After a Line)

*Observation,
not old age,
brings wisdom.*

— **Publilius Syrus**

OVERVIEW

Select a two- to three-person open scene. This exercise could be done with more than two or three characters, but since the focus is on timing it will be more practical to work with fewer actors. Working with the *same ground plan*, without altering or deleting the lines in any way, create *two* sharply contrasting scenes *with completely different situations* and characters. As usual with open scenes, create characters and a situation which fully motivate the dialogue, but the specific challenge in this exercise is to explore the *vast differences that can occur depending upon whether a movement comes before or after a line*. The pattern to follow in creating the two scenes is:

- Scene One: movement comes *before* each line.
- Scene Two: movement comes *after* each line.

Following these timing patterns doesn't mean that every line by every actor has to be accompanied by movement, but it does mean that when movement is used, these before and after patterns should be followed. In all cases motivate each and every movement.

SEE WHAT OTHERS NEVER SEE

Examples of before and after a line timing are everywhere, but most people couldn't care less whether someone moves before or after saying something. Yet directors are commonly asked to ponder aspects of everyday behavior that never happen to cross the minds of most people. Few people think in terms of "visual pauses," and yet they not only exist, but in the hands of a skillful director they can create very powerful dramatic moments. The same is true of the timing dynamics explored in this exercise. While the emotional outcome from before or after timing is most often clear enough, there is usually little thought given to what actually happened to bring it about. The challenge of this exercise is to get the director to think about movement far more intently than the casual observer.

The best preparation is observation — search for everyday examples of movement coming either before or after a line. After compiling examples of each, look to see if there are any common denominators, and this process alone will generate lots of possible scene ideas. The scale of the movements is an important factor to consider. Crossing from one side of a room to another is large scale compared to something as subtle as turning away from someone. Contrasting large and small movements can be effective, and creating progressions from smaller to larger movements or vice versa are definite possibilities as well. The cynic will argue that nobody moves consistently in a before or after manner, which is largely true, but this exercise deliberately pushes the norm as a means of getting the student director to become more sensitive to the timing of dialogue and movement in everyday, very real situations. In this respect, the intensive demands of consistently having to justify a before or after pattern make this exercise, as much as anything, a very advanced problem in justified movement.

Regardless of the scale, and regardless of whether the movement comes before or after the line, it has to have a purpose. Every movement must be carefully motivated. Movement captures the attention of the audience, making it a very powerful resource. Driven by insecurity and nervousness, the most common mistake from inexperienced actors is to make excessive, repetitive, and unfocused movements. But the fault of unfocused movement is not with inexperienced actors alone; directors can be just as guilty of creating excessive, unfocused movement. In an attempt to keep a scene from becoming static, inexperienced directors frequently fall into the trap of movement for movement's sake where a character will cross somewhere or sit somewhere for no apparent reason. Too little or too much movement can be a problem, but the biggest problem of all is when a movement doesn't have a specific meaning. When used correctly movement has an enormous communicative potential, such as:

- Expressing tension release by giving vent to strong emotions. Explosive lines encourage actors to move.

- Telling the story as clearly as possible by having people move meaningfully toward or away from each other. Sometimes people move toward those for whom they feel strong emotions and sometimes they move away from them.

- Articulating important transitions such as beat changes or changes in a character's tactics. Or possibly foreshadowing some new development.

- Expressing character, since body language — the way a person moves and walks — is always revealing.

- Establishing mood and clarifying the existing situation.

Since a moving actor attracts the audience's attention away from static actors, the general rule of thumb is for the actor to move only on his own lines, and not while another actor is speaking. Breaking this rule, as with all so-called rules, can create very effective moments, but the idea behind the rule is to avoid distraction caused by someone moving when someone else is speaking. Granted, sometimes distraction is exactly what the director wants, and sometimes when nobody is talking, movement between the lines makes a lot of sense. But in most cases the rule holds true. Moving only when speaking, however, does not necessarily mean that the actor should only move while actually saying the line. Moving before or after a line, can bring about very effective, yet very different results from movement that is strictly "on" the line. A character who has remained essentially unnoticed can capture the attention of the audience by moving before saying a line such as: "I'm the serial killer you've all been searching for." Without preliminary movement, the impact of even as strong a line as this one would very likely be lost. Even with a character who remains important throughout a scene, movement before a line can help to intensify the importance of the line.

Movement after a line can also be very useful. It can create a change in mood or clear the air for a new development in the scene. Or movement after a line has the potential of putting a "cap" or a period on a particular moment or sequence. A character who says, "I don't ever want to hear you mention that again," and then crosses to the other side of the room to sit at his desk is using movement to put an end to the discussion. Also moving after a line can help complete an incomplete thought. For instance, a character who exits in a huff after having said "I warned you — if you mentioned that again, I'd..." has clearly completed his unspoken ultimatum through movement.

TIMING

We often refer to an actor or comedian we admire as having "good timing." Timing may be dependent upon a great number of factors; examples of timing range from knowing exactly when to come in on a line after an applause to sensitively interacting with another actor. In this exercise we are experimenting with one of the mos pivotal factors of timing — the complex interplay between words and movement. Two rules of thumb will help get you thinking about this kind of timing:

- *Movement Before:* Movement *before* the line generally accents the line. If the actor moves *before* a line, then stops to say the line, the line itself is emphasized. For example, if the actor moves, then stops to say, "I'm leaving," the line itself is stressed.

- *Movement After:* Movement *after* the line generally accents the movement. If an actor says a line, and then moves *after* the line, the movement is emphasized. For example, if the actor says, "I'm leaving," and then moves, the motion is stressed.

These are simply rules of thumb and are by no means meant to put handcuffs on your imagination. As with any rule of thumb there are very meaningful exceptions, and the most important part of this exercise (as with all of the exercises in this book) is to explore through genuine experimentation. Maybe, for example, you will find in your own work, or from watching others work, exciting exceptions to these so-called rules. In actively exploring the dynamic difference between moving either before or after a line, avoid at all times just mechanically executing an action simply because it is part of the exercise. As always, carefully justify every choice — ***don't just make it work, make it work incredibly well***. As a final reminder, stick completely to the timing requirements — i.e., all movements should be either before or after the line, not just most of them. This does not mean that the actors have to move before or after every single line; it simply means that when they do move, they must conform to the timing demands. Although movement is the primary focus of this exercise, it is also worth observing that it's an advanced ground plan exercise as well. *Not only should the situations be different, but each should be as visually distinct from each other as possible*. Given that a ground plan encourages particular movement patterns, the director will have to work very hard to create scenes that are truly different from one another.

CRITIQUE

1. Were the *who*, *what*, and *where* effectively communicated? Did the situations seem well fitted to the before and after timing demands?

2. Was the ground plan effective? Keeping in mind that the director was using the *same ground plan*, were the two scenes contrasting enough? Was the director able to create enough staging variety between the two scenes, or were the scenes visually very similar?

3. Did the movements tend to be on a large or small scale? Was there any kind of progression from small to large movements or vice versa? Was the *before* (or *after*) a line timing accurately executed? Was the timing clean?

   • *Before Scenes:* Was the movement completed before the line was initiated, or were the movement and line timing blurred?

   • *After Scenes:* Was the line completed before the movement was initiated, or did the line and movement tend to be blurred?

4. What kind of *psychological moment*s or situations did the director create with the *before* or *after* timing? Did the following generalities prove to be true or false?

   • Movement before a line accents the line?

   • Movement after a line accents the movement?

5. Did the scene work overall, or did it seem like a class exercise?

6. Was the staging effective? What kinds of emphasis were used (direct, duoemphasis, secondary emphasis)?

7. Favorite moment? Least favorite moment?

RANT 'N RHYTHM
(Experimenting With Rhythm)

The larger the island of knowledge
the longer the shore line of wonder.

— Ralph Sockman

OVERVIEW

Rhythm, like music of which it is an integral part, is incredibly important because it has the power to work directly on the emotions of an audience. Rhythm also has a powerful effect on actors, which is also why directors need to be well versed with its possibilities. The fact that these rhythm exercises come relatively late in the training process is not an implication that they have less importance than other facets of the work; rather it attests to the fact that it is advanced work that requires proficiency in other areas before it can be fully appreciated. The intent of this exercise is to sensitize the workshop director to the scope and diversity of rhythmic work.

Working with the *same* three- or four-character open scene,[10] and the *same ground plan*, create *two* very *contrasting* scenes, with completely different situations. Let one scene be from category A, and one be from category B:

#	CATEGORY A	CATEGORY B
1.	Character rhythm contrast	Rhythm establishes the locale
2.	In and out of sync rhythms	Rhythm establishes atmosphere
3.	Prop punctuation	Rhythm establishes a change
4.	One against the group	Rhythm conveys a change in a character's tactic or beat

Using two of these different rhythmic perspectives, the challenge is to create two very different scenes with completely different situations from the *same ground plan and the same open scene dialogue*. Along with furthering an appreciation for rhythm, this exercise also demonstrates that the same ground plan can be used in very different ways. As much as possible, let the different approaches to rhythm be the guiding light in creating the two very contrasting scenes. Before presenting each scene, the director will be asked to beat the pertinent rhythm/s in the scene on a small drum.

---

[10]See pp. 162-165 for three- and four-person open scene possibilities.

189

RHYTHM AND TEMPO

Up to this point, the exercises have focused on how a director shapes the production in space, which involves composition and movement (i.e., blocking). With rhythm work, a director also has the possibility to shape a production in time (rhythm and tempo). When working with *space*, the director becomes the master sculptor relying on well-honed visual acuity, whereas when working with *time*, the director becomes a symphony conductor relying on his sensitivity to music. Blocking in and of itself helps to create a sense of rhythm. The use of the term "visual pause" hints at the power of a visual element to work rhythmically. Obviously, space and time (sight and sound) elements are inextricably connected, and our focus strictly on rhythm is a somewhat artificial, but very necessary task for the training.

Rhythm is all around us; each person has a characteristic rhythm which is revealed through both speech and movement. Likewise, each character in a play has his own rhythm and each play has an overall inherent rhythm. Good plays have failed miserably simply because the director and actors were never able to discover a convincing rhythm for the play; likewise mediocre plays have sometimes succeeded solely because the director and actors were able to tap into a theatrically exciting and convincing rhythm successfully. This is not to imply that a play can be interpreted rhythmically only one way; different rhythms will bring out different qualities, all of which play an important part in shaping the director's concept of the play. Observation of everyday events is an excellent way to increase your sensitivity to rhythm. Rhythm is a regular or irregular pattern of beats. Common to all rhythms are two special characteristics — *vitality and power of attraction*.

We instinctively fall into rhythm when listening to music, or when walking along the beach with the rhythmic ebb and flow of the surf. The pulsing quality in rhythmic experience is related to two fundamental life processes in nature: one is the beating of the heart, and the other is the breathing of the lungs. Both function in a rhythm of expansion and contraction which follow in endless sequence. Things which are rhythmic are associated with these processes, and thus have vitality. In his fifth century Chinese manual on painting, Hsie Hoe argues that the artist must identify so radically with the *ch'i*, the movement of life that animates all things in nature, that its spiritual rhythms resonate in his work and create "those spiritual rhythms of unbroken fluidity that mirror the mysterious reality of the universe."[11] Rhythm is strongly connected to the concept of tension and relaxation that is present not only in nature, but in manmade things as well. The fall, rise, and turning point of a pendulum is rhythmic, as is a bouncing ball or an automated bottling machine. Rhythm begins as something external, but "we grow to associate the rhythms that happen outside us with definite inner emotions or impressions."[12] Like music, rhythm gets immediately

[11]Frederick Frank, *Zen Seeing, Zen Drawing: Meditation in Action* (New York: Bantam Books, 1993), p. 153.

[12]For more discussion about this associative quality of rhythm, see Alexander Dean & Lawrence Carra, *Fundamentals of Play Directing*, (New York: Holt, Rinehart and Winston, Inc., 1974), pp. 229-230.

"soaked" into our systems where it becomes a direct tap to the emotions. Rhythm is an incredibly seductive force that when properly handled can lure an audience faster than anything else into the world of the play.

Many people confuse **rhythm** with **tempo**. Rhythm is a regularly recurring accent, whereas tempo is simply the rate of speed. The wrong tempo can be just as harmful to a moment in a play as it can to a particular movement in a symphony. Too often directors try to speed up the tempo out of fear that it will otherwise be too boring. George Bernard Shaw said that if a play is going too slowly it should be slowed down even more. This was Shaw's way of saying that only by slowing down a play will the director be able to discover the missing inner action and rhythms; once these are discovered, then, and only then should the tempo, if desired, be accelerated. Richard Boleslavsky, who made rhythm the sixth of his first lessons in acting, recognized that rhythm and tempo are often confused. He says if Shakespeare had used rhythm and tempo as characters, he would have written:

Rhythm = the *Prince* of the Arts
Tempo = his *Bastard* Brother[13]

One of the most common epithets used by critics to evaluate a director's work is tempo — the play was "well paced with rapid-fire delivery," or "too slow with actors hanging onto furniture," etc. Such evaluation is often clichéd and too general, but there's no question that sensitivity to tempo is vital to a director's work.

OPEN SCENE WORK AND RHYTHM:

The iambic pentameter of Shakespearean verse, with its five feet to a line, where each foot consists of a short (˘) followed by a long (´) syllable, has a definite rhythm as in the following phrase:

The clóck | strŭck níne | when Í | dĭd sénd | the nŭrse.

Although not as regular as iambic pentameter, normal conversation is naturally rhythmic; typically there is a rhythmic flow to everyday speech which is often punctuated by interjections such as "No!" and "Sure," "uh huh," "okay," etc. In her comprehensive study, *Rhythm in Drama*, Kathleen George feels that the deliberately pared down dialogue of open scenes make them ideal training vehicles for understanding the complexities of rhythm.[14] In addition to the rhythm inherent in each of the lines, she makes a perceptive observation that different rhythmic possibilities are created by the way the lines are clustered together. Lines are clustered together by

---

[13]Richard Boleslavski, *Acting: The First Six Lessons*, (New York: Theatre Arts Books, 1963), p. 112.

[14]She devotes an entire chapter to discussing rhythmic ramifications of the open scene. See Kathleen George, *Rhythm in Drama*, (Pittsburgh: University of Pittsburgh Press, 1980), pp. 17-28.

thoughts and/or actions, and these cluster patterns form a definite rhythm. To demonstrate her point she creates three different groupings (cluster patterns) from the same open scene. In Example 1, the cluster of lines is a 2-4-2-4-2-1-2-1-2 rhythm. The intent of this variation was to create the most possible changes while still keeping a sense of order. Along with the order there is a definite rhythmic progression (the fours become twos, and the twos become ones). The shorter segments with lines such as "Oh — Yes" tend to be more tentative (more hyperactive), as contrasted with the longer, more sustained sounding sections with lines like "Why are you doing this?" The clusterings, such as all of the twos, or all of the fours, suggest that there are parallels between them, and these parallels will inevitably affect the meaning and overall sense of the scene. The pattern gives the impression of repeated avoidance-confrontation, which steadily builds. In Example 2, there is still a suggestion of an avoidance-confrontation,

EXAMPLE #1

One:	Oh.	
Two:	Yes.	2

One:	Why are you doing this?	
Two:	It's the best thing.	
One:	You can't mean it?	4
Two:	No, I'm serious.	

One:	Please.	
Two:	What?	2

One:	What does this mean?	
Two:	Nothing.	
One:	Listen.	4
Two:	No.	

One:	So different.	
Two:	Not really.	2

| One: | Oh. | 1 |

Two:	You're good.	
One:	Forget it.	2

| Two: | What? | 1 |

One:	Go on.	
Two:	I will.	2

but its compactness into three almost equal divisions gives it, according to Kathleen George, a more classical feel.[15] The three-part division (a 6-6-8 pattern) is very familiar, conforming perhaps to Aristotle's notion that a play should have a beginning, middle, and an end. This second variation emphasizes more than anything else a cause and effect patterning, partly because each section includes a greater variety of responses and this, in comparison with the first variation, creates an even more pronounced sense of progression. The many changes of the first variation make us more aware of the relationship between the changes, hinting that the catalysts for changes are emotional. With fewer highlighted changes, the second variation makes us even more aware of the progression, hinting that the catalysts for the changes instead of being emotional are more likely to be from more "reasoned" tactical shifts of strategy.

[15]Kathleen George, *Rhythm in Drama*, (Pittsburgh: University of Pittsburgh Press, 1980), p. 21.

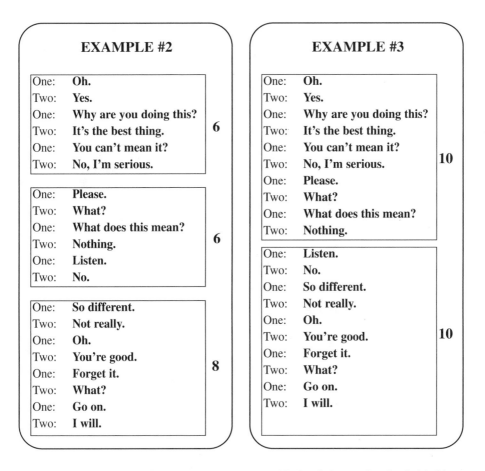

EXAMPLE #2

One:	**Oh.**	
Two:	**Yes.**	
One:	**Why are you doing this?**	
Two:	**It's the best thing.**	**6**
One:	**You can't mean it?**	
Two:	**No, I'm serious.**	

One:	**Please.**	
Two:	**What?**	
One:	**What does this mean?**	
Two:	**Nothing.**	**6**
One:	**Listen.**	
Two:	**No.**	

One:	**So different.**	
Two:	**Not really.**	
One:	**Oh.**	
Two:	**You're good.**	**8**
One:	**Forget it.**	
Two:	**What?**	
One:	**Go on.**	
Two:	**I will.**	

EXAMPLE #3

One:	**Oh.**	
Two:	**Yes.**	
One:	**Why are you doing this?**	
Two:	**It's the best thing.**	
One:	**You can't mean it?**	**10**
Two:	**No, I'm serious.**	
One:	**Please.**	
Two:	**What?**	
One:	**What does this mean?**	
Two:	**Nothing.**	

One:	**Listen.**	
Two:	**No.**	
One:	**So different.**	
Two:	**Not really.**	
One:	**Oh.**	
Two:	**You're good.**	**10**
One:	**Forget it.**	
Two:	**What?**	
One:	**Go on.**	
Two:	**I will.**	

The third variation is even more compact with the dialogue simply divided into two equal parts (a 10-10 pattern). This creates a comparatively more "irregular" rhythm, because each section is so crammed full of changes that they seem arbitrary. At first nothing seems to resolve, but a bit later suddenly everything seems to resolve. The ultimate effect with the third variation is that it comes off as too contrived and incomplete, giving it a "somewhat offbeat and tired-out flavor," all of which reminds Kathleen George of the double act structure used by Samuel Beckett.[16] There are many more variations than these three, but they are enough to demonstrate that open scenes are just as "open" to rhythmic possibilities as they are to other production elements. They also demonstrate that in any rhythmic pattern something has to remain constant while other things have to change. Changes are what distinguish a rhythm, but consistency is also critical in order to maintain a rhythmic pattern. Besides the multitude of clustering possibilities, there are also a great many stylistic variations.

[16]Kathleen George, *Rhythm in Drama*, (Pittsburgh: University of Pittsburgh Press, 1980), p. 21.

When the director perceives that every writer, including even an "open scene" writer, has his own rhythm as distinctive as his handwriting, then the director is ready to reap the rewards of rhythmic work.

CATEGORY "A" EXPLANATIONS

1. *Character Rhythm Contrast*:

Every person has a characteristic rhythm in both his or her movement and speech. Extenuating circumstances such as state of mind or situation may result in variations, but there will still be a characteristic rhythm. An aggressive salesman will have a very different rhythm than his grade school daughter or son. Some rhythmic possibilities might include:

- Jerky or smooth (staccato or legato)

- Volatile or even-tempered

- Impulsive or deliberative

- Ponderous or light

- Broken or continuous

For this scene, concentrate on creating characters with very different character rhythms. Let the rhythms be evident in both line delivery and movement. Before doing the scene, you will be asked to beat out on a drum the specific rhythms for each character.

2. *In and Out of Sync Rhythms*:

Watch people who are in sync with each other, such as lovers and very good friends and you'll see them stand exactly the same way while talking, or using similar phrases and intonation. There is a harmony to all of their interactions; watch the same people during a quarrel, and instead of harmony there is only dissonance. This kind of rhythmic interplay is hardly the exclusive rights of lovers; it can happen in a variety of relationships and circumstances.

For this scene, work with either an A-B-A or a B-A-B structure where A stands for synchronized rhythms, and B for unsynchronized rhythms. Work with both line delivery and movement to suggest whether the rhythms are in or out of sync.

3. *Prop Punctuation*:

Props may be used rhythmically, and oftentimes they become a symbolic extension of the character. For instance, think of the carrot chopping episode in *Joe's Not Home* or the mother making lemonade in *Lemons in the Morning*.[17]

Create a situation where one or more of the characters uses a prop as a direct extension of his or her personality. Concentrate on allowing the prop to punctuate lines and/or business for best effect.

4. ***One Against the Group***:

Think of the words "mob psychology" to savor the potential force of a group. Often a group rhythm is created where there is considerable pressure to fall in with the group.

Here the challenge is to create a situation where the rhythm of one person is dramatically at odds with the other two or three. The scene may keep this initial tension, or it may progress until the lone person falls in with the rhythm of the group, or the group falls in with the rhythm of the individual.

CATEGORY "B" EXPLANATIONS

1. ***Rhythm Establishes the Nature of the Locale***:

The locale for the play can definitely affect the rhythm. Each locality and country has a distinctive rhythm: We know that a totally different rhythmic sensation is experienced when we arrive in a metropolis after a stay in the country. A funeral parlor has a very different rhythmic pattern from a beauty parlor. Before the performance, you will be asked to beat out the specific rhythm for the locale.

2. ***Rhythm Establishes Atmosphere:***

Atmospheric details, as well as locale, can be a determinant of rhythm. The time of day, the season of the year, the kind of climate or weather determine rhythm. A scene at a breakfast table has a totally different rhythmic feeling from a scene at dinner time. A scene at the waterfront in a thick fog has a different rhythmic feeling from the same scene played in full sunlight.

3. ***Rhythm Conveys a Change***:

Besides a change in rhythm which might result from locale or atmosphere, a change in rhythm can also convey a change in the mood or chemistry of the group. Remember that rhythm and tempo are not the same thing. Before performing this scene, you will be asked to beat out the specific rhythms used in your scene.

---

[17]Both of these plays are from the *24 Hours AM/PM*, one-act play collections.

4. *Rhythm Conveys a Change in a Character's Tactic or Beat*:

This is similar to #3 on the previous page, except that instead of a rhythmic change in the group, there is a change in a single character's tactic or beat. As with each of the Category B choices, you will be asked to beat out the specific rhythms used in your scene.

CRITIQUE

1. Was the situation (the *who*, the *what*, and the *where*) well communicated in both scenes?

2. Even though both scenes used the same ground plan, was there an effective contrast? Was the ground plan effective? Did it help or hinder the scenes rhythmically?

3. Which of the following possibilities for categories A and B were selected?

#	CATEGORY A	CATEGORY B
1.	Character rhythm contrast	Rhythm establishes the locale
2.	In and out of sync rhythms	Rhythm establishes atmosphere
3.	Prop punctuation	Rhythm establishes a change
4.	One against the group	Rhythm conveys a change in character's tactic or beat

4. Were the rhythms convincing, or did they seem forced? Did they keep you interested in the scene? Were there any moments that seemed "out of" rhythm?

5. Did the scenes work overall, or did they seem like a class exercise? Did the scenes seem well rehearsed? Which scene did you like the best?

6. Was there a *visual* progression with one or both of the scenes? Was there a *rhythmic* progression with one or both of the scenes?

7. With the two scenes, did the director tend to favor the visual or the verbal elements, or was there a balance?

8. Favorite moment? Least favorite moment?

RIFFS OF RASHOMON
(Experimenting With Subjective Points of View)

I'm OK, you're a bit odd.

— Paul Chance

OVERVIEW

How do eyewitness accounts of three characters participating in the same event differ? Seeing the same event through the eyes of three different characters is the challenge of this exercise inspired from the Japanese film, *Rashomon*. Working with a three-character open scene, create a situation that centers around a particular event. Instead of simply justifying the given dialogue as is typical of open scene work, create three different variations of the same scene. At least one of the scenes should adhere to the given dialogue, but the others may vary as needed. Each variation becomes a separate scene, dramatizing a specific character's point of view. In other words, each variation is an eyewitness account of what happened. In each variation, one of the characters is the dominant figure while the others play supporting roles in the scene.

THE SUBJECTIVITY OF TRUTH

Time permitting, watching Akira Kurosawa's *Rashomon* can be an excellent introduction to this exercise. *Rashoman* focuses on four eyewitness accounts of a brutal rape. Each of the four characters directly or indirectly participates in the incident but their accounts differ greatly. The filmmaker's cynical vision centers around the idea that each of the characters demonstrates an indulgent evaluation of his own despicable behavior. The director refuses to select one truth as the definite one, thereby dramatizing the subjectivity of truth.

The revolutionary format and message of this classic film is the creative catalyst for the exercise. This is an excellent culminating open scene exercise because capturing a subjective point of view is very demanding work, frequently inviting stylistic treatment. While each scene centers around the same incident and characters, each enactment asks for a different character to be the dominant figure. This calls for very skillful work with all types of focus, and part of what will distinguish one version from another is the cunning use of direct, indirect, counter and duofocus.[18] Keep in mind that just because we are seeing the scene through a particular character's eyes, this dominant figure will not necessarily always be the one to have focus; who specifically has the focus depends very much on how the perceiving character is interpreting the event.

The exercise is complex because its very concept is a paradox. How can a director let us see something through a character's eyes when the character is present on stage? In this sense, filmmaking with its flexibility in camera angles and special effects has a distinct advantage in capturing a subjective point of view. But subjectivity can come alive on stage as well. For hints as to how subjective points of view can be effectively dramatized on stage, study the expressionistic plays such as Eugene O'Neill's *The Emperor Jones* or *The Hairy Ape*, or Elmer Rice's *The Adding Machine*.

The featured character is, in effect, telling us or personally experiencing his or her version of the story. Why and to whom the story is being told is a potentially important directorial choice. Is it a haunting inner vision that prompts the telling or is it a reenactment for a court testimony? Both cases would still be subjective, but one of them clearly has a more objective starting point. Maybe the three versions represent the three respective dreams, nightmares, or mental aberrations of the respective characters. Or maybe each of the three versions springs forth from the down-to-earth, everyday world of a raucous poker game where the players in their drunken stupor are compelled to dramatize for each other their version of the story.

A subjective point of view may mean that a particular facet of the incident is distorted or intensified, as frequently happens in expressionistic plays. But it could also mean that something is ignored, forgotten, or never consciously witnessed. Moment-for-moment interpretation shapes our every experience, which is part of what is behind the adage that "beauty is in the eye of the beholder." Most simply put, each person looks at the world differently. Moreover the psychological phenomenon known as projection may also very likely come into play. Something from within the perceiving character is unconsciously "projected" onto another character so that from scene to scene the same characters could come across very differently. Take this one a psychological step further and maybe each of the three characters is meant to be three different facets of the same personality! Many are the possibilities, as long as three contrasting viewpoints of the same event are dramatized.

---

[18]For a discussion of direct, indirect, and counter focus, see pp. 170-171 and pp. 174-175 See pp. 179-180 for an explanation of duofocus.

CRITIQUE

1. Was the basic incident worthy of three different interpretations? Were the interpretations contrasting enough to dramatically merit three distinct scenes? Was it clear why each of the scenes was happening, and to whom (if anyone) they were being played?

2. How did the staging for each variation clarify whose story was being told? Was it clear whose eyes we were looking through? What did each variation reveal about the dominant character?

3. Which variation was the most exciting? The least? Favorite moment and least favorite moment of each variation?

CHAPTER 6
CLOSED SCENE EXERCISES

Exit the *open scene* and enter the *closed scene*. The term "closed scene" means using a script (in full or in part) from an existing play. Just as the so-called "open scene" is never completely open, the "closed scene" is never completely closed since there will always be many ways to interpret the material.

Staging skills become most valuable when they are largely second nature. Assimilating and interrelating the layers of skills is no small task, and at times following the yellow brick road of the workshop seems to be a hopelessly frustrating journey. When the skills do finally come together, this frustration is replaced by an insatiable craving for longer scripts. Weaning the student director from open scene work is at this point hardly a problem, and cravings for bigger textual meals are definitely signs of a healthy appetite. More material may simply mean a ten-minute scene or very short play,[1] since after a steady diet of open scenes even a mere two- to three-page script becomes a welcomed quantum leap. Script analysis becomes an increasingly important part of the directorial vision, and while open scenes have been incredibly nourishing up to this point, it is now time to lustily partake from the horn of plenty.

Coming at the final phase of the workshop, these are very advanced exercises; success with these exercises is possible only because the student director at this point is able to tap into a wellspring of skills. Assuming a high level of proficiency, however, doesn't imply that the exercises are completely open-ended. They are consistent with the previous work in that they ask the student to solve very specific directorial problems. At first glance the exercises of this chapter might very well appear to be little more than traditional scene study exercises. Yes, they are designed to use scenes from actual plays, but that is where the similarity ends. Unlike traditional scene study work, where the student is simply asked to direct an overall great scene, the exercises from Chapter 6 have very specific agendas. In stressing this distinction, this is not to say that traditional scene study work is not beneficial; in fact, it can be of tremendous value at various phases of the workshop training in providing a barometer reading of the director's progress. Time permitting, it is often worthwhile to perform the scene "regularly" after working with the various exercises from this chapter.

An excellent way to introduce scene study of any kind into the workshop is to have everybody work on the same scene. Such an approach keeps everyone familiar

---

[1]Collections of very short (ca. 10 minutes) plays are listed on pp. 7-8.

with everyone else's work, which not only encourages in-depth criticism, but it also fosters an appreciation for the uniqueness of each director's work; it demonstrates in the most dramatic way possible the impact the director brings to a particular script. Collective participation with the same material (or the same problem, the same ground plan, or the same open scene, etc.) has been an ongoing through-line of the workshop exercises. An evolutionary step beyond the same scene approach is to have students select any scene they want from the same play. This has the continued advantage of keeping everyone familiar with the material, but it has the added benefit of creating a variety of scenes. And yes, there comes a time when separate scenes from separate plays, and even complete plays, are of value to the workshop. Each scene and each play has specific problems, and hearing a director articulate exactly what choices were made in solving them is a very worthwhile part of the training process.

Keep in mind that "closed scenes" could be easily applied to many of the previous exercises. Most of the open scene exercises from Chapter 5 could work effectively with closed scripts, and this is also true of some of the very early exercises such as *Scene 8: Serial Starters* or *Scene 10: Justified Patterns*. Closed scene material is what binds the following exercises together, since in all other respects they are a very diverse collection. The seven exercises in this chapter are:

SCENE	TITLE	DESCRIPTION
Scene 29	Picture Play	Creating a script, ground plan and staged scene from a single picture.
Scene 30	Musical Swap Stew	To experiment with creating a meaningful synthesis (a stew) of music, painting, and ground plan.
Scene 31	Superimposed Patterns	An advanced pattern exercise in which each character is associated with a particular part of the pattern.
Scene 32	Playing Against the Obvious	Exploring the complex interplay between the verbal (text) and the nonverbal (blocking).
Scene 33	Prop Physicalizing	To experiment with intensifying "inner action" or subtext through the use of physical metaphors.
Scene 34	No-Prop Physicalizing	Similar to prop physicalizing, except that the externalized expression of subtext is created without the use of props.
Scene 35	Inner Vision	Changing a totally realistic scene into a completely expressionistic work where everything is witnessed seen through the eyes of a central character.

PICTURE PLAY
(Creating a Picture-Generated Scene)

Every picture tells a story.

— Advertisement for Doan's Backache Kidney Pills, 1904

OVERVIEW

According to Chinese folk wisdom, a picture is worth more than ten thousand words; in this exercise, a single picture provides the inspiration for a fully developed five- to seven-minute scene. Pick *one* of the provided pictures to generate a scenario, ground plan and fully staged two- to three-character scene. For dialogue begin with an existing open scene,[2] but feel free to alter or embellish it in any way whatsoever. Whether the picture epitomizes the entire scene, or details a specific moment, let the picture be the prime creative mover.

INTRODUCTORY SCRIPT WORK

Picture Play is a perfect introductory script exercise because it is a creative outgrowth of the preceding open scene work. It serves as a transition from working with fully open to "closed" scripts. An open scene is still used, but suddenly the previous rules about never altering a single word are broken, and the dialogue is there to be embellished and edited as needed. This new freedom looks to the future of more fully developed scripts, but at the same time it doesn't ignore the richness of past work. This script could be created simply via improvisation, but keying off an existing open scene at this point should be no real problem, and it is a further source of ideas.

Letting a picture become the prime creative mover is perfect training for later production concept exercises and projects.[3] Later conceptualizing work might take the form of a question: If this play were a particular picture, what specific picture would it be? In other words, what single picture taps into the heart and soul of an upcoming production? In this particular exercise the picture does not necessarily have to convey the essence of the scene; it might, for instance, just convey the beginning picture of the upcoming scene or some other specific moment. Likewise, the picture can function as a metaphor for your scene, or it can be taken literally. Whatever the usage, however, this visual approach paves the way for the advanced conceptualizing work ahead.

---

[2]For "Open Scene" possibilities, see pp. 160-168.

[3]See *Scene 30: Musical Swap Stew*, pp. 207-212, and *Project D: Point Conception*, pp. 277-283.

VARIATIONS

If repeated, workshop directors might want to find their own pictures instead of relying upon those provided here. As a first time through, however, limiting choices is probably best, plus there is the built-in interest of seeing how others interpret the same picture. At any phase of the workshop training, there is always a fascination in discovering how different directors work with the same given material. Finding a meaningful connection between the picture and an open scene is the basic challenge of this exercise. In general, creative work is often characterized as bringing together ideas which are usually remote from each other; the union in this case is facilitated by the fact that for the first time in working with open scenes, it is now perfectly permissible to alter the dialogue. Even though text plays a substantial part in the basic exercise, an exciting possibility is to ignore the text completely and treat this exercise as an advanced silent scene. Still another interesting variation, with or without text, might be somehow to integrate the essence of two pictures, or selected details from two pictures, into a single scene.

PICTURE AS PRIME MOVER

Select one of the following pictures. Eventually a script is to be born from one of the pictures selected on pages 205 and 206, but remember that the "midwife" is an existing open scene. Let the open scene remain secondary, since the picture, not the text, is meant to be the primary catalyst for this exercise. Theoretically, an open scene could just as easily provide the creative spark, but for the sake of variety, let the inspiration for this exercise come from the picture. One way to generate ideas is to place yourself in the picture. This could take the form of identifying with a particular character in the picture, or just imagining that you've arrived as an additional person in the picture. Maybe you imagine a past or future self (or perhaps even an "alter-ego") placed in the picture. Questions to ponder as you place yourself in the picture might be:

- Where are you and what brought you here?
- Do you like being here?
- How are you related to other people in the picture?
- How do you feel about them?
- Do you plan on staying long?
- What has just happened, and what is about to happen?
- What are you planning to do there?

Besides these basic questions, there are many additional questions that a specific picture will inspire. Brainstorm several possible scenarios in this manner, and then search for an open script that best lends itself to one of your approaches. Another approach to consider in generating ideas is to title the picture. The title of the picture might refer to a dominant theme or function as an ironic commentary for the piece. Remember that the picture may be taken at face value and interpreted literally, or it may be interpreted more figuratively and treated as a metaphor. Remember also the wisdom of a Latin proverb: "*Mutum est pictura poema* (A picture is a mute poem)."

THE PICTURE POSSIBILITIES

PICTURE POSSIBILITIES *(Continued)*

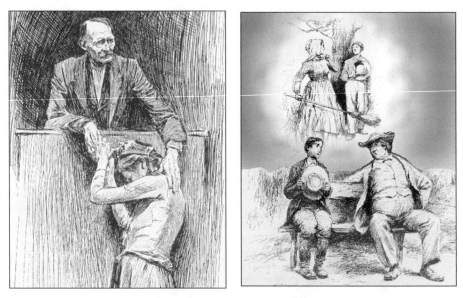

CRITIQUE

1. Was the situation (the ***who***, the ***what***, and the ***where***) well communicated?

2. Was the picture used literally or figuratively — as a metaphor or as a particular moment in the actual scene?

3. Was there a definite beginning, middle, and end?

4. Did the director rely more on the visual or the verbal elements, or was there a balance?

5. Favorite moment? Least favorite moment?

MUSICAL SWAP STEW
(Experimenting With Theatrical Stew)

*Without music
Life would be a mistake.*

— F.W. Nietzsche

OVERVIEW

Musical Swap Stew is an interesting exercise to do when the workshop directors are first preparing to work with closed scripts. This exercise is really two exercises, which are prepared at different times and which for convenience will be called *Part A* and *Part B*.

Part A: This is preparatory *paper work* instead of an actual performance. The intent of this part of the exercise is to help trigger your imagination to form a *production concept* for a play you are about to direct. Think of a production concept as the *seed* from whence all else (every detail, every prop, every casting choice, and every behavioral moment) will eventually grow. To get you thinking along these lines, Part A asks you to do three things:

- Find a *picture* that epitomizes your production. If your play were a picture, what specific picture would it be?

- Find a *musical selection* that epitomizes your production. If your play was a piece of music, what specific selection would it be?

- Create a scaled ground plan.

Part B: Working with a three- to six-person open scene,[4] create characters and situation which fully justify the dialogue. The challenge in creating the situation is to concoct a "musical stew" by combining three savory, swapped items:

- Ground plan
- Picture   } Swapped with *another director*
- Musical selection

Even if you happen to be familiar with your swapping partner's play, strive to create a situation very different from the actual play. Likewise, if you are savvy to

---

[4]See pp. 162-168. The other possibility is to write your own script for this exercise.

the ideas inherent in the ground plan, painting, and musical choices, attempt as much as possible to counter the intended usage. If you have absolutely no knowledge of your partner's play, so much the better. The multiple purposes of Part B are to:

- To discover which of these swapped items is best able to spark your imagination. Was the idea for your scene first inspired by a specific item, or were you energized equally by each of the items in the overall challenge of having to find a hidden pattern or connection among them?

- To explore the fine art of making stew — to see whether you're able to make a *meaningful blend* of ground plan, picture, and music.

- To compare and contrast your use of the swapped items with the director's original feelings about these choices.

- To evaluate the strength and weaknesses of another director's ground plan. For the director who created the ground plan, there is the advantage of seeing how someone else works in the space he has created. There is always the possibility that another director will use the plan in ways that the original artist hasn't considered. Plus if there are some major snags in the ground plan, there is still time to make adjustments.

CREATIVE STEW

Nothing better than *theatrical stew!* In general, being creative is kind of like making a stew, especially if you subscribe to the idea that a significant part of the creative process involves integrating oftentimes unrelated parts into a coherent whole — forming a new synthesis. Richard Wagner, the famous German composer/theoretician, loved to talk about theatre as being a "synthesis of the arts," and had he been slightly more tuned to his taste buds he might have used the word stew instead of synthesis. Creative breakthroughs which are oftentimes the result of juxtaposing elements or ideas that ordinarily do not go together (or detecting a hidden pattern of connection among things) are, in effect, psychic stews. Creativity begins to cook when ideas are combined and rearranged in a new way. Like a kaleidoscope which is able to reflect and refract its colored bits and pieces in a seemingly endless variety of novel combinations, our imagination functions virtually the same way with its boundless ability to bring all of our psychic "bits and pieces" into exciting new combinations. Think of the three swapped items of this exercise as the bits and pieces needed to conjure up fresh, dramatic reconfigurations.

While speaking of "stews," it is worth noting that there is an element of time inherent in all good stews; the more simmering time, generally the better the stew. Similarly, as psychologists remind us, there is oftentimes an *incubation period* needed for our creative work as well. When we say "we'll sleep on it," the wisdom of this folk expression refers to this incubation phase. It is not always necessary to actually go to sleep to incubate; sometimes it is as simple as putting the problem out of your mind for a while. By immersing yourself in a problem and then putting it on the back burner by focusing on something else, there is a very good chance that suddenly you will come up with a great idea that seems to come "out of nowhere" when you least expected it. Even though it seems like it came from "out of nowhere," odds are it came from a chance observation that magnetically connected itself to the incubating problem. Over three thousands years ago, the playwright Aristophanes sensed this very idea:

> If you strike upon a thought that baffles you, break off from that entanglement and try another, so shall your wits be fresh to start again.[5]

Knowing when to let go of a problem and allow it to incubate for a while is one of the best ways possible to get your stew cooking. What ultimately will get your stew really cooking is none other than **passion** for the work. In the lingo of psychology, this passion is called *intrinsic motivation* — "the urge to do something for the sheer pleasure of doing it rather than for any prize or competition."[6]

RECIPE SUGGESTIONS

There is always some mystery as to how ideas come about, and the specific stimulus for developing an idea will differ greatly between the individuals. While some people are inspired visually, others are first drawn into an idea through sound. And, in this exercise, maybe the spatial reasoning inherent in the ground plan work — how things are oriented in space — becomes the initial spark for your scene. And perhaps it is impossible for you to really decipher which of these items was the initial stimulus — the process itself might seem subliminal with "stew" right there from beginning. All this, of course, is food for thought for your journal. Important suggestions for each of your "recipe items" are:

The Music

Part A: Music is the soul of humanity. As we all instinctively know, music is a direct tap to our emotions and, unlike theatre, it easily breaks free of all language barriers. The language of music cannot be translated very well into the language of words — the meaning lies in the sounds themselves. Writer/director Barbara Damashek, co-writer and director of *Quilters*, explains when she directs any kind of a play, music becomes "her personal path into understanding a piece."[7] With all this in mind, search for music that epitomizes your play — in effect the play's "theme music." Any type of music is possible, with or without lyrics. Sometimes beginning

---

[5]Quoted from Ruth Noller, et. al., *Creative Actionbook*, (New York: Charles Scribner's Sons, 1976), p. 19.

[6]Daniel Goleman, et. al., *The Creative Spirit*, (New York: Penguin Books, 1993), p. 30.

[7]Jean Schiffman, "Barbara Damashek: A Moving Target," *American Theatre* 10, no. 12 (December 1993), p. 46.

directors find what they feel are perfect lyrics, and they love to read them out loud for clarity; keep in mind that if the lyrics aren't clear to begin with, it's pointless to read them to us, regardless of how meaningful you happen to think they are. The music, with or without lyrics, should speak fully for itself.

Part B: The musical selection needs *literally to play* at some point, if not all the way through your scene. There are a number of possibilities for integrating music into your scene. It can be used *realistically*, coming from a natural source, such as when a character turns on the radio, or it can be used more stylistically as *underscoring* (music underneath the text functioning as emotional emphasis to the text). Keep in mind that the underscoring *does not always have to be directly in sync with text*. There are wonderful possibilities for having the underscoring:

• Anticipate the tendency of the text.

• Hold onto a mood long after the text has seemingly taken a new tangent.

• Or suddenly bring into mind a previous mood or memory (Tennessee Williams in such plays as *The Glass Menagerie* or *A Streetcar Named Desire* loved to do this).

• Function as the *primary motivator* (in terms of such things as mood, movement, or overall rhythm) for either a *single* character, or all of the characters together.

Underscoring can be used constantly or intermittently. *The moments when you choose to bring in or out the underscoring, i.e. the transitions, can be as important as the musical selection itself.* A large part of this involves the art of sound level — sneaking the sound in or out, and making sure the music doesn't decibel out the dialogue. Also keep in mind, the potential of silence (referring to absence of text and/or music) to create a spellbinding moment. Too often people simply think of underscoring as simply "mood" or "background" music. Regardless of how you choose to use music, strive to make your music become much more than elevator-type "muzak," strive to make it the visceral core, the very soul and heartbeat of the performance.

The Painting

Part A: There is truth to the folk saying a picture is worth a thousand words; it is certainly the idea behind trying to find a single image (painting, photograph or graphic) that taps into the very heart and soul of your play.

• If the image you find is in color, make a *color* copy of it.

• If searching for a single image proves to be a problem, consider the possibility of creating a *collage*. With either a picture or a collage, search for an image that *transcends the obvious surface level* of your play. In addition to capturing the "essence" of the play, your picture might connect with the world of the play in any of the following ways:

≈ Texture (such as rough, smooth, hard, soft)

≈ A color scheme

≈ Overall feel or mood of the play

≈ Kinesthetic qualities (nervous, joyful, depressed)

≈ Specific imagery inherent to the play

Part B: Unlike the musical selection, the painting does *not* literally have to appear in the scene. What does the painting mean to you? How does it make you feel? Are there important motifs or themes inherent in the picture? Answering these kinds of questions will begin the process of connecting this picture to your scene. Besides the emotional/thematic elements of the picture, consider the *purely compositional elements of the picture* for possible inspiration. Does the artist tend to use straight lines or circles, triangles or rectangles? Where is your eye first drawn in the picture? Does the picture suggest much or little movement? These kinds of questions can easily be translated into your actual staging in very interesting ways. Incidentally, there is a distinct possibility that if you choose to relate to the picture strictly compositionally, the finished scene will bear little resemblance to the emotional nature of the original image. Such usage is not only fine, but your rationale for doing so could provide a very interesting journal entry.

The Ground Plan

Stick to the exact ground plan (the placement of set pieces), but use the plan in any way that you like. For example, if your partner gave you a plan with clearly marked kitchen items such as a stove and sink, by no means should you feel obligated to play your scene in a kitchen; maybe the plan is better put to use as a cave where the former sink is now a rock-hewn altar for some sort of sacrifice. This is relatively easy to do considering that we're only using the stock, black box rehearsal pieces. Likewise, entrances on the given plan do not have to be used as suggested.

While you may veer radically from the intended usage of the given ground plan, it is essential that for all intents and purposes, it should appear custom-designed for *your* scene. After the performance, part of the discussion will include your thoughts about the strengths and weaknesses of this ground plan.

CRITIQUE

To the originator of the swapped items

1. Which of the swapped items (music, painting, ground plan) was most important to you? In other words, which one was best able to spark

your imagination? Or were you equally energized by all of them?

2. Briefly explain your choices for each of the swapped items. How does your use of the swapped items compare with what you saw?

3. Were there any patterns used in the ground plan that you hadn't considered? Were there any of these you might consider using?

To the director of the scene we have just watched

1. Which of the swapped items (music, painting, ground plan) was most important to you? In other words, which one was best able to spark your imagination? Or were you equally energized by all of them?

2. Was the ground plan easy or difficult to work with? Were there enough acting areas and entrances? Were the axes of the ground plan effective, or were they in some way visually awkward or difficult to work with?

To the rest of the workshop

1. Which of the swapped items seemed to be the primary motivator of the scene? Was there a good stew? In other words, were the swapped items (music, painting, and ground plan) effectively integrated into the scene as a whole — was there a meaningful blend?

2. Were there any common denominators (or hidden patterns) between the swapped items that were discovered by the director?

3. Was the music in the scene effective? How was music handled (realistic or unrealistic source, underscoring anticipating the tendency of the text, underscoring holding onto a mood, underscoring suddenly bringing into mind a previous mood or memory, underscoring functioning as the primary motivator for a single character, or all of them)?

4. Were the transitions in and out of the music effective? Were the levels effective?

5. Did the ground plan help spotlight the important moments of the scene? What moments were spotlighted? What was effective or ineffective about the ground plan? Were there distinct psychological areas? If so, what were they?

6. Was there a visual progression? Was the staging effective?

7. Favorite moment? Least favorite moment?

SUPERIMPOSED PATTERNS
(An Advanced Pattern Exercise)

Christ! What are patterns for?

— Amy Lowell

OVERVIEW

With a specific scene in mind, pick one of the provided patterns. All of the available patterns are actually two patterns superimposed on each other, and the primary objective is to associate the characters with each of the respective patterns. With this in mind, create a ground plan which motivates the characters to move within their specific patterns. Stage the scene, adhering to the stipulation that each character becomes associated with a particular part of the overall pattern (one of the superimposed patterns), fully justifying all of the movement.

FINDING A SCENE

Associating each character with one of the superimposed patterns would at first seem to suggest that selections would have to be limited to a two-character scene. Keeping to a two-character scene the first time through with this exercise is probably a good idea, but it is possible to use three or more characters in this exercise, as long as they are relegated to one of the two patterns. For instance, suppose you are directing a three-person scene, and working with a ground plan generated from pattern #1; two of the characters might be associated with the rectangle, and the third character with the square. It is also possible in a three-character scene that the third character might function as a liaison between the two characters, in which case this third character would navigate the pathways of both patterns.

Do all scenes contain characters with sharply defined boundaries? No, of course not. But given that theatre loves conflict, a surprising number of scenes play well with a territorial game plan.[8] Sometimes the territorial boundaries are very subtly suggested, but even with the restraints of this exercise it is perfectly possible to underplay the boundary distinctions. All this is not to say that care should not be taken in selecting a scene; there are obviously some scenes which would not lend themselves very well to this exercise, such as an entire scene where two characters are in bed together. This is an advanced justifying exercise where pattern, text and

---

[8]See pp. 43-48 (*Scene 5: Breaking Silent Boundaries*) for a pertinent discussion about boundaries and psychological areas.

movement have to be skillfully interrelated with each other.

STAGING NOTES

As typical of pattern-generated ground plan exercises, the goal is not necessarily to have the ground plan end up looking like the pattern, but for it to inspire and help justify movement that conforms to the pattern.[9] Previous pattern work has demonstrated that the lines of the pattern are potential pathways for movement, and the challenge in designing the ground plan is to arrange set pieces so that the characters use the pathways inherent in the patterns. Stick to one of the provided patterns at first, but in subsequent attempts, entertain the possibility of making up your own superimposed pattern.

Each character needs to be associated strongly with a particular pattern, but this doesn't mean at strategic times one of the characters can't invade the territory of another. These "invasions" will be all the more potent if the territories have been firmly established beforehand. And as already mentioned, there is the possibility in a three-character scene of a third character functioning as a literal and figurative go-between for the other two. Several of the superimposed patterns suggest very specific places for invasion possibilities.

PATTERN POSSIBILITIES

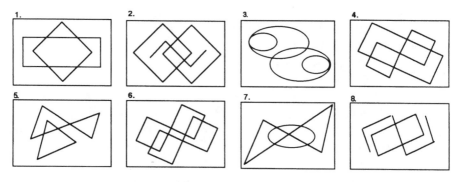

CRITIQUE

1. Was it clear which character was associated with which pattern?

2. Was there any effective boundary breaking?

3. Were all movements fully justified?

4. Favorite moment? Least favorite moment?

---

[9]It would be a good idea to review the previous pattern exercises (pp. 79-82 and pp. 135-138). Attempting this exercise without previous pattern work is not recommended.

PLAYING AGAINST THE OBVIOUS
(Exploring the Complex Interplay Between Text and Movement)

*The gods love the obscure
and hate the obvious.*

— The Upanishads
(800-500 B.C.)

OVERVIEW

As with the previous exercise, the sole objective of *Playing Against the Obvious* is to explore the complex interplay between text and movement. Exploring the ramifications of movement coming either before or after a line is for most student directors an eye-opening experience, but with this exercise the director is given many new doors to open in experimenting with the fascinating relationship between the visual and the verbal parts of the performance.

Select a *two- to three*-person scene. As in the previous exercise, the number of actors should be kept to a minimum in order to experiment most efficiently with what for most directors is a completely new way of thinking about blocking. In justifying the dialogue, *the overall objective is to create blocking that plays "against the obvious."*

BLOCKING AGAINST THE OBVIOUS

Most often a scene is staged to be in sync with the text, meaning that both the visual and verbal elements of a scene express the same meaning. A character says he is angry, and the anger is expressed visually as a vase is hurled at the wall and the character storms out of the room. A perfect example of the visual perfectly in tune with the verbal is described in the stage directions of Marsha Norman's *'Night, Mother*; Jessie tries throughout the play to convince her mother that she is going to commit suicide, and at one point when Jessie and her mother are struggling to put a slip cover on a sofa, the stage directions tells us that "the physical struggle somehow mirrors the emotional one in the conversation."[10] While the verbal and visual are usually in tandem, there are exciting theatrical possibilities when they are not. The objective of this exercise is to explore those times when the verbal and visual facets of performance are not the same.

---

[10]Marsha Norman, *'Night, Mother*, in Lee A. Jacobus, ed. *The Bedford Introduction to Drama*, Second Edition, (Boston: St. Martin's Press, 1993), p. 1271.

Sometimes playwrights are very sensitive to the interplay between text and movement. For instance, when the gentleman caller in Tennessee Williams' *The Glass Menagerie* announces his engagement, Laura is crushed — or as Williams puts it, "the holy candles in the altar of Laura's face have been snuffed out."[11] Williams senses the value of going against her obvious feelings by having her "bravely smile" as she offers Jim the broken glass ornament. Seeing Laura struggle against showing her true feelings creates a far more heart-wrenching moment than had she started to cry. Even when the playwright doesn't provide hints along these lines, the director can create staging that plays very effectively against the obvious emotional core of the scene. Robert Cohen and John Harrop in *Creative Play Direction* cite a recent production of *Romeo and Juliet* to demonstrate an instance of blocking against the obvious:

> In *Romeo and Juliet,* Paris finds Juliet apparently dead on her wedding day. In Mel Shapiro's production of the play at the Old Globe Theatre in San Diego, Paris came in with a hired group of strolling musicians, who played their joyous serenade right down to the discovery of the presumed corpse.[12]

Blocking against the obvious is very similar to what actors for ages have called "playing against the obvious." An actor playing a drunk who can't walk a straight line is more likely to succeed if he tries hard to suppress his fear of not being able to do so rather than going for the external effect. Similarly, a character who is supposed to cry, struggles instead to hold back the tears by laughing, but the tears show through the laughter creating a far greater emotional impact. Trying to cry by focusing on the desire to cry is destined to failure because this is not what the character would do. More than likely the character would want to save face or avoid the pain by trying to suppress an emotional display, and so when the actor tries to go against the crying he is simply doing what the character would probably be doing, and this process is more likely than anything else to allow the emotions to surface spontaneously.

Playing or blocking against the obvious capitalizes on the idea that there can be a difference between the verbal and visual facets of a scene. Theatre people are well versed in the distinction between *text* and *subtext* where a character may say to another, "what a lovely dress," but may actually be thinking "it looks hideous, but who cares as long as I make the sale." Skillful directors and actors are often able to provide hints about the real feeling — the subtextual level — through movement and stage business. Along the same lines, psychologists have noticed that in therapy sessions it was often possible to anticipate what the client thought about a topic even before the topic was discussed. For instance, psychiatrist George Mahl reported that in one of his therapy sessions a client, as she talked about her feelings of inferiority toward her husband, kept putting her fingers toward her mouth. Later she told him

[11]Tennessee Williams' *The Glass Menagerie*, (New York: New Directions Publishing Corporation, 1970), p. 108.

[12]Robert Cohen and John Harrop, *Creative Play Direction*, (New Jersey: Prentice-Hall, Inc., 1984), p. 125.

that as a child she felt that she was much less attractive than her sister because she had two buckteeth.[13] Sigmund Freud along with many other psychologists sensed that there was more than one level of communication:

> He that has eyes to see and ears to hear may convince himself that no mortal can keep a secret. If his lips are silent, he chatters with his finger tips; betrayal oozes out of him at every pore.[14]

After seeing a popular play of his time, Freud was quick to notice that one of the characters, a married woman who was having an affair, unconsciously revealed her true feelings by playing constantly with her wedding ring until finally taking it off before going to meet her lover.[15] Theatre artists since antiquity have recognized the communicative value of nonverbal behavior; they sensed that much can be learned about a relationship by watching how people look at each other, and how they stand and sit in relation to each other. In comparison to theatre artists, psychologists are way behind researching the relationship between verbal and nonverbal behavior. This doesn't mean, however, that there isn't something to be gleaned from some of their recent research. Playing against the obvious where the nonverbal behavior is contradictory to the text has been familiar to theatre practitioners for a long time, but psychologists Ekman and Friesen have pointed out that the relationship between the visual and verbal can be more than just contradictory.[16] Besides a simple relationship, where the verbal and visual are in sync with each other, they suggest that there additional relationships such as:

- The blocking can *anticipate* the text. That is, the blocking provides a preview of what is to come in the text. The example already mentioned of the woman who put her finger to her mouth before telling her analyst that she was ashamed of her buckteeth as a child exemplifies the visual anticipating the text.

- The blocking can convey meaning that is *contradictory* to the text. A person says he is not angry, but he looks and acts angry. Or a character who is on the verge of tears tries instead to laugh, yet his or her tears show through the laughter for greater impact.

- The blocking can be related to the more *global* aspects of the interaction, rather than specific parts of the verbal message. Two people may be

[13]George F. Mahl, *Exploration in Nonverbal and Vocal Behavior*, (London: Lawrence Erlbaum Associates, Inc., 1987), p. 40.

[14]Fragment of a case study on hysteria. In J. Strachey (ed. and trans.), *The Standard Edition and Complete Works of Sigmund Freud*, vols. 4 and 5, (London: Hogarth Press, 1905), pp. 77-78.

[15]Sigmund Freud. *The Psychopathology of Everyday Life*, in *The Basic Writings of Sigmund Freud*, (New York: Random House, 1938), p. 138.

[16]P. Ekman & W.V. Friesen, "Nonverbal behavior in psychotherapy research." In J.M. Shlien, ed., *Research in Psychotherapy*, vol. 3, (Washington, DC: American Psychological Association, 1968), pp. 295-346.

having a verbal disagreement, but their nonverbal actions toward each other indicate that their relationship is still a solid and satisfying one.

- The blocking can *accent a specific part* of the verbal text. The dialogue may branch out into other topics, but the blocking holds onto the specific moment.

- The blocking can be a *delayed registration of a previous verbal comment*. This often occurs in comedy; take the well-known scene in which a husband and wife are discussing some mundane topic, such as their next vacation, while the wife is calmly trying to tell her husband that she is pregnant. The husband continues talking in a normal conversational tone until the message sinks in: then he stops in the middle of a sentence and registers astonishment, amazement, glee, or dismay, depending on how he views the advent of a new progeny.[17]

These different relationships offer excellent staging possibilities. Plan on using *one or possibly two of these relationships in your scene*.

CRITIQUE

1. Was the situation (the *who*, the *what*, and the *where*) well communicated?

2. How was blocking against the obvious put into effect? What relationship between the visual and verbal was used?
    - Anticipating the text?
    - Contradicting the text?
    - Identifying more global aspects of the text?
    - Accenting a specific part?
    - Delayed registration?

3. Was the relationship between the visual and verbal elements of the scene convincing, or did it tend to be too obvious or gimmicky?

4. Was there a *visual progression*? Was the staging effective?

5. Did the ground plan help *spotlight the important moments* of the scene? What was effective or ineffective about the ground plan?

6. Were there distinct *psychological areas*? Were these areas enhanced by the director's selection in playing against the obvious?

7. Favorite moment? Least favorite moment?

---

[17]Ekman and Friesen also mention other relationships such as a nonverbal action substituting for a word or phrase in a verbal message, and the nonverbal functioning to regulate the communicative flow, indicating that one is listening, bored, ready to speak, etc. These can certainly be used to good effect, but since they come very naturally to most actors to begin with, the others listed above provide more interesting experimental possibilities.

PROP PHYSICALIZING

(Experimenting With Physical Metaphors — With Props)

Daring ideas are like chessmen moved forward;
they may be beaten,
but they may start a winning game.

— Goethe

OVERVIEW

A director's vision is sometimes very dependent upon an unrealistic or presentational production approach. Beginning with the early part of the twentieth century, there was an intense reaction against realism, which brought birth to a fine family of "isms." Even though many of these "isms" such as symbolism, futurism, dadaism, constructivism, expressionism, and surrealism were relatively short-lived, many of the techniques and trends lived on in mutated forms; for instance, as Cohen and Harrop point out in their discussion of aesthetic styles, "many of the most significant stylistic gestures of expressionism were incorporated into the post-1950s avant-guard, and the true value of expressionism — as with most of the 'isms' — lies in those new stylistic perceptions that it opened up to the theatre."[18] Despite their diversity, common to all of these approaches was the urge to transcend the "slice of li.`" approach associated with realism, and this urge is still alive and well in the contemporary theatre. In most workshops, there isn't enough time to do performance work in each of these aesthetic styles, so rather than target a specific "ism," this exercise and the following one are meant to function as a kind of theatrical "Esperanto" for all theatrical styles. Esperanto is an artificial language designed for use by people of all nations, just as prop physicalizing is meant to serve as an excellent foundation for exploring and creating a wide variety of aesthetic styles in the future. *Prop physicalizing* not only allows the director to experiment with an unrealistic (presentational) vision, but as a fringe benefit it also demonstrates a very valuable rehearsal approach for working with actors.

A two-person scene[19] is recommended when first approaching this exercise because the work is very likely to be a quantum leap into very new territory for most directors, and with additional actors, it will be harder to grasp the essence of *prop*

---

[18]Robert Cohen and John Harrop, *Creative Play Direction*, (New Jersey: Prentice-Hall, Inc., 1984), p. 260.

[19]See pp. 160-161 for two-person open scenes.

physicalizing. After directors have become more familiar with this kind of work, then the exercise can be effectively repeated with more actors. The two-person scene is performed *two ways:* **first realistically,** *and then as a* **prop physicalization**. First seeing the scene realistically performed has the advantage of allowing the workshop audience to understand the basic storyline better, plus it compares and contrasts in the most dramatic way possible, two very contrasting visions of the same situation. The intent of this exercise is:

- To experiment with creating an unrealistic production style that centers around a process which cuts through language to reveal the *essential action* of a scene.

- To demonstrate the value of *physical metaphors* in working with actors, a process which guides actors into experiencing the essential action of a scene through their bodies.

- To experiment with expressing and intensifying the "inner action" or *subtext* of a scene through the use of prop physicalizing. To discover through this kind of physical approach to the text that *a scene is about action*, not words.

- To experiment through movement and gesture with channeling impulses in unconventional, yet highly revealing ways.

PHYSICALIZING A PSYCHOLOGICAL REALITY

Even though the intent is to create an "Esperanto" style that theoretically bears no major allegiance to any specific style, this is easier said than done, and it will become increasingly clear that the concepts of this exercise are very much in keeping with the work of Artaud and Grotowski. This admitted bias does not negate the overriding "Esperanto" concept because the work of both Artaud and Grotowski are in themselves creative fusions of the many "isms" that came before them. The net result of prop physicalizing is symbolic or poetic, rather than realistic, and the intent is to distill intense human feelings into expressive physical images, or what are often referred to as "hieroglyphs." The term "prop physicalizing" was created to define this exercise, and help distinguish it from the following exercise, but the principles involved very much belong to Artaud and his followers.

Prop physicalizing is both a presentational performance style and a rehearsal technique. Used as a rehearsal technique, the fundamental advantage of prop physicalizing is that it allows actors to experience the essential action of a scene through their bodies in a very intensified form; the director and actors translate the actual dialogue of the scene into immediate *physical and symbolically intensified actions*. If, for example, in a scene where a character is verbally badgering another character, an actor might threaten or actually hit another actor with a pillow or a padded stick. In using this technique, even when working with a very realistic text, the visual elements of the scene will be extremely "unrealistic." Above all else, the objective is to capture the ***psychological reality*** of the scene. This technique allows actors to kinesthetically experience the psychological reality of their characters, and due to the inherent physicalized intensity of the exercise, it will be easy for them to recall these feelings when they perform the scene realistically. Cohen and Harrop provide an interesting example of how this kind physicalizing can be put to use as an acting exercise:

> There are a couple of scenes in *Othello* (III, iii and IV.i.) in which Iago is tempting Othello or poisoning him against Cassio and Desdemona. The kinds of physical metaphors that come to mind to encapsulate the essential action of the scenes might include a bullfight, a spider enmeshing its victim, or an angler playing a fish. Actually, the scenes are subtly different: in the first scene Iago is more tempting Othello; in the second, more goading him. Taking the angling image for the first scene (this might be reinforced by saying that Iago has Othello "on a string"), the actors can discover the physical dynamics of the scene if a rope is tied around Othello and put into the hands of Iago, who now, literally has Othello on a string and can play him like a fish. As he pulls on the rope, plays it out when he meets resistance, discovers when to strike and when to play along, Iago will discover the physical property of the lines and get a very strong sense of the physical relationships in space that the ebb and flow of the scene's action demand. Othello will also physically experience the pull of Iago's temptation, how strongly he needs to resist, and the way in which he is pulled into Iago's net.
>
> A similar exercise may be done for IV.i., using the bullfight image…Iago is given a cape and a stick with a padded end with which to physically goad Othello as the line suggests. The image of a trapped, maddened bull is also a useful one for Othello in this scene and will help the actor rise to the full dynamics.[20]

This is definitely an example of what is termed in this exercise as "prop physicalizing." Physical exploration of this type capitalizes on the idea that the body learns physically and communicates physically. Searching for subtext and inner action can get too introspective and static, and the advantage of prop physicalizing is that it can release energy, break down inhibitions, and provide a much better sense of the dramatic action; it gets it out of the head and into the body, which is vital for effective acting. As designed, this exercise is meant to be used with a scene from a longer work, but this approach has worked pretty effectively with open scenes as well. Actual scenes tend to be easier because there is more developed material to

[20]Robert Cohen and John Harrop, *Creative Play Direction*, (New Jersey: Prentice-Hall, Inc., 1984), pp. 208-209.

draw upon. Even if the final form is meant to be realistic, using prop physicalizing as a rehearsal exercise offers tremendous value because when performing the scene realistically, the actors will still remember dynamic feelings ignited in the physicalizing — their bodies will remember. A very important point to emphasize is that no matter how stylized and symbolic the actions become, the performances must remain *emotionally true to the original intent of the material*. For example, if a director of a serious scene physicalized tension by means of a pillow fight, it might very easily be interpreted as comedy, which would obviously be wrong for the scene. As always, the objectives behind the actual lines and actions are what are important; with the right objectives a pillow fight can easily become a very serious matter.

Everyday phrases such as "running scared," "choked up," or "standing firm" attest to the psychological fact that *emotion tends to manifest itself physically*. There are also numerous expressions such as "twist my arm" or "backed against a wall" that are physical metaphors for a particular situation. Searching for these kinds of expressions in your scene is a good source of ideas, but keep in mind that even these physical metaphors don't necessarily have to be taken literally — there are *many ways to channel a particular impulse*. For example, if one of your characters is *figuratively* trying to twist another character's arm, you might have the actor actually twist the other actor's arm, or perhaps twist the entire trunk of the other actor or maybe twist an object held by the actor — the physical possibilities for just this impulse are vast.

Work with either one or, at the most, two objects. If the prop has some degree of symbolic relevance to the scene, so much the better, but the primary function of the prop is literally to be a prop (i.e., an aid) in expressing intensified symbolic gestures. Since all impulses must be *real, intensified, and physicalized*, you need to select props that will in no way inhibit your actors from fully following through with their impulses. For this reason swords or knives, or other potentially dangerous objects are not good choices, whereas such objects as pillows, blankets, ropes, or balloons might work very well. Therefore, with *safety in mind*, select a prop, or props, that you feel will best able you and your actors to communicate the psychological reality of the scene. Search for multiple ways of working with the object/s, exploring both conventional and unconventional usage, and all the while translating the lines, beat by beat, moment by moment, into meaningful physical actions. Apart from the metaphorical level, a given prop can be used to punctuate an action or a line, and since all the impulses are intensified, this can be a tremendous aid in getting the actors "in touch" with the rhythms of the scene; the choice of whether to use the prop for pushing, stroking, knocking, twisting, etc. is as important as the prop itself.

A couple of examples will help demonstrate the scope of prop physicalizing. One workshop director started a scene from Peter Shaffer's *Equus* by having a light blanket completely cover Alan Strang's head. As psychiatrist Dysart slowly pulled the blanket off Alan's head, the troubled patient grabbed it at the last moment and the two of them slowly undulated the sheet, paralleling the hypnotic pencil tapping

action given in the text. After this, the blanket became a pathway, a bridle, a whip, and finally a bed for Alan to relive his story. Cohen and Harrop discuss two productions of the same play that clearly used prop physicalizing:

> In his production of *Marat/Sade*, for example, Peter Brook had Charlotte Corday flagellate de Sade with her hair. This is an essentially Artaudian image, more interesting, intense in impact, and broader of dramatic significance than any literal or stage whipping could be.
>
> In another production, a white sheet was used as a symbol through the piece, connecting images and denoting the action of the event. At different times the sheet was a cloak, the removal of which represented a physical stripping and metaphorical transfer of dominance. It was a serpent, representing sexuality and a threat, a whip, tantalizing and punishing, and a shroud, creating the image of death. It was also an umbilical cord, and passing through the crotch of one player to the crotch of another, it became the passage of semen in the sexual act.[21]

Although the outcome is symbolic and unrealistic, the beat changes in and of themselves should be extremely clear. Exactly how you delineate one beat from another is one of your major challenges; perhaps a change is marked by a completely new reaction to a prop, or a new usage of a prop, or by having the prop take on a new level of meaning, mood or rhythm. There are many possibilities, and as always, the creative challenge is in making what you feel is the best choice among many. What will help you immensely in getting ideas for beat changes and the work in general is if you take the time in rehearsal to brainstorm the usage of the prop or props *independent of the scene work itself*; by doing this, you and your cast will be developing a working vocabulary of physical metaphors to use in future work. Ultimately you need to make sure that each beat is expressed physically very clearly, and that each action is:

• Real   • Intensified   • Physicalized

Apart from the safety factor, a choreographed sword fight would not be "real," whereas hitting someone with a pillow, a piece of foam, a rolled up newspaper, a feather duster, or a balloon could be actually done with an intensified gusto. As simple as it sounds to physicalize an impulse, to the inexperienced performer who happens to be language bound, this kind of work can be both foreign and very threatening. Yet if the director can find a way to get a reluctant actor to participate fully in a physical confrontation with another actor, the payoff can be extraordinary. Some actors fear intensifying an impulse because they have been conditioned to tone down a performance for the sake of realism. But once the actor realizes that prop

[21]Robert Cohen and John Harrop, *Creative Play Direction*, (New Jersey: Prentice-Hall, Inc., 1984), pp. 272-273.

physicalizing is nothing other than physically connecting with the subtext, then it can do nothing other than intensify the inner life of the character. Plus, as any director is quick to learn, it is much easier to tone down a performance than it is to bring it up to a more meaningful level.

The scene should begin with a ***Psychological Tension Pose***. This means finding a contact pose with your actors that symbolizes the tension and the relationship for the entire scene. Keep in mind that the word "pose" does not imply an absence of motion in the usual sense; instead the idea is that there is *so much tension, that a temporary paralysis is the net result*. The scene may begin in one of two ways.

- Either start the dialogue in the psychological tension pose,

- Or break out of the pose *and then* begin the dialogue. That is, either before or someplace during the opening dialogue, your actors will break out of the pose at an appropriate point and then continue physicalizing the rest of the scene.

This prop physicalizing exercise is highly challenging, very advanced work that is new to most of the actors and directors alike. Both because the director is inexperienced and because it is inherently challenging work, it will require considerably more rehearsal than many of the previous exercises.

CRITIQUE

To the workshop

1. Was the situation (the *who*, the *what*, and the *where*) well communicated in both scenes?

2. What prop or props were used in the prop physicalizing scene? Were they effective choices?

3. Were all of the impulses of the prop physicalizing scene: *real*, *physicalized*, and *intensified*? Or were the actors at times holding back?

4. Was the psychological tension pose effective? What did it communicate?

5. How did the realistic version compare to the prop physicalized version? Was anything new brought out in the prop physicalized version?

6. Was the prop physicalizing an effective, psychologically true "translation" of the realistic scene? In other words, was the inner action effectively externalized? Was there a convincing psychological reality inherent in the physical actions?

7. Favorite moment? Least favorite moment?

To the director and/or actors

1. Was it difficult to find props and physical metaphors that channeled the impulses of the realistic scene?

2. Did the "prop physicalizing" prove to be an effective acting exercise? Did it ultimately help to improve their performance of the realistic version?

NO-PROP PHYSICALIZING
(Experimenting With Physical Metaphors — Without Props)

It's what you learn after you know it all that counts.

— Ethel Barrymore

OVERVIEW

As with the previous exercise, it is recommended that only a two-person scene be used.[22] Create characters and a situation which fully justify the given dialogue. Plan on performing the scene *two ways*:

- Realistically

- As a no-prop physicalization

For the no-prop scene, begin with a *psychological tension pose* which epitomizes the *psychological* reality of the relationship. Think of the term pose as a temporary paralysis which comes about from an excess of tension rather than simply an absence of movement; in other words, the absence of movement needs to be motivated. As with the prop physicalizing scene, either start the dialogue in the psychological tension pose, or break out of the pose and then begin the dialogue. At the end the actors may or may not return to their psychological tension pose. The purpose of this exercise is:

- To discover ways of creating an externalized expression of the character's inner state *without* using any props.

- To demonstrate the value of *physical metaphors* that don't rely on props as a *rehearsal exercise*.

NO-PROP PHYSICALIZING

As with prop physicalizing, the intent of this kind of work is to create an externalized expression of the character's inner state where all impulses are *real* (not realistic), *physicalized*, and *intensified*. The most significant difference between the two physicalizing exercises is that one uses a prop and the other does not; other than

---

[22]See pp. 160-161 for two-person open scenes.

this, the dynamics of this second exercise are identical. Think of *No-Prop Physicalizing* as a kind of **psychological gymnastics** and you should be on the right track for this kind of work. Search for meaningful physical contact points — in other words, make **real** contact. In those occasional times where real contact is inconvenient or even dangerous, a convention that works well in some circumstances is to create **long distance contacts** where a kick, a slap, or some other form of contact can happen when the actors are not actually touching each other; even though real contact isn't made, they both react as if it had. There is a danger of overusing this convention, and for the most part only real contact should be made. Although prop and no-prop physicalizing are conceptually very much alike, it is strongly recommended that directors try prop physicalizing before attempting this exercise.[23] The absence of a prop, where there is no physical buffer between the actors also makes this a more difficult exercise for the actors to perform. On the other hand, actors who have first experimented with prop physicalizing, usually find the transition to no-prop work fairly easy.

CRITIQUE

To the workshop

1. Was the situation (the **who**, the **what**, and the **where**) well communicated in both scenes?

2. What types of physical contact were used in the no-prop physicalizing scene? Where they effective choices?

3. Were all of the impulses of the prop physicalizing scene: **real**, **physicalized**, and **intensified**?

4. Was the psychological tension pose effective? What did it communicate?

5. How did the realistic and physicalized versions compare with each other?

6. Was there a convincing psychological reality inherent in the physical actions?

7. Favorite moment? Least favorite moment?

To the director and/or actors

1. Was it difficult to create physical metaphors and meaningful contact that wasn't dependent upon props?

2. Did the no-prop physicalizing prove to be an effective acting exercise? Did it help to ultimately improve the performance of the realistic version? After working with both prop and no-prop physicalizing, which do you prefer?

[23]See pp. 219-224 for a discussion of "prop physicalizing."

INNER VISION
(An Advanced Subjective Point of View Exercise)

Tunnel vision at times is terrific.

— Terry Converse

OVERVIEW

Transform a totally *realistic* scene (or very short play) into a completely expressionistic work where everything is seen through the eyes of a central character. Using the prop and/or no-prop physicalizing techniques previously experimented with,[24] create a scene in which everything is seen from a single character's viewpoint. Interpretation is based totally on projecting the subjective experiences of a single perceiving character.

A SINGLE POINT OF VIEW

Since every level of the action is meant to be seen from a single character's standpoint, the exercise is clearly a direct descendant of *Scene 28: Riffs of Rashoman*. However, now with the prop and no-prop physicalizing work on tap from the past two exercises, there is more opportunity than ever for capturing a completely subjective point of view. The only real distinction between this exercise and the previous physicalizing work is a subtle shift in point of view. Up to now, point of view has been deliberately open, but in this exercise absolutely everything is transmitted through the sensibility of a single character. While it may seem that an undue priority is given to a particular genre of theatre — namely expressionism — the exercise is a worthwhile extension of the previous work.

Perhaps the most stellar example of this kind of work is witnessed in the some of the recent work of director Charles Marowitz. As Artistic Director for the Open Space Theatre in London, Marowitz became known for his iconoclastic treatments of Shakespeare, Strindberg and Ibsen; in 1980, for instance, he created an expressionistic production of Ibsen's *Hedda Gabler* where everything was seen from Hedda's standpoint and transmitted through her sensibility. Prop and no-prop-type physicaling was used throughout the production to highlight the fact that all is emanating from Hedda's mind. For instance, when she talked of amusing herself with her father's pistols, Marowitz had a giant gun suddenly appear, which she immediately

---

[24]See pp. 219-228.

mounted and then spun around to threaten the others.[25] Assessing the pistol business, Marowitz said, "I wanted to represent the size of Hedda's aggression against her aunts, her husband, and the claustrophobic society in which she found herself."[26] In Ibsen's play, the manuscript is compared to a baby as she vengefully burns it. In Marowitz's production, however, Tessman the husband brings in not the manuscript, but a baby carriage complete with the bloodied body of a child. Says Marowitz, "I was trying to construct the theatrical imagery out of the literary imagery on which the play was founded."[27] Inner visions invite daring approaches because the mind is not bound by the comparatively polite rules of the outer world. But daring and extravagant action is folly if it isn't firmly rooted in the ideas of the text. Just the few examples mentioned above demonstrate Marowitz's ability to objectify the subjective and concretize the original metaphors of the Ibsen's text.

Apart from aesthetic considerations, physicalizing work needs as much open space as possible — usually the less realistic clutter of a real location the better. Open space is necessary in order to give the psychological gymnastics of physicalizing enough room to work. This is precisely the thinking of Marowitz in his approach:

> With Hedda, as soon as you start from the premise that you are going to project the experience of the central character, then you are in a completely different terrain. You are no longer in a room, no longer in a period. You are really in a state of mind which is always shifting. This exercise stipulates that we are in a single character's state of mind which is constantly shifting.[28]

Marowitz's *Hedda* was performed on an empty gray circular stage with one side masked by a tall black curtain. Of the space Marowitz said, "When you have a circle you are, in a curious sort of way, suggesting a mind or a brain." [29] As such the figures appeared on stage as though they were weaving in and out of Hedda's mind.

The text can be kept intact, or it can be altered to fit the extremely subjective vision. With his *Hedda*, Marowitz created a collage version of the play, using mixed-up fragments of the original text. But it is perfectly possible to create an "inner vision" without changing the text at all. Whether left alone or radically altered, the overall objective should be to throw some new light on the original.

---

[25]Charles Marowitz, *Sex Wars: Free Adaptations of Ibsen and Strindberg*, (London: Marion Boyars, 1982), p. 43.

[26]Kathleen Dacre, "Charles Marowitz's *Hedda* (and An Enemy of the People)," *The Drama Review* 25, (Summer 1981) no. 90, p. 7

[27]Ibid., p. 7.

[28]Ibid., p. 4.

[29]Ibid., p. 4.

CRITIQUE

1. Did the director rely more on prop or no-prop physicalizing techniques?

2. Did the director get us to see things strictly through the eyes of a single character? Was the inner action effectively externalized?

3. Favorite moment? Least favorite moment?

CHAPTER 7
SUPPORTING PARTS

The projects in this chapter are all devoted to "supporting" the performance work of the director. Support might mean supplying the know-how needed to break away from the picture frame stage, or it might mean providing the guidelines necessary to create a productive rehearsal schedule. The powerful support provided by these projects, encompassing practical advice about nonproscenium staging, script analysis and scheduling are meant to become the invaluable scaffolding for future performance work.

Scaffolding itself needs a firm foundation, and the projects in this chapter are very much dependent upon previous discoveries. *Project A: Thrust Staging*, for instance, given that it draws in a multifaceted way upon the principles of proscenium, would make little sense without the earlier foundation. There is a sequential logic to the seven projects of this chapter with *Project G: Scheduling* coming last because creating a master plan necessitates taking virtually everything into consideration. Three of the projects focus exclusively on interpretive concerns, and they work well together because they share the idea that all of a play's building blocks must interrelate with each other in a highly meaningful way. This idea of inextricably connected parts is really the thread that holds the entire chapter together — justification enough for calling the chapter "Supporting Parts."

Since the activities of this chapter are a means to an artistic end, rather than the performance itself, the word "project" is used to distinguish this preparatory kind of work from the strictly performance "exercises" of the previous chapters. Most of these projects require research or paper work, but the division between project and performance work is not necessarily precise, especially if the workshop facilitator requires the student directors to provide a written record — the blocking notation — for all of the scene exercises. The advantage for the facilitator of having blocking notes is that it can help in remembering specific details of the performance. Here it is important to distinguish blocking notes from "preblocking notes." The process of working out and recording the blocking in the prompt book before rehearsals begin is known as "preblocking," or "paper blocking" and even when a director has used extensive preblocking there is a strong possibility that between the paper planning and the performance many changes were made. The blocking notation given to the workshop facilitator should be a record of the performance itself, not the earlier planning.

There are sharply divided feelings about whether blocking should be preblocked in the sanctitude of the director's study or whether it should be worked out with the actors in rehearsal. There are advantages and disadvantages to both approaches, but in terms of training there are a lot of advantages to preblocking. The most obvious one is that it saves time. Actors forced to cool their heels while the director thinks through a blocking snag can get very impatient, resulting in an excess of tension and overall lack of concentration. Away from the pressure cooker of rehearsal, the director is able to consider many options, and paper blocking has the potential of opening up a director's imagination rather than closing it because many ideas are better than only a few. Instead of limiting the director to a single direction, preblocking has the potential of giving the director multiple approaches with which to experiment. Without advanced preparation, the director may just not be able to think fast enough and the actors will "run away" with the play, eclipsing for the most part the director's creative contribution.

All this is not to imply that a director shouldn't be flexible and shouldn't listen to suggestions from actors. Quite the contrary, and it is vital that the director keep in mind that the primary benefit of preblocking is that it frees rather than restricts the actor. At first the concept of imposing a blocking pattern upon an actor may seem constricting, but ultimately it can be liberating for the performer. When the actor senses that the patterns are nothing other than molds waiting to be filled with the life sustaining "soul" that only the actor can provide, then there is a fertile collaboration between director and actor. No matter what the approach, however, the director is ultimately fully responsible for the blocking. This debate over paper planning versus spontaneity is also paralleled to an extent in the activities of this chapter. Experienced directors may not always "formally" do this kind of work on paper, but very likely they will "informally" use many of the concepts as part of their basic preparation. The seven projects in this chapter are:

PROJECT	TITLE	DESCRIPTION
Project A	Thrust Staging	Learning the fundamentals of thrust theatre staging.
Project B:	Arena Staging	Learning the fundamentals of arena theatre staging.
Project C:	Script Analysis	Experimenting with Aristotelian analysis.
Project D:	Beat It	Experimenting with beats and objectives.
Project E:	Point Conception	Creating a dynamic production concept.
Project F:	Making a Promptbook	Creating a director's notebook.
Project G:	Scheduling	Creating a sequence list and rehearsal schedule.

THRUST STAGING

(Experimenting With Nonproscenium Staging — Part I)

Just as we can throttle our imagination,
we can likewise accelerate it. As in any other art,
individual creativity can be implemented by certain 'techniques.'

— Alex F. Osborn

OVERVIEW

In terms of training, the proscenium space is still the best starting point, but directors in training had better be prepared to travel well beyond the bounds of the traditional picture frame stage. Successful regional theatres such as the Guthrie in Minneapolis and the Arena Stage in Washington D.C. have been widely influential, and the increasing popularity of thrust and arena theatres means that, more than ever, today's director needs to have staging skills in nonproscenium spaces. The intent of this project and the following one is to provide the principles for staging in thrust and arena theatres.

Focusing on these two forms by no means implies that there are not other interesting nonproscenium staging possibilities; in fact the currently very popular "black box" space with its moveable seating banks is dedicated to the idea that there are numerous audience-actor spatial relationships worth exploring. Studied together, thrust and arena are the perfect training combination because proficiency in both of these spaces easily carries over into virtually any other form. Training for thrust and arena spaces is the best possible preparation for virtually any type of nonproscenium playing space. Even though the intent of this project is to break away, at least temporarily, from the confines of the picture frame theatre, it is important to stress that proficiency in proscenium staging is an absolute must before beginning this kind of work. The departures from the proscenium are still heavily dependent upon proscenium principles, and without this kind of a firm foundation, the new terrain of thrust and arena will present one pitfall after another.

Working with thrust and arena configurations requires a flexible playing space. The ideal working space for this project is probably a black box with moveable seat banks, but any large open space will work. Provided there is enough space, a single row of chairs can define the size and shape of the playing space, making it very easy to shift quickly between arena and thrust formations. Staging a short scene for thrust or arena is of value in itself, but an excellent way to master the nuances of proscenium and nonproscenium spaces is to *stage the same scene for two different performance spaces.*

Possible combinations to try are:

- Proscenium–thrust   • Proscenium–arena   • Arena–thrust

STARTING FIRST WITH THRUST STAGING

Why is it better to begin training in thrust rather than arena staging? Thrust staging permits the audience to sit on three sides of a stage that pushes or "thrusts" out into the auditorium, allowing the actors and audience to have a more intimate relationship. The division between actor and audience is greatly lessened because there is very much a sense that actors and audience share the same space. The actors are thrust into the midst of the audience, which puts an emphasis on them instead of the scenery, but no matter how far they are thrust forward, they are still "backed" by at least some scenic reinforcement. This back wall of the thrust theatre is what allows this very new space to retain at least a hint of the older proscenium form, and this is a significant issue as far as training is concerned because making a departure into new territory is always a little easier if at least a glimmer of the old territory is still in view. The new thrust space is a big leap forward, but still in view is the familiar old back wall — a focal point of the thrust space that provides at least some of the illusionistic potential of the proscenium stage.

This is not a recommended staging approach, but imagine taking a well-staged proscenium play, scooting it away from its picture frame housing so as to transform it into a thrust configuration; chances are there would be some problems, but a surprising amount of the play would probably be stageworthy from the sides. The reason for this is that good proscenium staging is by definition three dimensional, as is thrust staging. Were the same well-staged proscenium play completely surrounded by audience, the arena staging overall would probably be far less successful. This is why thrust tends to be the easier, and less threatening of the two. As a first stepping stone from the picture frame stage, a thrust configuration is the best choice — a choice that is consistent with the step-by-step training taken so far.

TYPICAL SHAPES OF THRUST STAGES

The thrust theatre is in many ways a cross between the Greek and Elizabethan theatre concepts. The raised stage jutting out into the audience is not unlike the Shakespeare's Globe Theatre, for instance, and the steeply banked seating in many thrust theatres is reminiscent of the Greek amphitheaters. Shapes of thrust stages vary considerably, with three of the most popular variations shown below:

Fig. 1

GROUND PLAN CONCERNS

To think of successfully transporting a well-staged proscenium play onto thrust space is, of course, a gross oversimplification because it completely ignores the major conceptual differences between thrust and proscenium ground plans. A conventional box set for a proscenium space, for instance, certainly wouldn't work very well on a thrust stage without considerable modification because the side walls would completely obstruct the right and left seating sections.

Three Invisible Walls: Instead of a single invisible "fourth wall" on the curtain line, the thrust space assumes three invisible walls, with a closed-off fourth side (the back wall). Architectural details such as window seats and cabinets can be used along the invisible walls as long as they are low enough not to obstruct sight lines. Compared to proscenium, the three invisible walls create a much more three-dimensional effect; despite the fact that the actors in a proscenium space are typically surrounded by three-dimension scenery, the net effect is an illusory two-dimensional quality very similar to painting, whereas thrust is three-dimensional and very similar to sculpture.

Entrances: Besides walls, another major difference between proscenium and thrust spaces has to do with entrances. Proscenium entrances for the most part stay within the picture frame. In thrust theatres, as shown in Figure 2, there are typically tunnels or *vomitoria*[1] at the downstage left and right corners that allow the actors to enter and exit from ramps or steps beneath

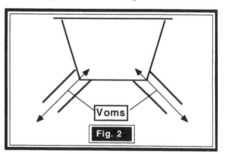

the audience. Vomitoria solve the problem of quick entrances and exits where many actors can be "vomited" onto or off the stage. In some cases the auditorium aisles are used as voms, or sometimes both aisles and voms become integrated into the staging.

Entrances, of course, can also be from the back wall area. The back wall area allows for architectural detail such as staircases and levels, which can be tremendously helpful in defining a sense of place. An important design consideration is whether or not to use one or both of the voms. If used, they create very *dynamic axes* (as shown by the arrows above) that have to be carefully integrated into the ground plan. An entrance or exit from a vom is much more dynamic than the equivalent proscenium entrance or exit because the pathway is directly to or away from the world of the audience. In some case, the audience can literally feel the whoosh of air as a group of actors rush onto the stage. The ground plan for *What the Butler Saw* shown in Figure 3 provides a good example of a set design effectively bringing into play a single vom entrance. Sometimes, it is effective not to use any voms at all, and rely only on the rear stage entrances, as is shown in the Figure 4 ground plan for *Antigone*.

[1]The singular of vomitoria is vomitorium, although most of the time this terminology is reduced to simply "vom" and "voms."

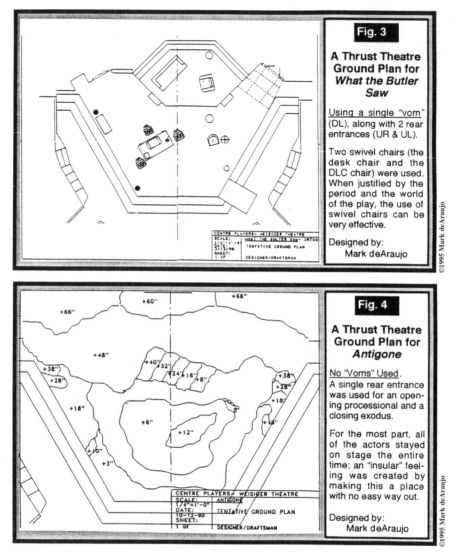

Fig. 3

A Thrust Theatre Ground Plan for *What the Butler Saw*

Using a single "vom" (DL), along with 2 rear entrances (UR & UL).

Two swivel chairs (the desk chair and the DLC chair) were used. When justified by the period and the world of the play, the use of swivel chairs can be very effective.

Designed by:
Mark deAraujo

©1995 Mark deAraujo

Fig. 4

A Thrust Theatre Ground Plan for *Antigone*

No "Voms" Used. A single rear entrance was used for an opening processional and a closing exodus.

For the most part, all of the actors stayed on stage the entire time; an "insular" feeling was created by making this a place with no easy way out.

Designed by:
Mark deAraujo

©1995 Mark deAraujo

BEWARE OF THE BACK WALL

Picture a thrust theatre with three separate, equally sized seating sections. Even when there is a completely democratic distribution of seats in each section, it becomes immediately obvious that *all seats in a thrust theatre are not created equal*; even before a single actor steps on stage, those seats in the center section, directly facing the back wall will be felt by most audience members to be the favored vantage point. Years of experiencing theatre through a picture frame have conditioned audiences into feeling that closer to the center means better seating. Directors and designers of thrust need to be aware of this built-in bias, and do everything possible

238

to reinforce the feeling that seating from all sides is equally interesting.

As previously discussed, the back wall is the common denominator between thrust and proscenium spaces, and this can help in making the novice director a little more at home in a very unfamiliar place. True enough, but the familiar back wall can also become a booby trap, lulling the unsuspecting novice director into thinking that staging for thrust is virtually the same as staging for proscenium. Thinking proscenium in a thrust space is the cardinal sin to commit in staging because it will inevitably lead to favoring the center section; instead of reducing, it reinforces the bias that most audience members bring with them to the thrust theatre. To treat a thrust theatre as a proscenium space is to disregard completely the sculptural potential of this unique type of stage. Favoring the center section in a thrust theatre is artistically fatal because it alienates at least two-thirds of the audience.

Preventing an overemphasis on the center section often begins with the ground plan. Figure 5 demonstrates the differences between thrust and proscenium in a typical living room setting. By turning the arm chair to face the sofa, a position far more typical than the side-by-side arrangement, there is visual interest created for all three vantage points.

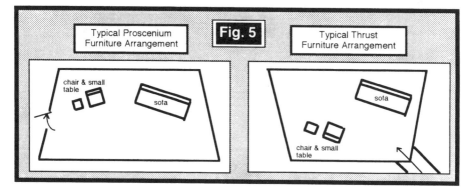

Had the proscenium ground plan on the left been used on a thrust stage, the message loud and clear from just the setting would be that the only good seats in the house were front and center. Using such a plan would make it extremely difficult to stage equitably among the three seating sections.

THREE VANTAGE POINTS

Think of a thrust stage as three separate, but obviously interrelated proscenium stages. In essence, in a typical thrust theatre, *each* of the *three vantage points* as shown in Figure 6 *becomes the equivalent of a proscenium theatre.* The director's ultimate staging challenge is to make the play visually engaging from all three perspectives. There will be times when a particular vantage point is truly favored over the others, but in the course of the entire performance, no single vantage point should be any better than the others overall. All this starts, as has already been mentioned, by designing a ground plan that is equitable to all three vantage points — it cannot be emphasized enough that successful thrust staging begins with a well thought out ground plan.

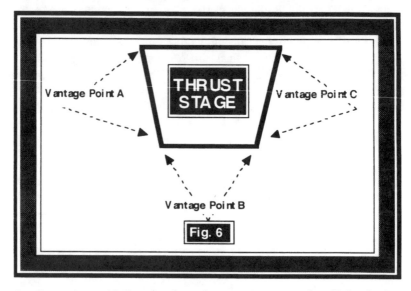

In rehearsals, avoid directing from the same vantage point. Sitting in the same place automatically encourages the actors to favor that perspective. Moreover, sitting and watching is the only way to know for sure whether or not a scene is working from a particular vantage point. Giving directions for thrust staging is problematic. For lack of anything better, most directors fall back on standard proscenium terminology (X URC, X DL, etc.). This is less than desirable because even with the best intentions, it throws everyone into a proscenium mind set. Because of the back wall, the center vantage point already has an advantage over the sides, and using proscenium terminology simply reinforces this bias. To counteract this problem, whenever possible the director is well advised to give directions by referring to the actual set pieces (X to the sofa, arm chair, table, etc.) instead of sticking to conventional terminology. The director of arena is already forced to do this because there is no such thing as right and left, and up and downstage in such a space.

Figures 7-12 demonstrate how the same specific movements range from strong to weak depending upon the given vantage point.

STRENGTHS AND WEAKNESSES

House left and right function as mirror images of each other, and here the terms "with the flow" and "against the flow" become meaningful.[2]

---

[2]"Flow" refers to conditioned eye movement. For a discussion about "with or against the flow," and the whole issue of right versus left movement, see pp. 35-38.

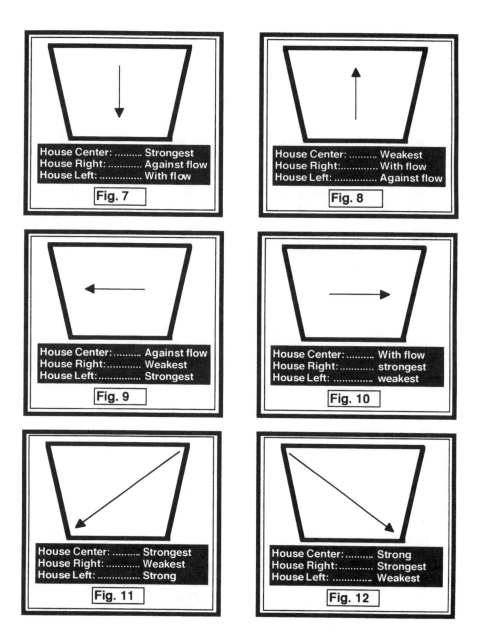

Fig. 7

House Center: .... Strongest
House Right: .... Against flow
House Left: .... With flow

Fig. 8

House Center: .... Weakest
House Right:............. With flow
House Left: .... Against flow

Fig. 9

House Center:.......... Against flow
House Right:............ Weakest
House Left:.............. Strongest

Fig. 10

House Center:.......... With flow
House Right:............ strongest
House Left: .... weakest

Fig. 11

House Center: .... Strongest
House Right: .... Weakest
House Left: .... Strong

Fig. 12

House Center:.......... Strong
House Right:............ Strongest
House Left: .... Weakest

STAGING TECHNIQUES

Two actors facing each other straight on can remain relatively open in proscenium staging, but not so in thrust staging. Whenever possible, use the *shoulder-to-shoulder* technique diagramed below in Figure 13 for basic conversations. Compared to the straight-on approach, shoulder-to-shoulder creates very little difference in the emotional effect, but it makes a very big difference in keeping the actors more open.

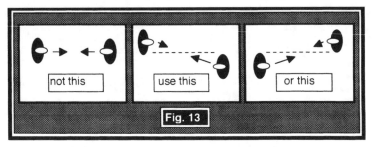

not this   use this   or this

Fig. 13

Actors staying in the same place and body position for very long on a thrust stage can create a problem in that they are apt to be closed off from a portion of the audience for too long. In thrust and arena, audience members will tolerate not being able to have a clear view of an actor a little longer than they would in proscenium because the intimacy of the space often allows them to see the reactions of other audience members who at the time are watching from a better vantage point. But even with this audience watching audience factor, it is important to shift perspectives fairly often. Two ways to accomplish this are to use *justified* "break-aways" and "rotations," as demonstrated in Figure 14:

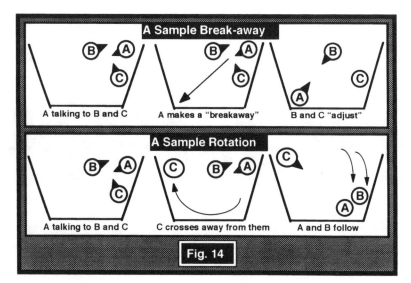

A Sample Break-away

A talking to B and C   A makes a "breakaway"   B and C "adjust"

A Sample Rotation

A talking to B and C   C crosses away from them   A and B follow

Fig. 14

ARENA STAGING
(Experimenting With Nonproscenium Staging — Part 2)

I think theatre in the round is the theatre of the future.
The proscenium is obviously two-dimensional in a way that film never was
and television isn't. Theatre in the round is more plastic, more fluid.

— Tom Courtenay[3]

OVERVIEW

Tom Courtenay's prediction (above) that arena theatre will be the wave of future is highly ironic given the fact that a group of spectators surrounding an event is one of the oldest activities in the world. Gathering around "the action" is a totally natural way for a group of people to witness or participate in something, whether it be watching a football game, a back alley fight, or a sacred tribal dance. Wanting to become one with, wanting to be included in, and wanting a clear view of are perhaps the basic urges that cause people to surround something of interest. Surrounding is a kind of closing off from the outside world that creates a circle of concentration unparalleled by any other form. This closing off, more so than any other type of performance space, creates a sense of "we're all in it together." Audience space is simply a radiating extension of the playing space, which results in a more collective feeling in comparison with the "us versus them" feeling of the proscenium. Rituals from every culture attest the power of the circular performance space; the early Greek theatre developed, for instance, out of the ritualistic dancing circle, and *the circus* can be traced back to the central playing area of the Roman arena.

Gathering around may be a highly natural group activity, but this does not mean that staging in such a space is perfectly natural. Some directors argue that arena staging comes closest to the real life experience, that the way an actor moves in an arena living room setting, for example, is identical to real life behavior. This may seem to be true, but it is really a fallacy because effective staging in arena is every bit as dependent upon the craft of the director as in any other playing space. The familiar back wall of the thrust is now taken away and at first the director in training will feel vulnerable — left to explore nonproscenium staging without any type of

---

[3]Tom Courtenay is an English actor who became an overnight star in his debut in the 1962 film "The Loneliness of the Long Distance Runner." Andrea Steavens, "A Couple of Vanyas Sitting Around Talking," *New York Times*, Sunday, 19 February, 1995, p. 25.

safety net. But the safety net is still there, provided this time by a firm grasp of thrust theatre staging. Many of the principles of thrust staging are applicable to arena, but the intent of this project is to learn what is also unique about this ancient playing space. If at all possible, staging the same scene in both thrust and arena could be tremendously valuable.

TYPICAL SHAPES OF ARENA STAGES

The claim to fame of the "arena" or "theatre in the round" is that it is the only kind of stage that is completely surrounded by audience. The action occurs in the middle of an arena surrounded by audience, and the actors enter from the aisles. As with proscenium and thrust stages, sizes of arena stages vary considerably. Shapes of arena stages tend to fall into one of the three shown below:

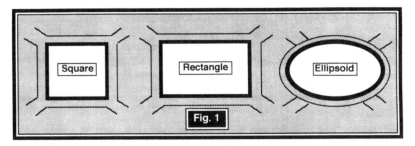

Perfectly square or round stages have the advantage of generally favoring equally sized seat banks, but they also share a disadvantage in that it is harder with these kinds of shapes to delineate different spatial qualities. *Generally it is far easier to create dynamic arena ground plans with the rectangular or ellipsoidal forms than it is with the more symmetrical shapes.*

FOUR VANTAGE POINTS

Regardless of the actual shape and size, all arena spaces can be thought to have *four distinct vantage points.* Each of these four vantage points, as shown in Figure 2, becomes the *equivalent of a proscenium theatre.* With either arena or thrust staging, the director must control the emphasis

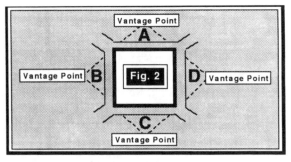

between and within the vantage points to achieve a performance that plays well in each. This means that for each vantage point, the principles of proscenium largely apply, but the art of arena staging is discovering how to direct four proscenium productions at the same time. Figures 3-8 show how different the same movement can be from the different views.

STRENGTHS AND WEAKNESSES

The four vantage points function as *paired opposites*. In other words, a strong movement favoring one vantage point automatically creates a corresponding weak movement from the opposite side. The designated North–South, East–West directions below in Figures 3-8 are for convenience only, and are not meant to imply that arena theatres typically label their seating banks in this way.

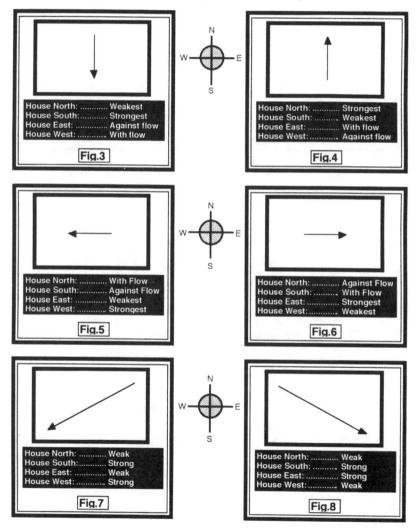

245

Figures 3-8 make it clear that movement is experienced very differently in each of the four vantage points. When mention is made in Figures 3-6 of "with the flow" or "against the flow," this is in reference to conditioned eye movement.[4]

BLOCKING TECHNIQUES

Power positions are created in arena staging primarily through the use of *space, level, direct and indirect focus.* No composition is going to be ideal from all parts of the house, but a good rule of thumb to follow is to make sure each vantage point is able to see at least one actor's face at any given moment.

Power in the Periphery. In a playing space surrounded by audience, a great deal of focus is naturally drawn toward the center. This, plus the fact that the entrances create imaginary axes drawing the eye to the center of the arena (see Figure 12), allow the center area of the playing space to take on considerable visual strength. Compared to proscenium staging, however, an actor in this center area is far less commanding since he will be seen by only half of the audience at a given moment. Therefore, moments that need to be seen by the vast majority of the audience at the same time need to be *played in peripheral areas.* Positioning an actor close to one of the aisles is the most effective way to keep that actor open to as much of the audience as possible.

Two-Person Staging. Many of the previously discussed thrust theatre staging techniques are applicable to arena staging. As with thrust staging, use "break-aways" and "rotations," and the "shoulder-to-shoulder" technique for basic conversations.[5] Similar in concept to the "shoulder-to-shoulder" idea, a *curved approach* has the advantage in thrust and arena spaces of keeping the crossing actor more visible to more parts of the audience. A curved cross is not always appropriate to the situation, but when merited, this type

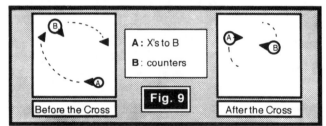

A: X's to B

B: counters

Fig. 9

Before the Cross   After the Cross

of cross is the better choice. Imagine one actor approaching a stationary actor, and it's obvious as demonstrated in Figure 9 that a curved cross will keep both the approaching actor and the stationary actor in better view because it prevents the continual covering of both actors that inevitably happens in direct crosses. Just as curved crosses keep both actors open to more of the audience, the same is true of keeping as much distance as possible between two actors. Space between two actors keeps them more visible, so a good general rule is to keep the actors as far apart from each other as can be justified. When they inevitably do come close to each other, figure out meaningful ways to break them apart.

---

[4]For a discussion about "with or against the flow," and the whole issue of right versus left movement, see pp. 35-38.

[5]For a discussion about "break-aways," "rotations," and "shoulder-to-shoulder" techniques, see p. 248.

Two actors sitting on a sofa pose an especially tricky staging problem for both arena and thrust. A sofa encourages both characters to face the same direction, which means that their backs will remain consistently turned to the same section of audience. To counteract this problem, the director needs to use contrasting body positions and head focus whenever possible (Figure 10); in general, for the same reasons that apply to sofa positioning, two actors should avoid facing the same direction at the same time. Keep in mind that many actors unfamiliar with arena or thrust are conditioned to favor a single vantage point, and they will constantly need to be coached that the audience is all surrounding.

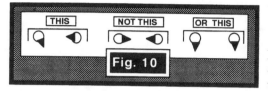

Triangular Compositions. Even more than with proscenium or thrust stages, triangular compositions in arena spaces *come across as very "natural"* (like people in a real room) because there is no single vantage point to favor consistently. Triangular compositions can be an excellent way to create compositions that *work effectively from several vantage points*. As demonstrated in Figure 11, typically, at least one performer in a triangular grouping will be relatively open to each of the four vantage points. Combining *different levels* in a triangular composition has the potential of further focusing the emphasis and opening the stage picture. Large compositions can be often effectively created by combining multiple triangular formations.

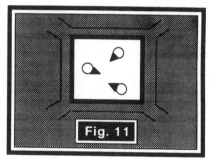

Triangular groupings also have the potential of keeping compositions keyed off the center area. For example, in Figure 11, if one of these actors turned away from the center to face the periphery, then this would create a dynamic counterfocus.

In certain cases compositions can be held longer in arena than in proscenium because of the audience-watching-audience effect. Even when a certain section of the audience cannot see a pivotal part of the action, they can become indirectly drawn into the action by watching reactions from the audience across from them. Audience watching audience is fine, and it undeniably exists, but the arena director is well advised not to rely on it very much. To the contrary, the director needs to vary the groupings as often as can be convincingly justified. Sometimes only very subtle changes are needed in order to assure a section of the audience that they have not been ignored. An actor who mechanically rotates from one section in one unmotivated movement after another, is asking to come across as a "pig on a spit." Movement in arena, as with any kind of stage, needs to be fully motivated, and the arena director is often required to be very inventive in creating justified movement shifts from one vantage point to another.

ENTRANCES AND EXITS

The typical arena theatre has four entrances, indicated in Figure 12 below as "*A, B, C, D*." Sometimes these entrances are simply the aisles used by the audience, and sometimes they are separate vomitoria. Actors enter and exit through these aisles or vomitoria. Besides these basic four, sometimes extra entrances, such as those indicated below as *AB-BC-CD-AD*, are either built into the architecture of the theatre or one or more of them are specially designed for a specific production. Note that all of these entrances create axes that meet at an imaginary point in the center, and these very dynamic axes need to be carefully considered in creating a ground plan.

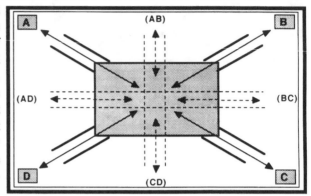

Of course, not all of these entrances need to be used in a given production. Whenever possible, position the entrances and exits opposite each other (such as using A and C or B and D). Evenly distributed entrances help to motivate an actor to move across the stage, or they help to balance the stage picture by bringing in a new character from the opposite side of the stage. *Diagonal entrances help balance and better distribute the use of space in the progression of the play.* At best this is simply a rule of thumb, since a ground plan is virtually always dependent upon the spatial logic dictated by the world of the particular play. Strategically placed entrances help safeguard against one vantage point acquiring more emphasis than the others.

GROUND PLAN CONSIDERATIONS

Since arena staging by necessity minimizes scenic elements, the viewer's imagination is stimulated into creating a convincing illusion. As with thrust stage settings, skeletal suggestion such as thin window frame hung from a grid can be used, but the audience is still called upon to fill in imaginatively the scenic background. Asking an audience to take an imaginative leap in appreciating the setting helps them to experience theatre actively, rather than passively. Look again at Figure 12, where the axes of movement are created by the four entrances. With arena staging, the director has the choice of designing the setting with or against the diagonal axes created by the four entrances. This choice corresponds to the raked or full-front setting of the proscenium stage;[6] there is a major difference, however, in that there is nothing equivalent in proscenium to the built-in diagonal axes of the arena. Figure 13 illustrates

---

[6]For a discussion of raked versus full-front proscenium settings, see p. 118.

the difference between playing with or against the diagonals in arena settings. Both ground plans use the same set pieces, and both are workable, but there is a big difference in the various blocking patterns that would come out of them. Playing with diagonals (as in the top ground plan) demonstrates that the design does not have to be dictated by the shape of the stage. Note how the swivel arm chair in both plans would be tremendously effective in shifting quickly from the sofa to the TV area; as with thrust, swivel chairs, when justified by the world of the play, can be enormously helpful in arena staging. The "Playing with the Diagonals" plan has an advan-

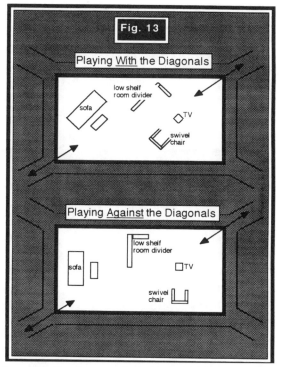

tage over the other plan because the sofa is lined up mostly behind an aisle; as a result, very few audience members would be faced with looking at the backs of seated actors. The primary objective is to create a dynamic playing space for the actors, while at the same time making sure that the audience has a clear view of the action.

Even though the arena stage is sometimes touted as true to real life, it is not any more real than theatre in any kind of space. Survey most interiors and the discovery will be that most people arrange their furniture against the walls. Survey most stage settings and regardless whether they are proscenium, thrust, or arena designs, seldom, if ever, will all the furniture be placed against the walls. Furniture placed against the walls in any kind of a theatre does not work very well, because it prevents the possibility of creating a dynamic "obstacle course." This is especially problematic in the arena because there are four "invisible walls," and furniture against the walls means a barricade between the actors and the audience. What works significantly better is to place the major furniture pieces away from the walls, with a few minor ones near the edges. A well functioning ground plan will also be an obstacle course, [7] and for this to happen some of the set pieces have to be moved away from the walls, as demonstrated in Figure 14:

---

[7]See pp. 114-118 for a discussion as to why a good ground plan needs to be an obstacle course.

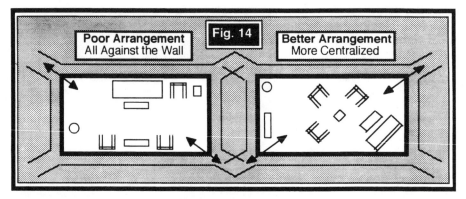

Both ground plans in Figure 14 use identical set pieces, but for most situations the plan on the right is the far better arrangement. It is impossible to say for sure whether a ground plan is good or bad because every ground plan has to be evaluated on the basis of how well it serves a specific production; but most directors, if they suddenly found themselves faced with these two ground plans and were totally unaware of the play they were about to direct (a director's nightmare, to be sure), would almost certainly prefer to work with the plan on the right. The ground plan on the left is probably more representative of a real room than the one on the right, but the one on the right offers the possibility for far more dynamic movement patterns. A stage setting is never a real place, only a symbolic representation of real place, and furniture against the walls has two major disadvantages:

- *Prevents the audience from having a clear view of the action.* The focus is thrown away from the audience. A player sitting in a chair, for example, has his or her back turned away from the nearest part of the audience. People gravitate toward the furniture in a room; sitting in chairs or standing around furniture is very typical behavior, but when the furniture is all against the wall, the furniture and the actors create little more than a blockade for the audience.

- *Prevents interesting variations in approaching and relating to a given set piece.* Furniture is most useful on stage when there is room enough to move around it. A chair placed away from a wall has a lot more potential for an actor than one shoved against a wall. Furniture moved away from the wall provides far more variety and flow of movement. If a chair, for instance, is away from the wall, it is very natural behavior for a character to cross to it and lean against its back, or rest a hand on it, all of which is next to impossible if the chair is backed up against an imaginary wall.

By thinking of the major set pieces almost as characters in need of being effectively "blocked," the director will have little difficulty creating imaginative, highly functional ground plans.

SIGHT LINES

Since the audience surrounds the playing area, sight lines are one of the major challenges of arena staging. With thrust staging there is at least a back wall to butt up against, which makes the sight line problem considerably easier. The overall ideal-istic objective of arena staging is to give each audience member the impression that he or she is in the best seat of the house. Among other factors, this means that each audience member needs to have an open, unobstructed view of the action. Large scenic units such as windows, mirrors and sometimes even doors can be suggested by a *skeletal treatment* (e.g. very narrow frames hung from the grid). Sometimes a window is suggested by a window seat only, or possibly nothing at all. The audience will accept the convention of a nonexistent window as long as the actors relate to it consistently and honestly. Avoid using solid set pieces that obstruct sight lines. When such solid pieces absolutely need to be used, such as tables, cabinets, and pianos, it sometimes works to position them in an aisle area that is not being used as an entrance. Make sure that set pieces such as sofas and chairs are low enough to keep seated characters fully in view of audience.

GIVING DIRECTIONS

Upstage and downstage along with right and left are *meaningless concepts* on an arena stage. Also meaningless are body positions (full front, profile, etc.) since an actor is always open to some section of the audience. Conventional proscenium ter-minology simply cannot work in an arena space. Some other system of orientation is needed in order to make sense out of the enclosed space. Sometimes naming the entrances makes them easier to remember, such as:

- *Alpha* (entrance A)
- *Bravo* (entrance B)
- *Charlie* (entrance C)
- *Delta* (entrance D)

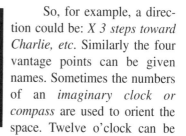

Fig. 15

So, for example, a direc-tion could be: *X 3 steps toward Charlie, etc.* Similarly the four vantage points can be given names. Sometimes the numbers of an *imaginary clock or compass* are used to orient the space. Twelve o'clock can be either oriented to the north, or towards some other reference point such as the entrance to the theatre, or the control room.

As with thrust staging, an excellent way to give directions is to key off actual set pieces (X to arm sofa, table, etc.) and to other characters (X toward Caliban, etc.). Using this kind of terminology also has the advantage of keeping the actors in touch with the reality of the play. Conventional stage terminology (X DRC, stay in a ¾ R, etc.) is abstracted and distanced from the world of the play, which at times can get in the way of the emotional crossfire of a scene. Figure 16 below demonstrates giving directions by combining:

- Set piece orientation

- Entrances orientation (Alpha, Bravo, Charlie, Delta)

- Character names (Characters A and B)

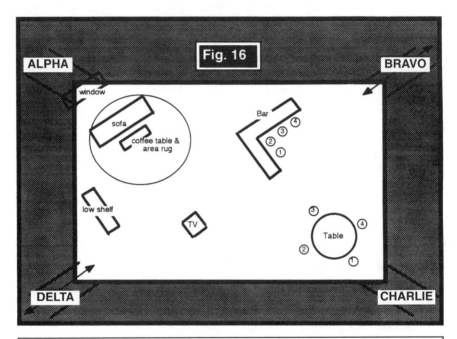

Entrances at "Bravo" (to outside) and "Delta" (to bedrooms)	
SAMPLE DIRECTIONS WITH THIS GROUND PLAN	
Character A:	Sitting on sofa (Delta side) watching television. Rises and Xs to TV, turning it off. "A" Xs toward Bravo a step or two, yells his line.
Character B:	Enters from Bravo, Xs to bar (stand by stool 3), gets a drink and Xs to table (sitting in chair 4); begins looking through papers on table.
Character A:	X to low shelf #1, gets a gun hidden in a box — starts cleaning gun. X to coffee table, glancing out window while cleaning the gun.
Character B:	Rises from table quickly to area between bar and TV. Glances first toward table, then to Delta and Bravo, and finally focuses on Character A.

SCRIPT ANALYSIS
(Experimenting With Aristotelian Analysis)

Theatre has to be about one thing first,
then it can be about a million things.

— **Robert Wilson**

OVERVIEW

Most likely, at some point in the workshop "closed scenes"[8] or full-length plays will be performed. The analysis of the formal elements of text is a valuable foundation for any production work. Aristotelian analysis is by no means the only effective way to interpret dramatic literature, but it is a good starting point because it gets the student director to look carefully at the parts of the play, and to understand how the parts interact with each other. Above all else, Aristotelian analysis helps the director to decide what needs to be emphasized in a particular script. Just as an actor has to learn how to emphasize key words in a sentence or speech, a director needs to learn how to emphasize important moments or scenes in a play. This type of analysis can be used with any length text, but using a short ten-minute play would provide excellent material for a first attempt at this kind of analytical work.[9] If, after being analyzed on paper, the play or scene could actually be brought to performance, so much the better as far as this underscores the practical value of script analysis for production.

ARISTOTLE'S SIX ELEMENTS

The essence of drama is conflict. Almost always a play depicts a conflict in which the main character is working toward an objective that is hard to reach and whose attainment is actively opposed. But how exactly does the playwright structure his tale of conflict? This was the very question that fascinated Aristotle and prompted him to write his *Poetics*, perhaps the most significant and influential work on dramatic criticism ever written. It was Aristotle who first described the elements of theatre as falling into six categories, which he listed in order from the most to the least important.

1. Plot	4. Language
2. Character	5. Music
3. Idea	6. Spectacle

---

[8]See pp. 201-202 for a discussion of "closed scenes."
[9]See pp. 7-8 for some specific short play suggestions.

253

PLOT

Aristotle considered plot to be the most important element of a play. Plot is a succession of carefully selected and arranged events designed to create an audience response. Most people are oblivious to the distinction between *plot* and *story*, but the art of playwrighting hinges on this very distinction. Plot is the particular way the writer decides to dramatize a story. Maybe the strategy is to withhold what we want to know, or maybe to delude us into thinking that we know more than we really do. Concealing or revealing, confusing or clarifying, along with many other storytelling techniques, can all take a part in the plot making process. *Plot is what gives shape to story, the particular way the playwright tells the story, not the story itself.* Studying the intricacies of plot will help a director determine what details are best stressed or subordinated in a production. According to Aristotle, the parts of the plot are:

Point of Attack	Foreshadowing	Climax
Exposition	Complications	Dénouement
Discovery	Crisis	Unity of Time and Action

POINT OF ATTACK

Where exactly to start the story? The beginning of a play is the specific point in the larger, extended story that the playwright felt was the best place to begin. In the extended story, Hamlet's father is murdered, but Shakespeare started with a ghostly aftershock rather than the deed itself. Play beginnings are maybe best understood by thinking of the plot as strategically placed stacks of dynamite. Each stack is bigger than the previous one, and setting off one stack automatically fires off the next closest one. The first explosion of the play becomes what is called the *point of attack* — a term which is not at all out of keeping with the metaphor of dynamite. The single event that sparks the first explosion is known as the *inciting incident*. The clearest definition for the inciting incident is "the event that lit the fuse before the curtain goes up."[10] We usually become aware of the inciting incident very early in the play. For instance, we learn through the Ghost that Hamlet's father was slain. If the inciting incident is the event that lit the fuse, the point of attack is the initial explosion caused by the burning fuse. The point of attack, therefore, is the moment when conflict first begins. Often the point of attack is when disequilibrium is created, destroying any existing sense of comparative calm. Thus, the inciting incident and point of attack are different from each other, but clearly interconnected. The pertinent critical question still goes back to asking why the playwright chose to start the play at a specific point. In an effort to grab our attention and keep to conventional time restraints, playwrights typically create a *late point of attack*, meaning that they begin the plot late in the story. It's all too easy for beginning directors to put either too little or too much emphasis on the

---

[10]Louis Catron: *The Director's Vision: Play Direction from Analysis to Production*, (Mountain View: Mayfield Publishing Co., 1989), p. 43.

point of attack. Creating a dud for a first explosion or shooting off all the fireworks at once does not make very good use of dramatic dynamite.

EXPOSITION

The part of the play that provides important background information is the *exposition*. Apart from generally introducing the audience to the everyday world of the characters, the single most important function of the exposition is to describe the inciting incident. The opening of Thornton Wilder's *The Skin of Our Teeth* mocks the old-fashioned, popular contrivance of gossiping servants telling each other, and of course the entire audience, what should to be perfectly obvious to them, but somehow is not. A little less obvious is the convention of bringing in a character who hasn't been around for a while and has to, along with the audience, catch up on current events. In such plays as *A Doll's House* and *Hedda Gabler*, Ibsen relies on this routine of the returning acquaintance, but he gets away with the artifice due to his skill in characterization. Exposition works most effectively when it comes out of convincing conflict. Writers who rebel against the restraints of realism might very well find even the best expository techniques too contrived; to them a projection or a slogan announced from a loudspeaker might be the best way to get across necessary background information. Just as playwrights have to handle exposition very carefully, directors in performance need to be aware of its many pitfalls. To a cast who has grown to know a play literally backwards and forwards, exposition may seem somewhat expendable. This brings an ever-present danger of rushing through the exposition, playing it as largely throwaway material. There is an equal danger of overstressing the exposition to the point that all subsequent action seems anticlimactic — all the dynamite has been detonated, greatly damaging the remaining dramatic landscape.

DISCOVERY

Imparting information to the audience needs to continue well past the formal exposition. Creating a dynamic flow of discoveries is a critical part of playwrighting. What usually works best is when discovery comes directly from the characters. In this way the audience is able to experience Oedipus' discoveries — his innermost revelations — with him. As the audience makes discoveries with the characters, the meaning of the play often becomes manifest. Related to discovery is the concept of recognition. This happens in *Oedipus Rex*, for instance, when the title character discovers the horrific truth about his past. Exposition is clearly part of the discovery process, but the obvious difference is that instead of just dealing with pertinent background material (antecedent action), discovery includes events that may happen in the course of the play on stage.

FORESHADOWING

Foreshadowing provides clues of future action; its function is to make subsequent events credible. Often it begins quite early in the play and, in addition to its general function in preparing the spectator for future developments, it also may help create tension and build suspense, or just generally help carry forward the momentum of action. Oftentimes foreshadowing reveals character; for instance, Jessie's cleaning of her mother's glasses in *'Night, Mother* is foreshadowing that she wants her mother to "see" clearly that her suicide makes sense from her perspective. Foreshadowing is the dramatist's way of ensuring that nothing about the play will seem superfluous or improbable. If nothing else, it alerts the audience to what the writer considers important. In this respect, by getting the audience to pay attention to foreshadowing, the director helps differentiate between major and minor events.

COMPLICATIONS

Complications are forces that change or intensify the course of the play. The first complication is the point of attack. Once the fuse has been ignited (the inciting incident), one dramatic explosion follows another. The first explosion is the point of attack, followed by a succession of additional explosions that may take the form of *obstacles* (barriers the protagonist must overcome) or *reversals* (actions that produce the opposite of what is intended or expected). All of these subsequent explosions in the play are known as complications. Ultimately the final explosion — the biggest bang from the biggest stack of remaining dynamite — is the climax. Directors must attempt to give each complication adequate emphasis. A play is like a series of building blocks in which each complication must contribute to the building process.

CRISIS

A crisis is a turning point when the tension reaches a peak and forces a change in events. A crisis is typically a clash of interests or a time of decision — a dramatic crossroads. It is the split second when Hamlet has to decide whether to kill or not to kill Uncle Claudius; it is the turning point when Oedipus makes up his mind to jab out his eyes. A crisis is not so much the completed action as it is fate hanging in the balance of the moment. Just as there is a series of minor climaxes leading to a major one (progressively bigger explosions), there is typically a series of crises growing out of the complications in the play. The major crisis can be thought of as the turning point of the action that leads directly to the climax. Crisis and climax usually occur very close to each other, but the difference is that a crisis capitalizes on the transitional moment, whereas a climax culminates in completed action — the moment before the explosion versus the explosion itself.

CLIMAX

Crisis bursts into climax, and the biggest stack of dynamite is finally detonated. All parts of the plot have conspired to bring about the chain reaction of explosions that consummate in a dramatic cataclysm. Climax is the point of peak emotional intensity, and the point of maximum disturbance. The climax often answers the question that was posed at the beginning of the play. For example, Ibsen's *A Doll's House* asks whether or not Nora will wake up to the fact that her marriage is hurting her. The answer is yes because she ultimately decides to leave him in what is clearly the climax of the play. Edward Mabley advises playwrights to write every scene with the climax in mind because the climax "is the lighthouse toward which the dramatist steers his ship;"[11] a play started without knowing the climax will flounder in an endless flow of revision and frustration. His advice for writers is every bit as applicable to directors. Without the lighthouse firmly in view, the director will be far less likely to chart a clear course to the climax.

DÉNOUEMENT

The dénouement is simply the final resolution of the action. Nora's climactic decision to leave her husband is fully resolved when she slams the door. Dénouement is a French word meaning "untying," which makes sense if the climax is thought of as the point where all the strands of plot are "knotted up." The dénouement, then, is the untying of the knot created by the complications. Conflict is over, equilibrium is restored, and the curtain can fall.

UNITY OF TIME, PLACE, AND ACTION

Aristotle stressed that the related events of a play must be unified into a logical beginning, middle, and end. During the Renaissance, over-zealous scholars argued that a dramatist should adhere to the so-called classical unities of *time*, *place*, and *action*. In point of fact, Aristotle mentions only time and action and, unlike the Renaissance scholars, he did not set down "rules" for dramatic composition because his primary objective was simply to observe the practices of the Greek playwrights of the preceding century.

Unity of Time: Aristotle felt that tragedy should strive to limit itself to a single revolution of the sun (i.e. a 24-hour period). Generally, the Greek playwrights adhered to Aristotle's observation, but there were several exceptions. Shakespeare took as much time as he wanted to tell his tales, as have many modern dramatists. Still, the basic concept (not the exact number of hours) is valid because all playwrights are more or less restricted to telling a story in a relatively short amount of time.

Unity of Place: Although it is frequently attributed to him, Aristotle never actually mentioned this unity. Many classical Greek writers confined their plays to a single setting, which is why scholars during the Renaissance stressed that adhering to the unity of place was every bit as important as those of time and action. Certainly there are many modern plays such as Marsha Norman's *'Night, Mother* that adhere to unity of place, but for the most part modern writers have felt very free to ignore the dictates of Renaissance scholars regarding place. Even though many plays have multiple locales, the basic concept is valid since a dramatist has to concentrate his action, at least to an extent, in order to maintain interest.

Unity of Action: Aristotle's unity of action meant that the dramatist should steer clear of nonessential material by focusing on a single course of events. Aristotle argued that the plot should be simple enough so that the viewer could easily keep it in mind. The important concept of this unity is that all parts of the play should function as

---

[11]Edward Mabley, *Dramatic Construction: An Outline of Basic Principles*, (Philadelphia: Chilton Book Co., 1972), p. 13.

dynamic, interrelated building blocks; one block creates the foundation for another block, and no block is ever extraneous. Just how a writer decides to construct his building blocks is very much open to interpretation, as the history of theatre aptly demonstrates. Here, as with most of his major points, Aristotle was functioning primarily as an observer, since most tragic Greek dramatists created simple, highly focused plots.

CHARACTER

Aristotle's second most important category is *character*. Whether plot should be valued as more important than character is debatable; certainly the distinction between plot and character is largely artificial and often blurred. It's impossible to discover anything significant about character except through actions, and yet it is these very actions that comprise the plot. Therefore, plot and character are inextricably connected. Aristotle described a tragic hero as an essentially good man whose downfall comes from a lapse of judgment due to a tragic flaw.

IDEA

According to Aristotle, the third most important category was *thought or idea*. Few would argue against the need of serious drama to grapple with intellectual issues, but many would question whether the ideas of a play should rank below those of character. Just as plot and character tend to blur together, making it impossible to prioritize one over the other, so do character and thought. The conflict of competing ideas cannot be reduced to the intellectual level alone, since the characters' beliefs are inevitably bound up with their feelings. A frequent error is to confuse the ethos of an author with those of the character. Shakespeare is often credited for saying something that, instead of himself, comes from one of his characters, and that may not at all reflect how Shakespeare really felt about the issue. Rather than random quotes, a much better way to tap into a writer's true feelings is to search for a basic recurring idea or topic, or in other words, the play's theme.

LANGUAGE — MUSIC — SPECTACLE

Next ranking in Aristotle's hierarchy is *language*. Besides speaking volumes about the characters who use it, language shapes the action and sets the tone of the play. After language, taking fifth place in the hierarchy, is *music and dance*. These two elements, which have been part of all world theatre from the beginning, are still very important. There is the obvious usage of music in opera and musical comedy, but even in the so-called "straight play," the power of music to evoke mood is widely used. Speech has the potential of soaring into song, just as human movement can burst into dance, and the theatre frequently capitalizes on both these capabilities. For Aristotle, the lowest rating went to *spectacle*. The low rating may have come from thinking about spectacle as simply an excuse to shock such as in the portrayal of dead bodies. But there is far more to spectacle than shock tactics. When well integrated into the production, scenery and costumes are invaluable assets in conjuring forth the world of the play.

BEAT IT
(Experimenting With Beats and Objectives)

The first thing I do with a script is divide it into beats
and measures — a measure being a sequence of beats —
to get a fundamental rhythm of the part before playing it in rehearsals.[12]

— Jack Nicholson

OVERVIEW

The value of creating a *beat analysis* is that it outlines the all important sub-textual level of the script. As shown on page 267, this type of analysis provides moment-for-moment detail work, as opposed to the more general approach experimented with in Project A. A beat analysis can be done for an open scene or script of any kind, but as with project A, using a short ten-minute scene for a first attempt is highly recommended.[13] Also highly suggested is that the paperwork culminate in an actual performance. A possibility would be to use the same scene or play that was used for Project A. In any case, after creating a beat analysis, the workshop director should begin to sense the harmonious interplay of the beat analysis system with Aristotelian concepts dealt with in the first project.

CREATING DYNAMIC OBJECTIVES

An *objective* is simply what a character wants. Seeking to satisfy a want, a character does something. Want motivates action; we do something (*the action*) because we want something (*the objective*). In real life we may be too caught up in the moment to be fully conscious about what we want, but onstage it is essential for an actor to grasp both the conscious and unconscious desires of his or her character. A director will rarely work out every single objective since this is mostly the domain of the actor. However, when an actor is unable to find the core of his character, or during problem spots when directorial interpretation needs to be explained on a moment-by-moment basis, the director will very actively work with objectives.

Types of Objectives

The term *objective* comes from the great Russian actor-director of the Moscow

---

[12]Ron Rosenbaum, "Acting: The Method and Mystique of Jack Nicholson," *New York Times Magazine*, sec. 6, July 13, 1986):17.

[13]See pp. 7-8 for some specific short play suggestions.

Art Theatre, Constantin Stanislavski. He referred to the major goal of a character as the *superobjective* and the subordinate goals as simply *objectives*. As the term implies, all of a character's wants (objectives) relate in an almost splinter-like fashion to the superobjective; in other words, one objective may be seemingly very different from another, but the common bond between them is that they are both reflections and refractions of the superobjective. As directors or actors divide a play into rehearsal units, the following gradations are recognized:

- *The superobjective*, which defines what the character wants more than anything else; the major motivating goal of the character for the entire play;

- *The scene or unit objective*, which defines the character's overall goal for a particular scene;

- *The beat objective*, which defines the character's goal for a particular sequence within a scene.

Formulating the Superobjective

A character's superobjective must encompass and justify every desire. The superobjective is the character's guiding light for every action. Each beat not only becomes illuminated by this light, but in a deeper sense each beat is a particle of this primary light. What is the best way to formulate a superobjective — search first for the whole (the superobjective) and then the parts (the objectives), or vice versa? The process of formulating a character's superobjective involves either searching directly for the guiding light with which to illuminate everything else, or searching indirectly for it by first finding and then identifying each of the individual specks of light.

Whole to Parts Approach: Superobjectives tell us what each character wants in the play, but the even bigger picture demands finding not just the guiding light for each character, but a guiding light for the entire production, or in other words finding the *theme* of the play. Theme is the relatively abstract, main underlying idea of the play that is usually expressed in a single phrase or sentence. Think of the theme as what the playwright wants to convey more than anything else — the playwright's point of view. Instead of using the word "theme," Harold Clurman preferred the word *spine*. Clurman, as one of the founding members of the Group Theatre, was directly responsible for popularizing Stanislavski's approach, and he asks the following kinds of questions as a means of discovering the spine of the play:

- What deep struggle gives the plot its shape and direction?

- What fundamental desire does the plot of the play suggest?

- What is the play's *core*?[14]

---

[14]Harold Clurman, "Principles of Interpretation," in *Producing the Play*, by John Gassner (New York: The Dryden Press, 1953), p. 277.

For instance, in directing Odets' *Night Music* for the Group Theatre, Clurman felt that spine was "searching for home." The spine of a play, like the spine of the body, is the crucial core or foundation which holds together the separate parts. The spine is the all-encompassing, unifying action which fully justifies the separate and subordinate superobjectives. An excellent place to find the spine (core or theme) of the play is the climax. Very often there are definite hints in the climax about what the writer, consciously or even unconsciously, wishes to convey. Besides focusing on the climax, there are two additional ways to discover the theme:

- *One is by looking at what is stated explicitly in the play itself*. For example, in *A Death of a Salesman*, there is the highly significant line, "he had all the wrong dreams, all, all wrong…He never knew who he was."

- *Another way to determine the theme is from what is shown explicitly through the action of the characters*. For example, in *The Cherry Orchard*, the characters are emotional, generous, impulsive, but never take positive action to save themselves.

Once the spine or theme of the play has been discovered, the next step is to determine a *superobjective* for each of the main characters. Directors sometimes refer to a superobjective as the *character's spine* which makes sense given that just as a play needs a core to hold it together, so does an individual character. Character spines need to be closely related to the spine of the play, and the metaphor works well in both contexts because just as the vertebrae of a spine are closely connected to one another, so are the individual character beats related to both each other and the theme of the play. The spine as a whole, with all of its interlinking, related parts, creates a central support system with an overall form — the perfect metaphor to play up the interdependence between the whole and its parts. Also implicit in the metaphor is the path-like progression suggested by the line of spine, and in this sense, the spine is an excellent metaphor to depict what Stanislavski meant when he insisted that there needs to be a *through-line-of-action* generated from the superobjective. Oftentimes the superobjective of the protagonist generates a basic course of action that is virtually identical to the spine of the play. The spines of the supporting characters, then, function as supports or obstacles to this basic action. For example, Elia Kazan, the first Broadway director of *A Streetcar Named Desire*, felt that the spine of the play was the cry of a dying civilization about to be "snuffed out by the crude forces of violence, insensitivity and vulgarity" and that the character spines or superobjectives were:[15]

- Blanche . . . . to find protection
- Stella . . . . to hold onto Stanley
- Stanley . . . . to keep things his way
- Mitch . . . . to get away from his mother

[15]Elia Kazan, "Notebook for A Streetcar Named Desire," in *Directors on Directing: A Source Book of the Modern Theatre*, ed. Cole and Chinoy (Indianapolis: The Bobbs-Merrill Company, Inc., 1963), pp. 364-379.

Parts to Whole Approach: Formulating character superobjectives for some directors works best by beginning with the parts themselves. For example, Paul Kuritz, in *Playing: An Introduction to Acting*, argues that an excellent way to discover a character's superobjective is simply to list all of the character's wants as they appear. Each want, when expressed in the form of an actual phrase, should stress the subtextual figurative level, rather than the more surface, literal level of the dialogue. Keep in mind that what a character says he wants may not be exactly the same as what he actually does, which reinforces the adage that "actions speak louder than words." Kuritz demonstrates his approach by listing the beats of the mother from Tennessee Williams' *The Glass Menagerie*. According to Kuritz, Amanda Wingfield's wants are:[16]

- To cling to the past
- To keep Laura pretty and fresh for marriage
- To escape the embarrassment my children cause me
- To shape a secure future for my children
- To get into the mainstream of life
- To protect my children from unpleasantness
- To convince my children to listen to me
- To force Tom to keep his job
- To instill in my children an appreciation of spiritual things
- To plan for my children's future

Generating such a list allows a director to see the common denominators, and from such a list it is a relatively easy second step to formulate the superobjective or spine of the character. A possible superobjective for Amanda from the above list might be "to secure success and happiness for my children." After the individual character spines or superobjectives have been discovered, the final step in formulating the play's spine is usually pretty easy to do.

Personal preference will ultimately determine whether a director wishes to work from the whole to the parts, or vice versa. The mind works very fast, and oftentimes very unconsciously, and so in truth, it is often very difficult for a director to really know what process is really being followed. Distilling coherent thoughts from the maelstrom of mental images and processes can never be reduced to purely rational explanation. Not being fully able to articulate the approach is hardly a problem as long as one way or another (or via bits of both ways) the director is able to formulate the superobjectives.

---

[16]Paul Kuritz, *Playing: An Introduction to Acting*, (New Jersey: Prentice-Hall, Inc., 1982), p. 152.

Scene and Beat Objectives

A scene objective is the all-embracing objective for a particular scene. Scene objectives are the major subdivisions of the character's superobjective. Scene objectives function as a chain of islands in a vast sea that the character strives to reach one at a time in order to eventually reach the mainland known as the superobjective. The spine or superobjective is the ultimate distillation of what the character wants, and the beats dramatize the *detailed ways in which the character tries to accomplish his goal*. If the scene objectives are like islands in a vast sea, the beats are the small stepping stones leading to, and ultimately forming the large islands. Stanislavski used the term "through-line-of-action" to spotlight the idea that each beat is related to the previous one — stepping stones solidify into islands, and the islands coagulate ultimately into the mainland. Ideally beats progress from weaker to stronger until a climax is reached, and the through-line-of-action insures a dramatically worthy pathway for each of the characters. Think of the scene objectives as chapters in a novel, and the beats as the individual paragraphs.

When you examine a scene for beats, you will find definite shifts or transitions built into the dialogue. A typical beat is about a half a page long, but this is obviously only a very rough rule of thumb. Sometimes, skillful writing creates an almost seamless shift of beats, but upon a closer look, the changes are definitely there for the finding. A new beat may begin:

- *With an entrance.* Typically an entering character will introduce a new want into the scene. This does not mean that every entrance signals a separate beat since it is possible for an entering character to continue with the flow of the present beat.

- *With an unsuccessful attainment of a wish.* If a character fails to get what he wants, a new idea, tactic, or activity might be tried. Maybe the character brings a new twist or topic to the conversation.

- *With the successful attainment of a wish.* After a character gets what he wants, the character will very likely shift to a new wish, or a new variation of the wish.

- *With a shift in power between characters.* The onset of a new beat may happen as a character begins to take initiative and "carry the ball." A power play that results in one character dominating the others may also determine "whose scene it is."

Phrasing Objectives

Objectives at any level (super, scene, or beat) are meant to be highly practical tools for actors and directors; they are not meant to be academically ladened nuggets of literary excellence; to the contrary, they should be phrased in the gutsy, dynamic lingo of the vernacular, which is meaningful to everyone. A direct simple statement structured to emphasize a strong, dynamic verb is the basic technique in phrasing an objective. In *An Actor Prepares*, Stanislavski argues that objectives should be:

- Directed *toward another character* rather than oneself or the audience.

- Directed toward the *inner life* of the character.

- Connected directly to *the main idea of the play.*

- Phrased in *the infinitive verb form,* as simply as possible, and from the viewpoint of the character.

Above all else, objectives should be worded so that they inspire the actor to act. Always use the infinitive form of the verb (such as "to badger" or "to needle"), and search for the strongest, most dynamic verb possible. An example of a poorly phrased objective for Laura in *The Glass Menagerie* might be "I want to withdraw from reality" because it would probably result in a weak, uninspired performance. Rework such an objective with a more positively oriented, dynamic verb choice such as, "I want to defend my fantasy world," or even more assertively, "I want to obliterate my bashfulness." Often directors and actors work with violent, or even sexual verbs as an effective means to goad the actor into action. William Ball, former artistic director of the American Conservatory Theatre, devotes an entire chapter in his *A Sense of Direction* to the fine art of phrasing objectives. Ball's first phrasing suggestion is to *eliminate nouns*:[17]

NOUN	VERB
I want a motorboat.	I want to EARN enough for a motorboat.
I want a wife.	I want to WIN Georgia's heart.
I want peace.	I want to ELIMINATE distraction.
I want attention.	I want to FASCINATE everyone.
I want order.	I want to ORGANIZE this mess.

His next suggestion is to *eliminate adjectives* and all *I am* type phrases:

ADJECTIVE	VERB
I am angry with her.	I want to DESTROY her.
I am nervous.	I want to FOCUS my attention.
I am frustrated.	I want to FIND a way out.
I am in love.	I want to TAKE CARE of her forever.
I am being charming.	I want to DAZZLE the guests.
I am confused.	I want to FIGURE OUT a solution.
I am giddy.	I want to CONTAIN my rapture.
I am drunk.	I want to PRESERVE business as usual.
I am friendly.	I want to WIN him over.
I am arrogant.	I want to BELITTLE him.

[17]William Ball, *A Sense of Direction*, (New York: Drama Book Publishers, 1984), p. 80-81.

Thirdly, he stresses the importance of using dynamic verbs or, as he says, "verbs that an ordinary person could get behind with his shoulder and push hard for at least ten minutes."[18] Further reminders are:

- Stay away from ***intellectual verbs*** such as *cogitate* or *reciprocate*.

- Avoid ***behavioral verbs*** such as *sleep, laugh, sneeze, cry, wait,* or *stand,* which suggest a state of being.

- Avoid ***existential verbs***, which include those vast activities that go on and on without our volition such as *to exist, to become, to live.*

- Avoid ***trigger verbs*** such as *shoot, slap, kick,* or *touch* — in other words, verbs that depict actions that occur so quickly that the doer could not pursue them for ten minutes.

Listed below are a number of frequently recurring "actable" verbs:

I want to CONVINCE.	I want to HELP.
I want to ENCOURAGE.	I want to SEDUCE.
I want to PREPARE.	I want to IGNITE.
I want to ENLIGHTEN.	I want to BUILD.
I want to ANNIHILATE.	I want to HURT.
I want to GET EVEN.	I want to AWAKEN.
I want to OVERWHELM.	I want to MOCK.
I want to REASSURE.	I want to CRUSH.
I want to BOMBARD.	I want to INSPIRE.
I want to SUPPRESS.	I want to DESTROY.
I want to BELITTLE.	I want to INCITE.
I want to LAMBAST.	I want to TEASE.

After a strong, actable verb has been found, there are two further refinements that Ball recommends. In addition to the verb itself, the objective should also specify:

- To whom the want is directed (i.e., *the receiver*)

- The desired response sought from that person (i.e., *the desired response*)

[18]William Ball, *A Sense of Direction* (New York: Drama Book Publishers, 1984), p. 86.

	VERB	RECEIVER	DESIRED RESPONSE
I want	to WIN	Gloria's	admiration.
I want	to AWAKEN	my father's	enthusiasm.
I want	to REDUCE	my lover	to tears.
I want	to IGNITE	the crowd	to riot.
I want	to PERSUADE	Ann	to kiss me.

Including the receiver and the desired response is the most sophisticated and effective way of phrasing an objective. As Ball emphasizes, "the actor's power is increased when his want is directed to a specific person."[19] All that really needs to be added to Ball's suggestions is the reminder that whenever possible phrase the beat with a sense of progression from the weaker to the stronger. A script builds through a series of minor climaxes to a major one, and the phrasing of the beats should reflect this dramatic structure.

To summarize, all objectives should be expressed as positive goals in the infinitive verb form by action choices that are consistent with the overall interpretation of the *entire* play. A well phrased objective will include:

- A strong, dynamic verb

- A receiver

- A desired response from the receiver

The phrasing of beats should parallel the progression inherent in the script. Each beat, each with a well-chosen verb, receiver, and response, is phrased in the character's wording to match the building momentum of the text.

SAMPLE BEAT ANALYSIS

This sample analysis is based on the *Time to Let Go* scene we have previously worked with (see pages 151-153).

---

[19]William Ball, *A Sense of Direction*, (New York: Drama Book Publishers, 1984), p. 80.

Time To Let Go
(Sample Page)

Begin BEAT #1: (happens before any dialogue) She: I want to distract mysef into calmness. **End BEAT #1:**	(script page taped on a piece of paper)

Begin BEAT #2: She: I want to lambast my husband's interference. He: I want to make her under- stand my plan. **End BEAT #2:**	One: Oh. Two: Yes. One: Why are you doing this?
Begin BEAT #3: She: I want to awaken his feelings so that he will change his mind. He: I want to prepare her to let go of the toys. **End BEAT #3:**	Two: It's the best thing. One: You can't mean it. Two: No, I'm serious.
Begin BEAT #4: She: I want to arouse his grief. He: I want to ignite her into talking about it. **End BEAT #4:**	One: Please. Two: What? One: What does this mean? Two: Nothing.
Begin BEAT #5: She: I want to ensnare him into remembering better times. He: I want to obliterate her need hold on. **End BEAT #5:**	One: Listen. Two: No. One: So different.
Begin BEAT #6: She: I want to bombard him with guilt. He: I want to win her sympathy. **End BEAT #6:**	Two: Not really.
Begin BEAT #7: She: I want to comfort him so that he'll comfort me. He: I want to assure her that she now has the strength to let go. **End BEAT #7:**	One: Oh. Two: You're good. One: Forget it. Two: What. One: Go on. Two: I will.

POINT CONCEPTION
(Creating a Production Concept)

The creation of a thousand forests
lies in one acorn.

— Ralph Waldo Emerson

OVERVIEW

Create a production concept for a play, preferably one that either will be performed in full, or partially in the form of a scene. ***The project will take the form of a formal oral presentation, which is to be no longer than twenty minutes.*** The premise for the talk is a hypothetical first meeting in which the director discusses his concept with his set and costume designer. Members of the workshop will assume the actual roles of the designers, with the rest of the workshop fulfilling the roles of potential investors or visiting artists; this comes as close as possible to simulating an actual production meeting.

THE STARTING POINT — THE CONCEPT

Finding a production concept means flying in a fog for a while, knowing the landing strip is somewhere below, but not knowing exactly where. The fog is frustrating but valuable in forcing you to keep all options as open as possible. But suddenly the fog breaks away in burst of sunlight, and you see your landing strip below in brilliant clarity. Searching with a production team of designers for the best landing strip possible is very similar to formulating a production concept. The germinating image or idea from which all aspects of theatre blossom forth is referred to as the production concept. This central image or idea can be expressed in several different forms; sometimes the concept becomes expressed in a metaphorical sentence.

- Tennessee Williams' *The Night of the Iguana* is the interaction of lunatics in a mental asylum.

- Rupert Holmes' *The Mystery of Edwin Drood* is a period version of *Noises Off* where the fun of the show is the distinction between onstage and offstage, and where production clichés in putting on a play are pushed to the hilt.

- Eric Overmyer's *On the Verge* is an insular, yet shifting dreamscape where new things float upward instead of downward, representing the *inner journeys* of the three Victorian ladies.

Metaphors can be very helpful in providing a unifying image for a production. Most of the time the metaphor is deliberately kept as a metaphor, but some of the most daring concepts are those that allow the metaphor to become literal. For example, there is a world of difference between saying that *The Night of the Iguana* is like a lunatic asylum versus actually putting the characters into a literal asylum. There are certain instances when the production concept may even go against or even mock the playwright's intention. Bringing Thornton Wilder's 1942 sermon on survival, *The Skin of Our Teeth*, into the 1950s in order to create a "cave man meets the atom bomb" vision, would definitely be an example of a concept going against the playwright's intent. Exactly how much freedom should directors be given in putting their signatures on a production? Too little "signature" may pave the way for a stillborn museum piece, while too much may wash away all traces of the writer's work. In most instances, finding a balance between these two extremes is probably best, but all sorts of factors, not the least of which is whether or not the play is in public domain, need to be taken into consideration. The line drawn as to what's ethical and legal can become very fine when the production takes a conceptual leap which flies in the face of what was seemingly the original intent of the writer. Evocative metaphors can be invaluable in conjuring up a special vision for a production, but they are not without potential perils. What might seem to be a terribly exciting idea at first can later prove to wear thin after the first half hour of the show. Metaphors can easily become stale and trap a show, so the challenge is to find a metaphor that can maintain excitement and interest clear through to the climax.

Besides a metaphorical sentence, a production concept can also take the form of a picture or a musical selection. Both painting and music can give the director and designers a feeling for the period or an aesthetic point of view. Sometimes just the general style of a piece such as the surrealistic paintings by Dali or the dreamy music of Debussy is sought, but at other times very specific selections are used to capture a unique look or approach. Notice how important music is to Tyrone Guthrie and Jacque Coupeau in the following quotes:

> The performance of the play is clearly analogous to the performance of a symphonic piece of music. By the time the play is ready, if it is properly rehearsed, the diverse voices, the group of people who are playing the thing, will have found a music for their parts.
>
> — Tyrone Guthrie[20]

> We have found that a good script, a play that is well written for acting on the stage, contains time spans — movements and rhythms — which are comparable to those in music.
>
> — Jacque Coupeau[21]

---

[20]Toby Cole and Helen Krich Chinoy, *Directors on Directing*, (Indianapolis: The Bobbs-Merrill Company, Inc., 1963), p. 222.

[21]Ibid., p. 248.

Paintings, photographs, or graphic images can likewise provide a general feel for the production or it can help bring about specific ideas for colors or composition. Notice how pivotal paintings are to the setting and lighting designers in a recent production of Lorca's *Yerma* at the Arena Stage.[22]

> Using Dali as my beginning point, I was trying to use surreal colors that take you past reality. The moon became a very strong image of Yerma's isolation. She's alone and isolated in the evening and in the daylight she's under the spotlight, in the harsh brightness of sun.
>
> — Nancy Schertler, Lighting Designer

> I was intrigued with the idea of doing a variation of Georgia O'Keefe's bone paintings, using that sort of tunnel effect. So I created two planes using the idea of paper, crumpled paper, with the edges singed and ripped apart. I think much of Lorca is about ripped emotions, blood. The moon is also central to Lorca's pieces for me personally, so I designed a moon which Nancy could light as a sculpture — she could create the idea of a crescent moon, an eclipse or even a full moon.
>
> — Loy Arcenas, Set Designer

Some directors create collages or musical mixtures to communicate the concept. And a director is by no means limited to one form or another; some directors will use everything available as a means of defining their vision of the play. No matter what the form, the production concept is meant to be the starting point for the production process. Concept statements are usually relatively brief because the intent is not to explain every detail of the prospective production, but to provide inspiration and unity for the work ahead. Zelda Fichandler, artistic director and producer of Arena Stage, Washington, DC, eloquently defines concept:

> Concept is the penetration of the very root or conflict of the play, and then its opening up. It's almost like a cubist painting where all the areas are laid open by a penetrating eye who sees through the entire object. You have to circle, circle, and circle the play for a long time to find the concept natural to you… Everything springs from concept rightfully used: every prop, every light cue, every behavioral moment of an actor, the casting, the rehearsal method. Your concept invades every detail and triggers your imagination; it pierces the heart and circulates through the whole body of the work. Concept means fertility, birth of the work, the uniting of opposite impulses to form one that is generative: like conception.[23]

---

[22]Nichelle Pearce, "Behind the Design: A Portfolio," *American Theatre* 10, no. 10 (October 1993):30.

[23]Quoted from N. M. Boretz, *The Director as Artist: Play Direction Today*, (New York: Holt, Rinehart and Winston, 1987), p. 161.

In theory, a production concept could just as easily spring from a designer as from the director, but convention places the ultimate responsibility for overseeing the production in the hands of the director, which is why it is frequently called the *director's concept*. Each director finds something important about a particular play that he wants to particularly emphasize, and this emphasis or slant is usually what crystallizes into a production concept. Different concepts will yield very different productions of the same play which, of course, is precisely what makes theatre an exciting art form. Concept is a means of turning script into action, which is why a director's concept differs from the playwright's vision. The playwright has skillfully put thought, action, and message into the text, but the director and his fellow artists have to figure out how best to bring the playwright's work to birth.

SAMPLE CONCEPT NOTES

1. KING LEAR

Lear will happen two or three centuries after the great atomic holocaust, when the few survivors have worked themselves up to a feudal scheme of things. Not much is left of the earth where anything will grow — that's the reason both for the violent storms and for greediness. The heath is one of the direct-hit, infertile areas. There are only two classes of people: those at the "courts" and those who live like animals on the heath. The latter are "mutants," and Kent and Edgar "in disguise" look like them. The "human" survivors occupied the remaining parts of buildings and subsequently built onto them with whatever they could find. This means a disquieting juxtaposition of styles. They used stone, mostly, because there wasn't much wood. Their clothes — they'd have wool, but not silk; I can't think they'd have many dyes. Clothes distinguish the haves from the have-nots, but they're stiff and hard, giving a sense of not belonging on the body, but worn to disguise it and to state rank. Their style is a combination of archaic and spaceship. The general scenic effect is of coldness, hardness, the earth returning to barren rock, man having destroyed it and himself. "This great world shall so wear out to naught." There is no comfort anywhere. The characters are constantly wrenched and tortured by surprise, fearful discoveries, pain; a recurring pattern is their seeing each other in a new, shining light. The only pain relievers in this shattered world are power and sex. The music is futuristic (the storm too), except for the Fool's songs. He sings them to the traditional, remembered melodies: Tea for Two, Alexander's Ragtime Band, etc.[24]

---

[24]This concept was designed for a production at the University of Hawaii. See Hardie Albright, *Stage Direction in Transition*, (Encino: Dickenson Publishing Co., Inc., 1972), p. 105.

2. CELEBRATION (by Tom Jones & Harvey Schmidt)

The concept could be based on a *dream of Orphan's*. A dream is a warning from the unconscious that something is wrong in the self's waking life. Orphan is at a crisis point in his life, and a decision has to be made. His orphanage has been sold to a rich man in New York and Orphan has set out to find this man and salvage the Orphanage. In scene one Orphan searches to find a warm and safe place to sleep on a freezing night in the outskirts of New York City. Orphan has no place to go. He has nobody and he has no money. As a result he is thrust into a *convulsive dream which exposes his conscious fears and his repressed drives*.

• *Potempkin:* is Orphan's seer into the unconscious. Potempkin represents what Orphan represses the most: aggressiveness and self survival at any cost. Potempkin uses people to get things (material items). He is in his prime. His redeeming quality is that he admits his evil.

• *Rich:* represents Orphan's most conscious fear — success through materialism without any regard for other human beings. Rich is ruthless, and refuses to admit that evil to himself, consequently causing his own destruction.[25]

Further ideas: for color maybe pinks, lavender, blues; in terms of the set, perhaps a circular circuitous feeling, generated by a ramp — maybe a raised horseshoe effect.

3. ENDGAME and THREE SISTERS[26]

JoAnne Akalaitis ignored Beckett's stage directions and the set the action of *Endgame* in a *subway station littered with debris*. This 1984 American Repertory Production (Boston) was defended by artistic director Robert Brustein: "To insist on strict adherence to each parenthesis of the published text...threatens to turn the theatre into a waxworks."

Andrei Serban found similarities between the master realist Chekhov and the existentialist clown Samuel Beckett in his 1983 production of *Three Sisters*. His minimal, imagistic staging underscored the dispossession and despair that overtake the women as, one by one, they lose their dreams.

---

[25]For more information, see N. M. Boretz, *The Director as Artist: Play Direction Today*, (New York: Holt, Rinehart and Winston, 1987), p. 134.

[26]Quoted from Milly S. Barranger, *Theatre: A Way of Seeing*, (Belmont: Wadsworth Publishing Co., 1986), color insert, p. 214.

4. LONG DAY'S JOURNEY INTO NIGHT

Ingmar Bergman's 1988 production was staged as part of the centennial celebration of Eugene O'Neill's birth. In his production the veritable museum of realistic details that fill up the Tyrones' summer house in O'Neill's stage directions was methodically dismantled. Bergman set aside the conventions of psychological naturalism with which this play has, until recently, seemed inextricably bound up. What the audience saw, in this freer, less closed interpretation, was a performance space for visions, memories and dreams — above all, the memories of the poet Edmund, with his black book, at once prisoner and the note-taker of his life's bitter experiences. In a limbo, cut off from the world of reality, on a small lighted platform furnished with a scattering of significant objects, the interlocked spiritual and psychological histories of the four Tyrones was enacted, or perhaps, reenacted as if the play was Edmund's dream. Nothing, in the words was "real" except for the intense spiritual reality and torment of the characters themselves. Projected images (the facade of a house, a window, a door, clouds and, at last a tree of silent promise) appeared and imperceptibly disappeared, like fleetingly glimpsed bits of world beyond the stage world. Even the "foghorn" and the "bell" in the harbor were snatches of atonal music.

SUGGESTED PROCEDURE

1. A production concept should evolve from a basic analysis of the play, but it is important to understand that analysis and concept are *not* the same thing. Part of the preparation for creating a production concept should include an analysis of the play. Be able to identify:

    - Inciting incident
    - End of exposition
    - Point of attack
    - Foreshadowing
    - Reversal
    - Crisis and climax

2. Be able to state the ***theme*** of the play in a single sentence. Remember that an excellent place to attempt to discern the theme is the climax, since it is often at this point in the play that the author reveals, perhaps even unconsciously, what interpretation he or she puts on the play. Foreshadowing may also provide good hints as to what a writer feels is important thematic material. Again, theme and concept are intimately related, but they are also not the same thing; theme can be thought of as largely the playwright's point of view, whereas concept is the ***director's point of view*** toward the play. In your talk to the

workshop, you should definitely discuss the theme of the play, but depending on time and your priorities, you may decide to not discuss such things as foreshadowing, point of attack, etc.

3. In terms of actually creating a concept, begin by thinking of your production concept not as a description of the final form of production, but rather as the seed or starting point for the evolutionary process that will be generated through your interaction with your hypothetical designers and production crew. The production concept is really a way of communicating to your fellow artists in a way which assists them in aligning their efforts with yours.

4. Bring in a *single picture* that somehow epitomizes the entire play. In other words, if this play were a picture, what *specific* picture would it be? As an optional activity, or instead of doing a single picture, prepare a *collage* using drawing, bits of fabric, wood, metal, paper, or pictures cut from magazines which express either the outer world of the play, or its inner psychological landscape. Search for visual statements beneath the obvious surface of the play. The picture can relate to:

> • *Texture* (rough, smooth, hard, soft)
>
> • A possible *color scheme* for the play
>
> • Overall *feel or mood* of the play
>
> • *Kinesthetic qualities* (nervous, joyful, depressed)
>
> • *Specific imagery* (a fortress, a tavern, and so on)

5. If this play were music, what would the *specific* musical selection be?

THE PROMPTBOOK
(Creating a Director's Notebook)

Everything is relevant;
making things relevant is the creative process.

— William J. J. Gordon

OVERVIEW

A promptbook is a director's personal notebook. Along with the script itself, it contains notes on blocking, character, costuming, set design, properties, lighting, sound, script analysis, concept and publicity, etc. It ultimately becomes the "score" for the entire theatrical production. As with any art form, revision is a major part of the process, so the promptbook is always in draft form. It is a record of the director's latest working draft of the production.

Just as each person has his or her own specific way of organizing a desk, each director ultimately finds his or her own particular way of organizing a promptbook. The specific method suggested for this project is merely a starting point for what will ultimately be a highly personalized directorial tool. For workshops culminating in a final performance project, such as a one-act play, a promptbook is a vital part of the process, but there is no reason that making a promptbook for even a five- or ten-minute scene couldn't also be a worthwhile pursuit.

WHAT'S IN A NAME?

Why is it called a "promptbook"? The term is hardly precise, since today's director will rarely "prompt" from it. Instead of calling it a "promptbook," Brecht used the term *Arbeitbuch* (workbook), which is a far more accurate description. The term "promptbook," outmoded and inaccurate as it may be, is still very much in usage. Call it a "promptbook" to keep with tradition, but think of it as a "workbook," and you'll be well on your way to appreciating it as the very valuable, ongoing tool that it is meant to be. The "workbook" is a tool to be used both in and out of rehearsals and, above all else, it should grow with the production. Think of the promptbook as a vessel to be filled rather than a vintage wine ready to be uncorked. The promptbook is at first only the rough notes of what will ultimately become the accurate record of your production. It is meant to be more word processor than great novel, more toolbox than fine furniture and, as it is gradually filled, the promptbook becomes a continual reminder of the developing vision, where its most important function is to aid in that process rather than to just accurately record the finished work.

277

In its earliest phases, the promptbook might simply contain a collection of research articles relating to issues raised in the play. Meaningful pictures, poems and music might also be found or created during this research phase. Obviously, not everything can be conveniently placed into the book; a collection of tapes and CDs, for instance, won't fit very well into a notebook, but the promptbook might very well be used to list the various selections. As rehearsals are about to begin, besides the script itself, a promptbook might typically contain:

- *Contact Sheet*, which is a typed list of phone numbers for everyone (cast and crew) involved with your production. For each person, include:
  - Name
  - Role or function
  - Home *and* work phone

- *Sequence List*, which is a breakdown of the play into workable rehearsal units. Each sequence should be given a name that best expresses the essence of the sequence, and which best helps identify this particular moment in the play from the rest of the play. Sequence names become useful rehearsal vocabulary, such as when the stage manager calls, "places for the 'Time Capsule' sequence.[27]

- *Rehearsal Schedule*: a detailed, day by day agenda for the entire project from first rehearsal to performance.[28]

- *Ground Plan(s)*: Reduced to fit onto an 8" x 11" sheet of paper.

- *Research Notes*, including notes about the period of the play, the playwright, critical commentary about the play or playwright, the director's own interpretive notes.

PROMPTBOOK FORMAT

Original Manuscript Method: If you're beginning with a typed, *single-sided original manuscript*, the bulk of formatting is done because, as the book is opened, the page on the right contains the text whereas the page on the left is blank. The completely blank page provides ample note-taking space for the text on the right as shown in Figure 1.

---

[27]See pp. 285-286 for an explanation and sample sequence list.

[28]See pp. 295-296 for an explanation and sample schedule.

Published Script Method: More likely than not, you'll be starting with *standard acting edition* from a play-leasing agent such as Samuel French or Dramatists Play Service. Even when this is the case, the intent is to create a notebook with the same kind of format (blank page, script page) as illustrated in Figure 1. This is done by simply taking apart two existing scripts, and pasting or taping each page onto a single sheet of paper, resulting in the back of each page being left free for notes. Either transparent tape or a glue stick work fine for this, but if tape is your choice, make sure to use the kind that allows itself to be written upon. Because the script page is smaller than the 8" x 11" sheet of paper it is attached to, there is additional space to make notes on the script page as well as the completely blank page on the left. The only disadvantage to this system is that it, in effect, doubles the thickness of the given text. This double thickness disadvantage can be alleviated by photocopying each page after the smaller script page has been attached. Photocopying, of course, in most instances, requires permission from the publisher, but it is oftentimes well worth the effort, since it allows for a much more manageable notebook, not to mention the fact that it saves tearing apart two scripts.

The obvious goal of this formatting is to create additional space for note-taking. Because of the ample space, the completely blank page created on the left works best for blocking notation. A system for creating detailed blocking notes is explained on pages 5-6. Besides this completely blank page, there is also considerable extra space created in the margins of the script page. The generous margins on the right page are perfect for making notes relating to lights, sound, and props.

Use a Spring-Back Notebook: The type of notebook is also significant. A standard three-ring binder will do, but it has the disadvantage that it is difficult to hold in one hand, which makes it awkward in many types of rehearsal situations. Oftentimes, the director needs to be on his feet, onstage, referring to the book, but keeping a completely free hand to communicate better with the cast. Only a *spring-back type notebook* allows for this kind of one-handed use. To insert the pages, the notebook covers are folded backwards in order for the loose-leaf pages to be inserted. No hole punching is needed with a spring-back notebook.

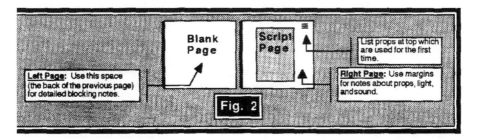

As shown in Figure 2, props used for the first time in the play, regardless of whether they are called for by the script or invented by the director, can be listed on the top right-hand corner of the page. Arrows drawn from the text into the margins can list light and sound design ideas. Some directors put all lighting notes on the right side of the page, and all sound cue notes are on the left. In any case, keeping the technical notes confined to the right-hand page makes it very easy to ultimately create a master lists for props, lights and sound. The right-hand page is also very useful for making character notes, defining specific beats and objectives, and other relevant observations.

Use Tab Dividers: Once the script itself is set up so that the left page of the book is blank for blocking notes, consider increasing the efficiency of the notebook by using tab dividers. These dividers allow easy access to designated parts of the promptbook. They can be used to locate specific acts, scenes, or sequences. Plus in the *back of the notebook*, following the script itself, tab dividers can be useful in creating separate sections for:

• Character notes	• Properties
• Sound	• Lights
• Costumes	• Publicity
• Set notes	• Research notes

A particular play might very well call for other pertinent categories as well, but these are typically the basic ones. At first many of these categories will merely contain empty sheets of paper, but if they're there at the beginning, an efficient system has been set up for further use.

It's often handy to have the very first page be the *contact sheet* (a complete listing of all phone numbers for the cast and crew). This list, which is usually prepared by the stage manager, should also include emergency phone numbers (police, hospital, etc.). Following the contact sheet, *before the script itself begins*, consider placing:

• The ground plan(s) (reduced for an 8" x 11" sheet of paper).

• The calls (i.e. the rehearsal schedule).

• The sequence list.

Make Miniatures: An excellent idea is to place a miniature ground plan on the back side of each script page. Usually these miniatures are no more than around 1" x 2" — just large enough so that there is enough room to notate the position of each character on stage at the start of that page. Once the blocking is recorded, this scheme allows the director to turn to any page in the book and quickly figure out where everybody on stage should be as the first line on that page is spoken. Miniatures can be pasted or taped directly onto the blank page but, as with the script, its better to photocopy the miniature onto each page.

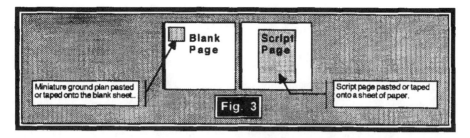

Blank Page

Script Page

Miniature ground plan pasted or taped onto the blank sheet..

Script page pasted or taped onto a sheet of paper.

Fig. 3

Miniatures sometimes are specially drawn but, more often than not, it is usually possible to make them via successive photocopied reductions. When working with a detailed ground plan, it may be necessary to white out unnecessary detail such as elevation markings, labels and the like. As the full-scale ground plan is gradually reduced, this kind of detail will probably become illegible anyway, and whiting it out simply makes the miniature look cleaner. Miniatures need only show the basic orientation of the set pieces — just the basic outline — in order to be effective. Figure 4 shows a

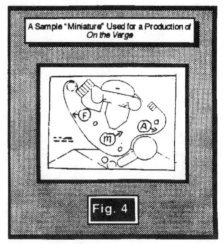

A Sample "Miniature" Used for a Production of *On the Verge*

Fig. 4

miniature ground plan (the exact size used) for a production we did of Eric Overmyer's *On the Verge* at Washington State University.[29] The miniature shows Mary (M) DRC in a ¾ left position, Fanny (F) ULC in profile right at ULC, and A₁ (A) DRC in a quarter left. Rather than having to write down all these specifics, the miniature says this much more simply in a single picture.

Incidentally, once a miniature is made, it's very easy through photocopying to paste seven or more of them on a single page. Then the paste-up page full of miniatures can be used to make as many additional copies as needed. The diagrams can then be cut from these pages and pasted anywhere in the script they are needed to clarify the blocking, and quickly glancing at a diagram is much easier than wading through a lot words in order to find out what's happening at a particular moment. Once a page full of miniatures is made, this original can then be photocopied as often as necessary. Scratch pages of miniatures allow you to take "visual notes" as you're working through various blocking possibilities. Miniatures are also great for visualizing complicated set shifts. Using miniatures makes it possible to see all the ground plan changes or variations on a single page or two. For instance, in the production of *On the Verge* mentioned above, we used a unit setting with mechanically shifting

[29]This 1991 production of *On the Verge* was designed by Richard Slaubaugh and directed by Terry Converse.

281

platform elements to represent the multiple locales; by using miniatures, these seven variations were able to be shown on a single page.

BLOCKING NOTATION

A large portion of the promptbook is used to make detailed blocking notes. With the promptbook opened, the page on the left (the back of the previous page) is completely free for blocking notation. On this blank page, number each movement consecutively, and place corresponding numbers at the exact place in the text where these movements occur. A significant advantage of this system is that it is possible to be very accurate in terms of where the exact movement happens. An important movement, for example, might happen during a pause in the middle of a sentence. *Begin again with #1 when starting a new page*, otherwise numbers soon get unmanageably high, making inevitable revisions unnecessarily confusing.

Abbreviations save time and space in recording the blocking. Use the first initial to designate a particular character to save space. If, by chance, there are two characters with the same first letter, then the first two letters of the name can be used. Figure 5 lists some useful abbreviations, although each director will probably want to create a personalized set of symbols. When somebody, such as an assistant, needs to consult the book, it is fairly easy to relay to them the "code." In blocking, I find it very *useful to distinguish between the everyday meanings of "to" and "toward."* A world of difference exists between crossing all the way "to" something, compared with moving only "toward" something. Therefore, a typical direction might be:

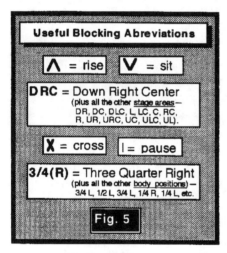

Useful Blocking Abreviations

Λ = rise   V = sit

D RC = Down Right Center
(plus all the other stage areas—
DR, DC, DLC, L, LC, C, RC,
R, UR, URC, UC, ULC, UL).

X = cross | = pause

3/4(R) = Three Quarter Right
(plus all the other body positions)—
3/4 L, 1/2 L, 3/4 L, 1/4 R, 1/4 L, etc.

Fig. 5

Cross 2 or 3 steps *toward* the window.

In some cases, where the blocking is very complex, even the completely blank page on the left may not be enough space. The solution to this problem is to cut the script page in half horizontally and designate one page by number and the letter "A," and the next page the same number and the letter "B." (i.e. p. 24A, 24B). This technique literally doubles the space available for blocking notation and increases available space for technical annotation. Figure 6 on page 283 summarizes the formatting and blocking concepts suggested in this project:

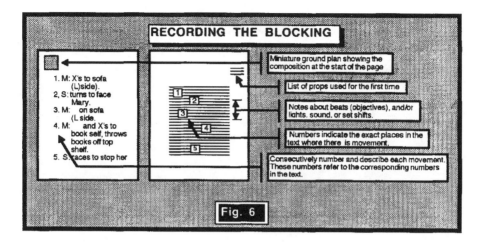

RECORDING THE BLOCKING

1. M: X's to sofa (L)side).
2. S: turns to face Mary.
3. M: on sofa (L side.
4. M: and X's to book self, throws books off top shelf.
5. S: races to stop her

Miniature ground plan showing the composition at the start of the page

List of props used for the first time

Notes about beats (objectives), and/or lights. sound. or set shifts.

Numbers indicate the exact places in the text where there is movement.

Consecutively number and describe each movement. These numbers refer to the corresponding numbers in the text.

Fig. 6

SCHEDULING REHEARSALS
(Creating a Sequence List & Rehearsal Schedule)

*Questions are the
creative acts of intelligence.*

— Frank Kingdom

OVERVIEW

Artistic concerns will always be a director's top priority, but absence of an effective schedule will prevent artistry from happening faster than any other single factor. Creating an environment where actors, designers and crew can do their best work is of critical importance to the director. Even when the director is assisted by a stage manager in creating "the calls," the director still needs to be the mastermind behind the scheduling because artistic vision is completely dependent upon the structure that brings it into being. This is why different directors of the same play are very likely to create very different schedules. The intent of this project is to provide guidelines for creating highly productive rehearsal schedules. In most workshop situations, it will probably be a one-act play that precipitates the first need for a rehearsal schedule, but the concepts are applicable to works of any length.

BREAKING DOWN THE SCRIPT INTO SEQUENCES

In order to create a rehearsal schedule, the script must be separated into practical rehearsal units. A play may already be divided into acts and scenes by the writer, but usually the director needs to make a more detailed breakdown. Think of a scene as similar to a chapter in a book, and a *sequence* as a separately titled subdivision of the chapter. Following through with this analogy, the book's individual paragraphs are then comparable to the individual beats of the play. Sequence lists are usually based on two kinds of divisions:

- *French Scenes* are those divisions based on the entrance or exit of a character. The term derives from neoclassical French playwrights who structured scenes around the entrances and exits of major characters. Each time a new character enters, a new scene is indicated in the text.

- *Action Units* are those divisions based on relatively complete interactions between characters. Since there are bound to be disagreements as to what constitutes a "complete interaction," action units are less clear-cut than French scenes, but figuring out the transition from one action

285

unit to another is very similar to working with beats. Each action unit functions as a necessary building block of the production, complete insofar as it is seen as a particular part of the play's infrastructure.

Many times directors use a mix of French scenes and action units to create a sequence list. Regardless what type of approach is used, *each sequence should be given a meaningful title*. As signposts, the titles create practical reference points, making it easy for everyone to remember each of the major building blocks of the play. Titles also help director and cast keep the pivotal points of the sequences in mind, which is not always easy to do when so much of rehearsal process is focused on finding nuance within nuance; in such instances, titles can become very useful signposts that guide the actors away from the maze of minutia and back to the bigger picture. Below is a sample sequence list using Peter Shaffer's *Equus*:

SAMPLE SEQUENCE LIST
ACT I: Equus Sequences

#	Name	Pages	Featuring								
1.	Horse Heads	7-8	Dysart	Alan			Nugget				
2.	No More Patients	8-11	Dysart	Alan	Nurse	Hester					
3.	Alan's Arrival	11-13	Dysart	Alan	Nurse						
4.	Behave Yourself	13-14		Alan	Nurse						
5.	Dysart's Dream	14-15	Dysart	Alan							
6.	Ek Discovery	15-20	Dysart	Alan	Nurse	Hester		Frank	Dora		
7.	Strang House	20-26	Dysart	Alan				Frank	Dora		
8.	Nightmare	26-27	Dysart	Alan							
9.	My Turn	27-29	Dysart	Alan							
10.	Beach	29-34	Dysart	Alan			Nugget	Frank	Dora		
11.	Dora's Visit	34-37	Dysart						Dora		
12.	Dalton's Visit	37-39	Dysart						Dora		
13.	Tape Recorder	39-40	Dysart	Alan	Nurse						
14.	Frank's Visit	41-44	Dysart	Alan				Frank			
15.	Electric Shop	44-47	Dysart	Alan	Nurse					Dalton	
16.	Grooming	47-50	Dysart	Alan			Nugget			Dalton	Jill
17.	Bet You Don't	50-52	Dysart	Alan							
18.	A Normal Life	52-55	Dysart			Hester					
19.	Blink	55-60	Dysart	Alan							
20.	Riding Prep	60-61	Dysart	Alan			Nugget				
21.	Ha–Ha Ride	61-65	Dysart	Alan			Nugget				

The sequence list shows at a glance who is in what sequence, and how many sequences separate a character's different appearances. Such a listing makes it much easier to design a rehearsal schedule so that actors are called only when they are needed. Requiring actors to sit around for long periods of time when they are not needed will likely create serious morale problems. Moreover, making efficient use of each actor's time allows them needed time away from the rigors of rehearsal for private character work.

Consolidating time for actors is reason enough to create a sequence list, but once created it can be a fine tool for devising rehearsal strategies. For instance, suppose the actor playing Frank in *Equus* is having difficulty finding the flow and progression of his character, a problem not unusual to fragmentary plays of this type, and that the director is trying to solve the problem by running all the Frank sequences in succession, one after the other, without any of the normal interruptions. Here a sequence list such as the one on page 286 is invaluable in quickly identifying all of the Frank sequences (#6, 7, 10, & 14). Or maybe, there are purely practical reasons for running all the Frank scenes together due to the fact the actor is unable to attend certain rehearsals. Moreover, a sequence list could be tremendously helpful to the costume designer in figuring out possible changing problems, and character combinations. It could also help the property master, lighting designer and sound designer better grasp the interrelated parts of the play from their perspectives.

Besides facilitating the time and rehearsal strategies, a sequence list has the added advantage of becoming an analytical aid. For example, studying the *Equus* sequence list shown makes it perfectly clear that the play centers around psychiatrist and patient (Dysart and Alan), and so just the titles of these numerous Dysart-Alan sequences can help determine the differences between them. Similarly, there are three scenes that focus around Dysart and Hester (#2, 6, & 18), and here as well the list encourages the director to ask what is different about each one of these sequences. Taken together, the titles of the sequences create a kind of "rough-cut" road map for everyone to use. A sequence list visually captures the interrelated building blocks of a play, allowing us to see both the parts and the whole at the same time. In this sense, a sequence list captures almost pictorially the essence of Aristotelian analysis.[30]

TYPES OF REHEARSALS

With sequence list in hand, the director is ready to create a master schedule. It is important to *plan the entire rehearsal schedule before rehearsals begin.* Without a master schedule it becomes altogether too easy to spend too much time on a particularly difficult sequence while precious time slips away. Planning helps ensure that all sequences will be given adequate rehearsal time. Problems can arise with or without a plan, but a master schedule helps minimize the consequences, plus it becomes the

---

[30]See *Project B: Script Analysis*, pp. 243-252 for a discussion of Aristotelian Analysis.

best tool available for solving them. Different plays require different approaches, and there is obviously a world of difference between scheduling a one-act studio play using stock set pieces versus a full-scale main stage musical, not to mention that there can be tremendous differences in the skill levels of particular groups. Differences notwithstanding, most schedules break down into the following four major phases:

• *Orientation rehearsals*   • *Polishing rehearsals*

• *Blocking rehearsals*   • *Technical and dress rehearsals*

Orientation Rehearsals: This phase introduces everyone to each other and to the journey about to be undertaken. Perhaps most important of all is for the director to pass along his or her enthusiasm for the upcoming project. During these introductory sessions, the play is discussed to stimulate ideas, and to suggest possible pathways for the exploration ahead. Designers frequently help cast and crew visualize the look and feel of the play by bringing sketches or models into these early sessions. Possibilities for musical underscoring might be played by the director or sound designer to tap further into the spirit of the production. Anything at all, from videos to poetry, is fair game so long as the material helps to bring people closer to the world of the play and to each other. The wise director will bring in not only designers, but crew heads and as many other related production people as possible, because this helps send the all-important message that everyone is working as an ensemble toward the common goal of producing quality theatre.

Typically the orientation phase includes round table readings of the play, although to what extent, and whether done at all, varies greatly from director to director. Those in favor of round table readings believe that an actor cannot be expected to assimilate very much if he is actively engaged in movement. At the other extreme is the argument that actors, like dancers, create best kinesthetically, and sit-down readings are either a waste of time or downright damaging because they encourage an overly analytical approach, more suited to the literature class than to practical theatre. Actors do best acting, not discussing or analyzing, goes the argument, and so some directors feel that sit-down readings set the tone for lots of talking that continues into the blocking rehearsals ahead. Do round table readings prevent dreary intellectualizing by purging the group early on of the need to do so, or do they set a dangerous precedent for future work? Generally I like to get actors on their feet as soon as possible, oftentimes completely eclipsing round table readings, but this is not to say that certain types of plays don't lend themselves perfectly well to sit-down work. Round table readings for period plays make a lot more sense than they do for contemporary plays, but even this has to be balanced against the skill level of the group. Some directors use ensemble exercises and improvisations instead of round table readings. Creative warm-ups along with specially designed exercises, improvisations and games can work well in getting the cast to explore the world of the play, as well as going a long way toward making the cast comfortable with each other.[31] Many directors do warm-ups religiously at the beginning of every rehearsal, and many use improvisations and exercises at various times throughout the rehearsal period.

How many round table rehearsals to have is also a great debate. At the extreme is someone like the late French director Jean Villar who devoted more than half of his total rehearsal period to sit-down sessions. Similarly, American director Marshall Mason advocates having his actors memorize all their lines at the table before any blocking at all begins. At the opposite extreme is the late Tyrone Guthrie who wanted his actors on their feet from the onset without any reading at all. Most directors settle for simply one or two reading rehearsals, but even when this is the case there is no conformity as to the specific type of reading rehearsal. For instance, for a first reading sometimes directors have actors alternate reading lines around the table without regard for the actual casting; this has the advantage of starting democratically with everyone equally sharing in the process and putting a check on actors who have a tendency to push too early for results. Subsequent sit-down rehearsals may shift to the actors reading their actual roles, but typically directors will ask the actors to read mostly for content, downplaying performance whenever possible.

Blocking Rehearsals: Orientation rehearsals ultimately create the scaffolding necessary for staging the play — getting the play "on its feet." Before the first blocking rehearsals begin, typically the stage manager has taped out the ground plan, in full scale, on the rehearsal room floor. Substitute set pieces and props are also typically secured for the first "walking rehearsal." Starting with a functional ground plan is definitely the norm, but there are exceptions. Some groups feel that a ground plan handed down from the heavens is far too prescriptive, and a better approach is to let it organically evolve with as much actor input as possible. Such an approach is obviously far more time consuming and expensive, plus it necessitates a scene designer willing to observe rehearsals frequently. But for some theatre companies this is the only really effective way to work.

Most directors prefer to work through the blocking sequentially, from the beginning to the end of the play, saving nonsequential work, if needed, for later. In certain cases, however, blocking nonsequentially is a better way to work; in a play pivoting around a traumatic incident, for instance, blocking the trauma first might create a meaningful emotional context for the actors to use in subsequent blocking rehearsals. A director must also decide how much detail to block at a given time. Some directors like to rough block the whole play in very broad strokes, blocking the entire play in a rehearsal or two, and then gradually filling in the details in subsequent rehearsals.

---

[31]An excellent source for theatre games is: 1) Christine Poulter, *Playing the Game*, (London: Macmillan Publishers Ltd., 1987). Other very good references are Augusto Boal, *Games for Actors and Non-Actors* (New York: Routledge, 1992), Marsh Cassidy, *Acting Games: Improvisations and Exercises* (Colorado Springs: Meriwether Publishing Ltd., 1993), and Viola Spolin, *Improvsation for the Theatre: A Handbook of Teaching and Directing Techniques* (Evanston: Northwestern University Press, 1964).

Others fill in the detail right from the start, bit by bit, working much more slowly, but getting considerably more finished results. Blocking rehearsals, whether sequential or nonsequential, rough sketched or detailed, are usually handled in one of two ways:

- *Prescriptively*, meaning that the actors write into their scripts movement given to them by the director. This requires the director to preblock the movement in varying degrees.

- *Organically*, meaning that much of the movement is allowed to grow out of the spontaneous impulses of the actors, with the understanding that the blocking will eventually get "set" as various patterns become more valued than others.

Working different ways requires different time commitments and planning. Directors who know in advance how they will conduct their blocking rehearsals are far more likely to devise a realistically based working schedule. Some directors like working out all the details of blocking in the privacy of their studies with a scale model and miniature figures to represent the characters. Other directors believe that when blocking is worked out spontaneously it is much more organic and character driven. The popular conception that genius reveals itself through spontaneous outbursts of creativity is countered by Louis Pasteur's famous quote that "Inspiration is the impact on a well-prepared mind" or the equally famous saying of Thomas Edison that "Genius is one percent inspiration and ninety-nine percent perspiration." Those against preblocking feel that it is an inhibiting millstone on the actor's creative input and spontaneity; they believe that a far better approach for actors and directors is on-the-spot, improvisational creativity. Great directors work both ways, and it's impossible to say which method works the best. There's also nothing to say that a director could not, even within the same production, use both methods.

The issue of prescriptive versus organic blocking is further complicated by the fact that there are many variables to consider: the complexity of ground plan and the play itself, the cast size, the experience level of the actors, the length of the rehearsal period, and the director's self-confidence. There are actually few extremists currently in practice; even the most hard-core advocates of preblocking will allow the actors some leeway in working out stage business and will make changes based on actor suggestions. Likewise, those that advocate pure spontaneity are still bound to the pressure of deadlines and the need to "fish or cut bait" in terms of making final decisions. A compromise for the spontaneous director is to decide only where each character will enter and exit and the general area where a scene will be played. This method can work well with experienced performers, but it's pretty ineffective with inexperienced actors. Detailed blocking creates a foundation or structure to build from and it provides the inexperienced actor with a very needed sense of security. A compromise for the preblocking director is to limit preblocking to scenes with more than two actors.

Time permitting, my favorite way of working for most situations is to schedule

290

around a three-phase process of ***previewing, blocking, and reviewing***. A day or so before a sequence is to be blocked, a "preview" rehearsal is held where actors are allowed to freely associate with the material in any way they wish. Movements are improvised and spontaneous impulses are encouraged in a free-form rehearsal of exploration and experimentation. The director, along with everyone else, offers suggestions, but a large part of what the director does is to take notes of moments or approaches that seem to work well. In some cases, as long as it keeps from becoming intrusive, an assistant might videotape the rehearsal for the director's later perusal; videotaping has the advantage of allowing the director to stay actively engaged in the exploratory work at all times.

Ideas gleaned from this preview work are then formally "set" in the upcoming blocking rehearsal. Sometimes just the slightest spark from a preview session, something almost barely noticeable, will burst into brilliant fireworks during the actual blocking rehearsal. Searching for a creative spark, knowing how to keep it alive and glowing, and figuring out how to fan it into theatrical fireworks is a big part of the director's job. It matters not whether the capturing and cultivating of sparks is done in the privacy of the director's study or in the heat of the actual blocking rehearsal because either way the spontaneous impulses from the actors are highly valued and put to work.

The final phase of the three-part process is the "reviewing" of the blocked material. Reviewing reinforces the blocking for the actors, plus it provides a breather before moving into new territory. Always leave time at the end of a rehearsal to review blocked material because the time taken is well worth the improved retention. Fail to do this and you'll be amazed at how much has been forgotten at the very next rehearsal. While on the subject or reviewing, beware of making the fatal mistake of thinking that once a sequence is blocked and reviewed, the actor will forever remember it. Review regularly to prevent everyone from realizing just how ephemeral the theatre can be.

Once the staging of a sequence has been relatively "set," it is an ideal time to require memorization because at this point the actor is able to associate the lines with specific movements, and learning by association is far easier and more meaningful than learning by rote. I prefer to assign deadlines for lines in short segments — that is, block and a review a short segment of the script, and then make it clear to the cast that by the next rehearsal this much material (say two to three pages) should be memorized. This three-phase process of previewing, blocking, and reviewing may only cover eight to ten pages of the script at a time, and so the process is repeated as needed in order to finish blocking the play. The beauty of this system is that since it starts from the spontaneous impulses of the actors, it integrates the normally opposing schools of prescriptive and organic blocking into a highly productive process.

Polishing Rehearsals: The purpose of polishing rehearsals is to fine tune the performance into a finished form. By this point the play has taken shape; it has crystallized, but remains a rough-cut diamond desperately in need of having each of its facets smoothed and polished. Polishing can range from discovering nuances in mood and expression to finding more dynamic rhythms and tempos. Bits of business may need cleaning up, more economy of expression might still be wanted here and there, and flow from one sequence to another may still be a problem. Directors who have planned poorly may well discover that they've run out of time for any possible polishing, and without polishing even the best of gems look little better than plain old rocks.

During the polishing process, the director *juggles "work-throughs" with "run-throughs."* Work-throughs mean lots of stopping and starting, whereas run-throughs are comparatively uninterrupted. Work-throughs have the advantage of allowing on-the-spot fixing of problems, providing the director immediate gratification in getting each problem solved as soon as it surfaces. Since the problem is dealt with immediately, there is no confusion as to where the trouble spot happens to be, which is not always the case during run-throughs when communication is usually limited to notes given afterwards. Run-throughs, on the other hand, have the advantage of providing continuity, allowing actors to get a better feel for rhythms and tempos, and better approximating for actual performance conditions.

Directors differ considerably in how they prefer to give notes, and the differences can impact scheduling considerably. Some directors feel that actors are often too tired after a run to concentrate on notes, and so they prefer to write them up and present them the following day. This also has the advantage of saving everyone's time, giving the actor a "hard copy" of the notes for future reference, and allowing the director more time for reflection; sometimes with an especially sensitive issue, the director can benefit from a little extra time to figure how to best approach the problem. The disadvantage of writing up notes to be given the day afterwards is that not only does it consume a great amount of the director's time, but it also limits possible study time before the next rehearsal. It also frequently becomes awkward when there are notes that pertain to several actors at once and require a coordinated effort to solve. Other directors feel it is best to give notes to the gathered group, which solves the problem of coordination, but it can be incredibly time consuming. We have all witnessed the plight of the poor soul with a bit part who has to sit through a seemingly endless litany of notes, only to discover not a single note pertained to him. A good strategy is to take a few moments to organize the notes so that group notes are given first, and those without any individual notes can be dismissed. Different note-giving strategies require very different time demands, all of which need to be taken into account when scheduling.

Run-throughs are easier said than done. At first, running through a single section or two nonstop is challenging enough, but gradually more and more of the play can be rehearsed effectively without interruption. Sometimes a highly effective method of rehearsing is to pick a section of the play that will allow time for it to be rehearsed three times: first as a nonstop run-through to warm up the actors, then as a work-through fixing specific problems as they arise, and finally once again as a run-through to coalesce for the cast what has been accomplished. In many ways this *three-part polishing process* is very similar to the three-part process of the blocking rehearsals — previewing, blocking, and reviewing. As rehearsals get closer to opening, run-throughs will increasingly dominate the schedule, increasingly preparing the cast for performance conditions. Even when run-throughs are the primary modus operandi, the director may still want to spend ten to fifteen minutes on trouble spots at the beginning of the rehearsal, ultimately enabling a smoother run.

Technical and Dress Rehearsals: As the title suggests, the purpose of technical rehearsals is to integrate sets, lights, sound, costumes, properties and all other technical details into the production. Months of planning during regularly held production meetings that bring together the director, technical director, stage manager, designers, and crew heads are necessary in order to prepare for tech week. Lots of mistakes will happen at the first tech, but by this point it is essential that everyone understands the ideal effect that is being sought. The tradition of throwing set, lights, sound, costumes, and everything else together at the last possible moment is fine provided that the show is incredibly simple technically. But a complex show is disaster bound if the production team has not gradually integrated the various elements into the actual rehearsal work.

The more things tested and experimented with before the actual technical rehearsal the better. Complex musical scores need to be worked out well in advance, with the sound designer or director bringing in selections to experiment with during run-through rehearsals; often just a simple "boom box," with tape and CD player, is sufficient to make choices about selection and timing concerns. Similarly, spending one-on-one time interchanging ideas with the lighting designer during various run-throughs is well worth the effort. Early explorations, rather than last-minute panic attacks, are a far more creative way to work. In any case, by the first tech all cues should be set to go; this is not the time to program computers or make the sound tape, or paint scenery; it is the time to rehearse the cues and fine tune the effects as needed. All this does not magically happen; careful planning and scheduling are essential.

Remember that technical rehearsals for designers and crews are the equivalent of working rehearsals for the director and performers. Technicians need to stop and start, run and rerun cues in order to feel secure in what they are doing. Typically there are two ways to conduct technical rehearsals:

- ***Cue-to-cue rehearsals***: Cues are practiced one by one, asking the actors and crew to skip ahead a few lines before the actual cue takes place. Once everyone is confident the cue is working, all are asked to jump ahead to the next cue, and this continues on through to the end of the production. A cue-to-cue rehearsal may single-mindedly focus only on a particular type of cue, such as a cue-to-cue for lights only, or a cue-to-cue rehearsal can focus on coordinating all the various cues (set shifts, lights, sound, etc.) as they actually occur. If various types of cues overlap each other, such as a sound effect keying off a specific shift in the lights, then this type of coordinating cue-to-cue work is at some point essential.

- *Barrel-on-through rehearsals*: As the name implies,[32] cues are executed primarily in a run-through with minimal stops. This has the advantage of communicating to everyone the continuity of the production, along with clarifying how much time there actually is between cues. Notes are taken instead of actually stopping. For this kind of a rehearsal to work lots of advanced planning and "dry-teching" is needed. Light cues have been roughed into the computer, providing a respectable "rough draft." The sound tape has been put together and leadered (or programmed, depending upon the equipment), and many of the costume problems have been solved in a previous "costume parade." All of the technical aspects have had a trial run *before* the formal technical rehearsal.

What kind of tech rehearsal to run highly depends on the specific demands of the production. Sometimes safety concerns alone dictate that a cue-to-cue approach would be best, whereas at other times, in say an easy tech show, the far better choice would be a barrel-on-through approach. Another option is to do both, beginning the first tech as a cue-to-cue and progressing to a barrel-on-through for the final tech. Above all else, have an arsenal of contingency plans because technical rehearsals, especially the first technical rehearsal, is virtually guaranteed to make "Murphy's Law" — *whatever can possibly go wrong, very definitely will* — into an understatement! As with everything in theatre, technical details need to be worked and reworked for perfection.

The climax of the production process is the dress rehearsal, when truly everything is seen together, uninterrupted, as it will be in performance. With the exception of emergency safety concerns, it is absolutely essential that the dress rehearsal runs without any stops whatsoever. This is the time for the actors to collect themselves after the rigors of the technical rehearsals, and a time for the crew to practice their work under performance conditions. At this point the stage manager is fully in charge of the production and, as much as possible, the director should wait until afterwards to communicate with all of the technical personnel. Usually the norm is two or three dress rehearsals, but keep in mind that the more opportunity the actors have to get used to their costumes the better. As with the earlier run-through work, notes are given at the end of the rehearsal, or the next day.

FORMAT

Format may seem like a trivial concern, but more than once a poorly designed,

---

[32]This tongue-in-cheek terminology, which perfectly describes this kind of technical rehearsal, comes from William Ball, founder/director of the American Conservatory Theatre (A.C.T.). Ball presents a very convincing argument for this type of approach; please see William Ball, *A Sense of Direction: Some Observations on the Art of Directing* (New York: Drama Book Publishers, 1984), pp. 131-142.

hard-to-read rehearsal schedule has been responsible for a communication breakdown. Some directors and stage managers prefer a calendar format, which has the advantage of presenting a very familiar schema, but it also has the disadvantage of not providing very much writing space. Other directors prefer a simple, day-by-day listing of activities. My favorite format is shown below:

SAMPLE FORMAT			
Equus Calls			
Week 2			April 9-15
Date	Time & Sequences	Characters	Notes
Sun. 9	7:00 - 7:30 *block* pp. 34-37 (Seq. 12: Dora's Visit)	Dysart Dora	Deadline Lines, pp. 8-20
	7:30 - 8:00 *block* pp. 37-39 (Seq. 13: Dalton's Visit)	Dysart Dalton	Deadline: Substitute
	8:00 - 9:00 *block* pp. 41-44 (Seq. 14: Frank's Visit)	Dysart Alan Frank	Props for Act II
	9:00 - 9:30 *review* pp. 34-44 (Seq. 12-13-14)	Dysart Alan Dalton Frank	
	9:30 - 10:30 *preview* pp. 44-50 (Seq. 15: Electric Shop) (Seq. 16: Grooming)	Dysart Alan Nurse Dalton Nugget Jill	
ETC.	ETC.	ETC.	ETC.

SAMPLE SCHEDULE

Obviously a rehearsal schedule has to be custom designed for a specific group and a specific play. Use the generic schedule below only as a very rough guideline for working out your own schedule. Outlined below is supposedly a "typical" schedule for a one-act play, based on the following assumptions:

- *A 30-45 minute play*
- *A 40 page script*
- *2-3 hours per rehearsal*
- *4 weeks of rehearsal*
- *3 rehearsals per week*
- *Minimal technical demands*

Sample Schedule

	Week 1	
1st Rehearsal	**2nd Rehearsal**	**3rd Rehearsal**
• *Read through* entire script • Discuss play and characters • Establish schedule for the entire rehearsal period • Have the stage manager get everyone's business and home telephone numbers	• Warm-ups & theatre games • Discuss ground plan • *Preview* . . . . .full play (a free association type rehearsal – the intent is to get used to the space, and for the director to get staging ideas)	• Warm-ups & theatre games • Block . . . . pp. 1-5 • Preview (free association, trying suggestions from everyone) . . . . . pp. 6-15 • *Review* . . . . pp. 1-5
	Week 2	
1st Rehearsal	**2nd Rehearsal**	**3rd Rehearsal**
• Warm-ups • Review . . . . pp. 1-5 • Block . . . . pp. 6-15 • Review . . . . pp. 6-15 • Preview . . . . pp. 16-20	• Warm-ups & improvsations • Review . . . . pp. 1-15 • Block . . . . pp. 16-20 • Review . . . . pp. 1-20 • **Deadline for lines pp. 1-15**	• Warm-ups • Run-through . . . . pp. 1-15 • Work-through . . . pp. 1-5 • Run-through . . . . pp. 1-15 • Review . . . . **pp. 16-20**
	Week 3	
1st Rehearsal	**2nd Rehearsal**	**3rd Rehearsal**
• Warm-ups • Run-through . . . . pp. 1-20 • Review trouble spots from earlier material • Preview . . . . pp. 20-30 • **Deadline for lines pp. 16-20**	• Warm-ups • Block . . . . pp. 20-30 • Review . . . . pp. 20-30 • Theatre games and improvisations for character work • Preview . . . . pp. 30-40	• Warm-ups • Run-through . . . . pp. 15-30 • Run-through . . . . pp. 1-15 • Speed *through* . . pp. 1-30 (where actors do all their lines, business as fast as possible)
	Week 4	
1st Rehearsal	**2nd Rehearsal**	**3rd Rehearsal**
• Warm-ups • Block . . . . pp. 30-40 • Review . . . . pp. 1-15 • Review . . . . pp. 30-40	• Warm-ups • Review . . . . pp. 30-40 • Trouble spots • Work-through . . . pp. 15-30 • **Deadline for all lines**	• Warm-ups • Run-through . . . . pp. 1-40 • Trouble spots • Speed through of entire play

Note: The intent of the above schedule is to have a cast fully prepared to enter the technical, and dress rehearsal period.

QUESTIONS TO CONSIDER BEFORE SCHEDULING

Answers to the following questions will have considerable impact on your rehearsal schedule. Consider each carefully before putting together your final schedule.

1. Will divisions for a sequence list be based on *French scenes* or *action units*, or both?

2. In what ways will my sequence list:

    • Help consolidate time for the actors?

    • Help create rehearsal strategies?

    • Help as an analytical aid?

3. When would it be effective to bring in musical selections, models, sketches, and the like to better introduce everyone to the look and the feel of the production?

4. Will round table readings be used? If so, how many, and how will they be conducted?

5. Will warm-ups, games or improvisations be used during the orientation rehearsals? If so, how many, and when? Will they be used beyond the orientation phase?

6. Will you want the ground plan to be taped down, and rehearsal furniture ready to go for the first blocking rehearsal?

7. Will you block:

    • Sequentially or nonsequentially?

    • Prescriptively or organically?

    • In broad strokes at first, and filling in the details later?

    • In detail, bit by bit, right from the beginning?

    • Following a process of previewing, blocking, and reviewing?

8. Once sequences are blocked, what system will you use to insure that sequences are reviewed often enough to keep them "on tap," not forgotten?

9. How will working rehearsals be juggled with run-throughs?

10. Will you tech:

    • Cue-by-cue?

    • Barrel-on-through?

11. When do you intend to set deadlines for the completion of: lines, sets, sound, properties, costumes, and lights?

12. How many tech and dress rehearsals do you intend to have?

The point of all this discussion is to consider carefully each step of the rehearsal process. Scheduling is a direct reflection of the director's process, and a director's survival kit had better include superb scheduling skills. In many ways, a well-structured rehearsal schedule resembles a well-structured play — each piece is a contributing part of the whole helping to build to a climax of interest. With all phases of the rehearsal process it is wise to keep the advice of Tyrone Guthrie firmly in mind:

> The all-important thing for a director is not to let rehearsals be a bore. The chief practical means to this end is to keep people busy...seeing that work proceeds at a good brisk pace, not at that of the slowest wits. Better to rush the dullards off their feet than to bore and frustrate the brighter spirits.[33]

---

[33]Tyrone Guthrie, *A Life in the Theatre*, (New York: McGraw-Hill, 1959), p. 153.

AFTERWORD

So, well-seasoned traveler, what happens when all the exercises and projects have been completed? We have traveled far, but keep in mind that to know what we do not know is the real beginning of wisdom. Much of the educational process encourages us to think that once we've done it, once we've reached the end of the road, often with degree in hand to prove it, that we've "mastered" or "doctored" our art. But there is a single remaining exercise left, and this is perhaps the most important exercise of all. The final exercise is to believe beyond all doubt in the following:

Exercising Never Ends

Performances and plays end, classes and workshops end, but a director is always in training — always exercising. The end of any journey should always be a call to begin another one. Directing can be thought of as a series of problem-solving journeys where each play is a fascinating net of new exercises waiting to lead us deeper and deeper into uncharted territories. Even when we think we know exactly where we want to go, we may discover fascinating side trips along the way. Side trips are often what separate the tourist from the well-seasoned traveler and, besides, who can actually say beforehand whether a path taken is a direct route or a side trip. Sometimes the side trips are extraneous to the production and sometimes we are too much on the run to fully enjoy them, but we know they will be waiting seductively in the wings, ready to possess us at a moment's notice. Even when not actively in production, a director is preparing for the next journey, arranging the itinerary, gathering tools and equipment for the open road ahead. At all times, enjoy getting caught in the web of discovery — a web even farther reaching than the world-wide web of the internet. Thread from a single exercise can spin into many fine theatrical tapestries. And as I write this paragraph an as yet unformed exercise is "exercising" in my mind, wanting to be born, but ready for only an ultrasound:

Netscape

Create a net of human tensions in which the movement of any person in the net results in a change in each of the others. A movement from any one person necessitates from all the others a corresponding readjustment of position.

No problem figuring out where this exercise came from — the associations are obvious, and yet it is very new and very untried. Now is the time to close your eyes and begin a wonderful walk in the dark.

LIST OF WORKS CITED

Albright, Hardie. *Stage Direction in Transition*. Encino: Dickenson Publishing Co., Inc., 1972.

Arnheim, Rudolph. *Art and Visual Perception: A Psychology of the Creative Eye*. Los Angeles: University of California Press, 1974.

Barker, Clive. *Theatre Games*. New York: Drama Book Specialists, 1977.

Barranger, Milly S. *Theatre: A Way of Seeing*. Belmont: Wadsworth Publishing Co., 1986, color insert, p. 214.

Ball, William. *A Sense of Direction*. New York: Drama Book Publishers, 1984.

Boal, Augusto. *Games for Actors and Non-Actors*. Translated by Adrian Jackson. London and New York: Routledge, 1992.

Boleslavski, Richard. *Acting: The First Six Lessons*. New York: Theatre Arts Books, 1963.

Boretz, N.M. *The Director as Artist: Play Direction Today*. New York: Holt, Rinehart and Winston, 1987.

Cassady, Marsh. *Acting Games: Improvisations and Exercises*. Colorado Springs: Meriwether Publishing Ltd. 1993.

Catron, Louis. *The Director's Vision: Play Direction from Analysis to Production*. Mountain View: Mayfield Publishing Co., 1989.

Cirlot, J.E. *A Dictionary of Symbols*. New York: Philosophical Library, Inc., 1962.

Clurman, Harold. "Principles of Interpretation," in *Producing the Play*, by John Gassner. New York: The Dryden Press, 1953.

Cohen, Robert. *Acting Power: An Introduction to Acting*. Palo Alto: Mayfield Publishing Co., 1978.

Cohen, Robert & Harrop, John. *Creative Play Direction*. New Jersey: Prentice-Hall, Inc., 1984.

Cole, Toby and Chinoy, Helen Krich. *Directors on Directing*. Indianapolis: The Bobbs-Merrill Company, Inc., 1963.

Dacre, Kathleen. "Charles Marowitz's Hedda (and An Enemy of the People)." *The Drama Review* 25, (Summer 1981) no. 90, 3-16.

Dean, Alexander & Carra, Lawrence. *Fundamentals of Play Directing*. New York: Holt, Rinehart and Winston, Inc., 1974.

Frank, Frederick. *Zen Seeing, Zen Drawing: Meditation in Action*. New York: Bantam Books, 1993.

George, Kathleen, *Rhythm in Drama*. Pittsburgh: Univ. of Pittsburgh Press, 1980.

Goleman, Daniel, et. al. *The Creative Spirit*. New York: Penguin Books, 1992.

Gordon, William J.J. *Synectics: The Development of Creative Capacity*. New York: Harper and Brothers, 1961.

Hall, Edward T. *The Silent Language*. Greenwich: Fawcett Publications, 1959.

Hammarsjold, Dag. *Markings*. Trans. Leif Sjoberg & W. H. Auden. New York: Alfred A. Knopf, 1964.

Henshaw, Wandalie. "The 'Open Scene' as a Directing Exercise." *Educational Theatre Journal*, v. 21, Oct. 1969: 275-284.

Hodge, Francis. *Play Directing: Analysis, Communication, and Style*. Englewood Cliffs: Prentice-Hall, 1988.

Freud, Sigmund. *The Basic Writings of Sigmund Freud*. New York: Random House, 1938.

Guthrie, Tyrone. *A Life in the Theatre*. New York: McGraw-Hill, 1959.

Hofmann, Charles. *Sounds for the Silents*. New York: Drama Book Specialists, 1970.

Hollingshead, August B. and Redlich, Frederick C. *Social Class and Mental Illness*. New York: John Wiley & Sons, Inc., 1958.

Jacobus, Lee A. Ed. *The Bedford Introduction to Drama*. Second Edition. Boston: St. Martin's Press, 1993.

Jaworski, Adam. *The Power of Silence*. London: Sage Publications, 1993.

Johnstone, Keith. *Impro: Improvisation and the Theatre*. London & Boston: Faber and Faber, 1979.

Kazan, Elia. "Notebook for A Streetcar Named Desire," in *Directors on Directing: A Source Book of the Modern Theatre*, ed. Cole and Chinoy. Indianapolis: The Bobbs-Merrill Company, Inc., 1963.

Kuritz, Paul. *Playing: An Introduction to Acting*, New Jersey: Prentice-Hall, Inc. 1982.

Mabley, Edward. *Dramatic Construction: An Outline of Basic Principles*. Philadelphia: Chilton Book Co., 1972.

Mann, Thomas. *The Magic Mountain*. Trans. H.T. Lowe-Porter. New York: The Modern Library, 1927.

Mahl, George F. *Exploration in Nonverbal and Vocal Behavior*. London: Lawrence Erlbaum Associates, Inc. 1987.

Marowitz, Charles. *Sex Wars: Free Adaptations of Ibsen and Strindberg*, London: Marion Boyars, 1982.

McKim, Robert H. *Thinking Visually*. Belmont: Wadsworth Publications, 1980.

Mekler, Eva. *New Generation of Acting Teachers*. New York: Penguin Books, 1987.

Noller, Ruth. et. al. *Creative Actionbook*. New York: Charles Scribner's Sons, 1976.

Ornstein, Robert. *The Psychology of Consciousness*. New York: Viking Press, 1972.

Packard, Vance. *The Status Seekers*. New York: Simon and Schuster, Inc., 1966.

Parnes, Sidney J., et. al. *Guide to Creative Action.* New York: Charles Scribner's Sons, 1977.

Pearce, Nichelle. "Behind the Design: A Portfolio." *American Theatre* 10, no. 10 (October 1993): 30.

Picard, Max. *The World of Silence.* Chicago: Henry Regnery Co., 1952.

Point of View (Fall 1993), a newsletter published by the UCLA School of Theatre, Film, and Television.

Poulter, Christine. *Playing the Game.* London: Macmillan Publishers Ltd., 1987.

Rice, George. "The Right to Be Silent." *Quarterly Journal of Speech* 47, 1961: 349-354.

Ron Rosenbaum. "Acting: The Method and Mystique of Jack Nicholson," New York *Times Magazine*, sec. 6, (July 13, 1986):12-21.

Schiffman, Jean. "Barbara Damashek: A Moving Target." *American Theatre* 10, #12 (December 1993): 46-47.

Shlien, J.M. Ed. *Research in Psychotherapy*, Vol 3. Washington, D.C.: American Psychological Association, 1968.

Spolin, Viola. *Improvisation for the Theatre: A Handbook of Teaching and Directing Techniques.* Evanston: Northwestern University Press, 1973.

Steavens, Andrea. "A Couple of Vanyas Sitting Around Talking," *New York Times*, Sunday, 19 February, 1995, p. 25.

Strachey, J. Ed. and Trans. *The Standard Edition and Complete Works of Sigmund Freud* (Vols. 4 and 5). London: Hogarth Press, 1905.

Tannen, Deborah & Savelle-Troike, Muriel. Ed. *Perspectives on Silence.* New Jersey: Ablex Publishing Corporation, 1985.

Unknown author — clipping on the studio wall of Spokane artist, Harold Balazs. See Andrew Strickman, "Art's Renaissance," *The Pacific Northwest Inlander.* Vol. 2, #33, May 31, 1995, p. 11.

Van Ekeren, Glen. *Speaker's Sourcebook II.* New Jersey: Prentice-Hall, 1994.

Williams, Tennessee. *The Glass Menagerie.* New York: New Directions Publishing Corporation, 1970.

INDEX

T

U

V

W

Y

About the Author

Dr. Terry Converse is a Professor of Theatre in the Washington State University School of Music and Theatre Arts, where he teaches all levels of Directing and Script Analysis. He holds an M.F.A. in Directing from the University of Minnesota and Ph.D. in Theatre Arts from the University of California at Los Angeles. Prior to coming to Washington, he taught at Centre College in KY, the University of North Dakota in Grand Forks and Livingston University in Alabama. Additionally Dr. Converse has directed works for the Long Beach Grand Opera, the Guthrie Other Place Theatre, The Arkansas Arts Center, Cherry County Players, Peninsula Players and Theatre By The Sea. He has presented papers and all day workshops at the National Convention of the Association for Theatre in Higher Education and at the Northwest Drama Conference. He has directed twenty-eight plays with university students and thirteen plays/musicals/operas in professional settings. Dr. Converse lives in Pullman with his wife, two children, a large dog and a cat. When not teaching or directing, he loves to escape to the water to wind surf.

NOTES

NOTES

ORDER FORM

MERIWETHER PUBLISHING LTD.
P.O. BOX 7710
COLORADO SPRINGS, CO 80933
TELEPHONE: (719) 594-4422

Please send me the following books:

_____ **Directing for the Stage #TT-B169**   **$14.95**
by Terry John Converse
A workshop guide of creative exercises and projects

_____ **Great Scenes From Women Playwrights**   **$14.95**
#TT-B119
by Marsh Cassady
Classic and contemporary scenes for actors

_____ **Characters in Action #TT-B106**   **$14.95**
by Marsh Cassady
Playwriting the easy way

_____ **The Theatre and You #TT-B115**   **$14.95**
by Marsh Cassady
An introductory text on all aspects of theatre

_____ **Acting Games — Improvisations and**   **$12.95**
Exercises #TT-B168
by Marsh Cassady
A textbook of theatre games and improvisations

_____ **Truth in Comedy #TT-B164**   **$12.95**
by Charna Halpern, Del Close and Kim "Howard" Johnson
The manual of improvisation

_____ **The Scenebook for Actors #TT-B177**   **$14.95**
by Norman A. Bert
Great monologs and dialogs for auditions

These and other fine Meriwether Publishing books are available at your local bookstore or direct from the publisher. Use the handy order form on this page.

NAME: _____

ORGANIZATION NAME: _____

ADDRESS: _____

CITY:_____ STATE: _____ ZIP: _____

PHONE: _____

  ❑ **Check Enclosed**
  ❑ **Visa or MasterCard #** _____

                           Expiration
Signature: _____ *Date:* _____
          (required for Visa/MasterCard orders)

COLORADO RESIDENTS: Please add 3% sales tax.
SHIPPING: Include $2.75 for the first book and 50¢ for each additional book ordered.

  ❑ *Please send me a copy of your complete catalog of books and plays.*

ORDER FORM

MERIWETHER PUBLISHING LTD.
P.O. BOX 7710
COLORADO SPRINGS, CO 80933
TELEPHONE: (719) 594-4422

Please send me the following books:

_____ **Directing for the Stage #TT-B169**   **$14.95**
by Terry John Converse
A workshop guide of creative exercises and projects

_____ **Great Scenes From Women Playwrights**   **$14.95**
#TT-B119
by Marsh Cassady
Classic and contemporary scenes for actors

_____ **Characters in Action #TT-B106**   **$14.95**
by Marsh Cassady
Playwriting the easy way

_____ **The Theatre and You #TT-B115**   **$14.95**
by Marsh Cassady
An introductory text on all aspects of theatre

_____ **Acting Games — Improvisations and**   **$12.95**
Exercises #TT-B168
by Marsh Cassady
A textbook of theatre games and improvisations

_____ **Truth in Comedy #TT-B164**   **$12.95**
by Charna Halpern, Del Close and Kim "Howard" Johnson
The manual of improvisation

_____ **The Scenebook for Actors #TT-B177**   **$14.95**
by Norman A. Bert
Great monologs and dialogs for auditions

These and other fine Meriwether Publishing books are available at
your local bookstore or direct from the publisher. Use the handy
order form on this page.

NAME: _____

ORGANIZATION NAME: _____

ADDRESS: _____

CITY:_____ STATE: _____ ZIP: _____

PHONE: _____
   ❑ **Check Enclosed**
   ❑ **Visa or MasterCard #** _____

                                  Expiration
Signature: _____ *Date:* _____
        (required for Visa/MasterCard orders)

COLORADO RESIDENTS: Please add 3% sales tax.
SHIPPING: Include $2.75 for the first book and 50¢ for each additional book ordered.

   ❑ *Please send me a copy of your complete catalog of books and plays.*